World War II & the media

A Collection of Essays

World War II & the media

A Collection of Essays

Edited by

Christopher Hart

Guy Hodgson

Simon Gwyn Roberts

Midrash Publications

First published in 2014

Published by Midrash
Email: midrash@mac.com

A catalogue record for this publication is available from the British Library.

ISBN 978-1-910481-00-4.

World War II & the media

A Collection of Original Essays

Contents

edited by *Christopher Hart, Guy Hodgson and Simon Gwyn Roberts*

Introduction

This collection came about as a result of a conference held at the University of Chester in June 2011. Its title was 'World War Two and the Media', and it would be the cause for self-congratulation if the organisers could claim it had been the end product of a beam of inspiration. We were working, however, in the North West Media Centre, Warrington, which is a building converted from a theatre that used to entertain Second World combatants. Looking across a Padgate Campus vista that once was filled with British and Canadian airmen and still bears the archaeological traces of old runways and hangers, it would have been a serious case of academic neglect if we had not stumbled on the subject. The only question was the date and, like the theme of the conference, it became apparent with only a little teasing of the facts: June 22 was the 70th anniversary of Operation Barbarossa, the German invasion of the Soviet Union, arguably the turning point of World War Two.

Like a meal, a conference is only as good as its ingredients, and while it was not a surprise how much the subject of World War Two resonated in the UK, the interest from abroad was a especially pleasing. Seven decades on, media representations between 1939 and 1945 remain at the heart of debates about what it means to be British, but the massive role the conflict played in the self-narrative of nations extended across the globe. This was reflected at the conference where 11 researchers from six nations delivered inter-disciplinary studies of both factual and fictional representations. This book includes several of these papers – including contributions from Canada, Germany, Latvia and the Netherlands – and other work that explores the many nuanced effects of the media and nationhood in times of war. The subjects range from film, radio, television, newspapers and music, and the time span from 1939 to the late twentieth century.

Chapters in this volume

In Chapter 1, Michael Paris (University of Central Lancashire, UK) examines the initial response from Hollywood, to the attack on Pearle Harbor. Paris looks at the 'hate movies' such as *Remember Pearl Harbor*, *China Girl*, and the documentary *Menace of the Rising Sun* that vilified the Japanese. Despite The Office of War Information's manual recommending filmmakers to avoid portraying the Japanese as "little buck-toothed and treacherous" and to remember America was fighting a "system and not a race", Paris shows these guidelines were effectively ignored by film-makers. Racism was, he argues, endemic in the American psych and, therefore, provided the frame of reference for many Second World War films. However, the irony Paris points out is that films in this period were perhaps the single most important channels for the dissemination of American propaganda throughout the Second World War, and much of that propaganda focused on the democratic nature of American society - a timely reminder of the need for national unity in order to wage total war. Films like *Bataan* took the hyphen out of American identity, albeit temporarily, and taught valuable lessons about the nature of democracy and willing collaboration. Yet the irony is that almost within months of the end of the Second World War, the Cold War ushered in a period of fear, repression and censorship in which America almost completely forgot the meaning of democracy and a free society.

In Chapter 2, Christopher Hart (University of Chester, UK) takes a popular wartime film, *Mrs. Miniver* (1942) and analyses is from a Simmelian (derived from the work of Georg Simmel) frame of reference. Taking the assumption that *Mrs. Miniver* is a 'why we fight' film, Hart looks closely at this categorization to make visible for analysis the essentially moral messages in the narrative. Through a detailed examination of several social forms including, value exchange, time and temporality, Americanisation, and conflict Hart argues that categorising *Mrs. Miniver* as a 'why we fight' film is overtly simplistic and misses the purpose of the film and its director William Wyler. *Mrs. Miniver* is, Hart argues, a narrative about the future of civilization. *Mrs. Miniver* was aimed at the American audience, some of who when the film was being made, were advocating isolationism. *Mrs. Miniver* presents the Americans with a moral choice between supporting the moral choice already made by the British not to capitulate to the 'evil of Nazism' or to do nothing and allow Nazism to establish itself as a world order. On 7th December, 1941 with the Japanese attack on Pearle Harbor this moral choice was largely lost and Mrs. Miniver became, regardless of its widespread popularity, classified as a 'why we fight film'.

In Chapter 3, Phylomena H. Badsey (University of Wolverhampton UK), examines the popular BBC comedy television series *Dad's Army*, written and produced by Jimmy Perry and David Croft, first broadcast between 1968 and 1977, comprising of 80 episodes in nine series and three Christmas specials. It was the first British television situation comedy series made about the Second World War. All the principal characters are men. Women appear or are referenced in all but four of the 80 episodes of *Dad's Army*, in many cases as significant characters, and some women's characters appear frequently throughout the series. This chapter, therefore, extends the traditional cultural studies approach to examine the representation of women in this popular comedy, showing how rather than being periphery to storylines are, in fact essential to the core comedy and characterization of men during this time.

In Chapter 4, Kristina Meier (Freie Universität Berlin, Germany) argues that few people have explored the leading opponent of Goebbels' propaganda machine - the German Service of the BBC. Fewer still have acknowledged that the BBC's radio transmissions to Germany entailed not only news and comment but also drew upon an unusual and unprecedented method of British psychological warfare - satire - as a form of counter-propaganda. Hitherto, the combination of radio and satire as part of a propaganda effort had never been exploited. Meier analyses the different attitudes towards the BBC's unexpected and revolutionary take on propaganda, drawing extensively on documents from the BBC Written Archives Centre (WAC) as well as The National Archives (TNA). A brief introduction to the satirical programmes and their historical context will be followed by more specific examples of the approach to satire and the heated debate this inspired within the BBC. The paper concludes with a brief discourse on satire as a morally appropriate measure for the fight against Nazism. Was it acceptable "to laugh amid the hell's noise of the war machinery" (Lucas, 1978:455, own translation), as one of the programme's authors phrased it?

In Chapter 5, Chris van der Heijden (University of Applied Sciences, The Netherlands) examines the role the newspaper *Vrij Nederland* in and during in the post-war decades. In May 1965, *Vrij Nederland* extensively interviewed a number of students of an Amsterdam high school about World War Two and its aftermath in the Netherlands. Their elders thought, so the students said, that they had liberated Europe from the Nazis. That was untrue. The Allied forces and a small group of Dutch resistance fighters liberated them: they were liberated. The majority of the Dutch had done nothing but wait and see. It was one of the reasons why they, according to the interviewees, were also responsible for what had happened to the Dutch during the war. *Vrij Nederland* was founded at the beginning of the war and is typical for the Dutch resistance: they fought by words instead of by arms. Van der Heijden explores the current day confusion over the role of the Dutch during the war in an attempt to map shifting images and perspectives during generations when the only constant was *Vrij Nederland*.

In Chapter 6, Guy Hodgson (University of Chester, UK) takes as his starting point the phrase "We're all in this together" - originally said by Winston Churchill and used by David Cameron in August, 2010. Hodgson looks at the veracity of the unity of purpose, one of the myths deriving from the Blitz, and show that people had a more nuanced experience between 1939 and 1945. It will look at the social conditions in Britain in the Second World War, the support for the war, the anti-German and Italian backlash and the psychological consequences of the aerial bombardment. It will explore the relatively neglected area of the north of England in the Second World War, with Manchester as its focus. The chapter uses Manchester's Blitz in December 1940, when nearly 1,000 people died, as the starting point to monitor unity in the weeks that followed at a time when the sense of togetherness was given its most severe test. It will do so by examining contemporary accounts in the Home Intelligence and Mass Observation archives and by monitoring the city's newspapers to see if the highly censored editions of wartime Britain reflected the tensions brought by severe bombing by the *Luftwaffe*.

In Chapter 7, Aimé-Jules Bizimana (Université du Québec en Outaouais,

Canada) examines the role of hundreds of Canadian and foreign war correspondents and how they reported on the military events on the battle fronts. On December 10, 1939, Gillis Purcell of the Canadian Press (CP) and Robert T. Bowman of the CBC were the first Canadian war correspondents dispatched to sail to England with the First Canadian Contingent. However, the captain of the flagship *Aquitania* refused to allow Bowman on board until authorities in Ottawa intervened. The initial reserve at the beginning of the war gave way to a greater but more controlled acceptance of war correspondents on the front. After presenting the censorship system in Canada and the war correspondent accreditation process on the front, Bizimana analyses how the censorship of war information worked, the role of Canadian Army Public Relations, and the coverage of large-scale Canadian military operations.

In Chapter 8, Helen Southall (University of Chester, UK) surveys the popularity of local musicians from the North West during the war. Basing a history of popular music scenes at that time purely on the available recordings may be appropriate for those artists that did record their music but Southall argues, for local, jobbing musicians another approach is needed. Fortunately there is plenty of evidence of music-making at that time which is more durable than the music itself, such as contemporary newspapers and periodicals, which are particularly useful for confirming facts, figures and locations. In addition, the personal testimony of individuals who were directly involved in popular music performances has its own specific advantages, especially in giving viewpoints which contemporary published sources tended not to cover, such as that of part-time musicians in provincial towns and cities like Chester and Warrington. Southall looks at the music scene from the standpoint of the local scene, at bands that would have been familiar to the troops and locals living during the wartime years in the North West of England.

In Chapter 9, Brian Machin (University of Chester, UK) looks at the recoding on film and photographs of non-white soldiers who fought for the combatant forces involved in the Second World War. Soldiers from many Commonwealth countries fought for the British during the war. However, few images of them exist except for those standard portraits of smiling young men in new uniforms taken in studios and sent home to families. Machin notes that research for his chapter found more images of black French colonial soldiers – about one in ten French soldiers was of colonial origin, mostly North or West African. While there are images of African men in French recruiting material, more often than not, any photographs Machin found were taken by Germans. The French deployed approximately 150,000 Black African soldiers. Given the Nazis beliefs about race these men could expect to be placed in the thick of the fighting and to be treated harshly if they managed to surrender – in itself a difficult task for any soldier in the heat of battle; for a black African soldier an extremely hazardous one. Nazi soldiers and professional photographers working in Propaganda Kompanies (PK) of the Wehrmacht (German Army) exploited the photograph as a means to show the 'negro' in service of the German propaganda machine.

Chapter 1

The Values We Are Fighting For
Propaganda and the World War Two Combat Film

Michael Paris
University of Central Lancashire, UK

Introduction

Towards the end of the Second World War the film producer Walter Wanger, reflecting on Hollywood's contribution to the war effort, rather smugly claimed, "When future historians write the story of World War Two, a bright chapter will be assigned to the contribution of America's motion picture industry in winning the war" (Furhammer and Isaksson, 1971:66). In the main, Wanger was correct, for popular cinema had become, arguably, the single most important channel for the dissemination of Allied propaganda. Film propaganda played a significant part in boosting morale, encouraging the work force to strive for maximum production, explaining the cause of the war, exposing the true nature of the enemy, and reconstructing the visual image of the battlefield for home front America. Perhaps the single most important element in this list was the focus on the essentially democratic nature of American society – a timely reminder for the American people after the extremism and trauma of the Great Depression of what the Republic was intended to be by its Founding Fathers, and crucial reinforcement of the need for national unity in order to wage total war against a vicious and totalitarian enemy. It was also a crucial message of hope for both those who suffered under the heel of the Axis Occupation and those brave enough to resist. This essay examines how propagandist messages operated in the combat film and specifically how the 'democratic way' was promoted in the combat film. The focus is particularly on *Bataan*, directed by the veteran journeyman director Tay Garnett, and released in June 1943; and Howard Hawk's *Air Force*, released in the same year.

On 7 December 1941 the Japanese attack on the American naval base at Pearl Harbour took the Americans by surprise, despite a number of indications from their allies and their own intelligence services that the Japanese were planning for war. The inherent racism of the Americans ensured that they had continually underrated Japanese war technology and their ability to wage modern warfare throughout the 1930s. Thus the successful attacks on the American fleet at Pearl Harbour and on US army bases at Wake Island and in the Philippines created a mood of near panic among the American people. The rapid conquest of Wake and the Philippines, and the simultaneous Japanese invasions of British and Dutch possessions in the Far East, simply increased the panic, suggesting, for many Americans, at least, that the Japanese advance was unstoppable and that for the first time the United States might be facing a major military defeat.

Hollywood Responds to Pearl Harbour

In Hollywood the initial response to the crisis was to turn out a number of cheaply- produced B movies exploiting the situation in the Pacific and vilifying the Japanese and their treacherous 'unprovoked' attack on Pearl Harbour. These hate movies included hastily-put- together productions like *Remember Pearl Harbour, China Girl,* and the documentary *Menace of the Rising Sun.* Shoddily made and with second-rank actors, these films offered little entertainment or enlightenment. The first in this sub-genre was MGM's *A Yank on the Burma Road,* in which Barry Nelson played an American trucker taking supplies along the dangerous Burma Road to China to supply the partisans fighting the Japanese. The Chinese cause means nothing to him for he is interested only in money and girls. However, Japanese brutality and the suffering of the Chinese force him to reassess his values. Still in production in December 1941, Pearl Harbour caused the Studio to undertake a hasty re-write to include the Japanese attack – the final factor to arouse the innate patriotism of our hero and which ensures that he leads the Chinese in a successful attack against the 'dirty little Japs'. The film was released on 28 January 1942. Richard Strauss, writing in the *New York Times,* called it "irresponsible stuff…in making a serious business the background for preposterous action" and denigrated its patronizing attitude towards the Chinese (Morella and Epstein, 1973:63).

Through 1942 these so-called 'Beast from the East' movies continued to flood American movies theatres. Perhaps the most unpleasant was the racist *Little Tokyo USA,* from Twentieth Century Fox and set in the Japanese-American community of 'Little Tokyo' in Los Angeles. The film played to the worst elements of American racism, suggesting that virtually every Japanese American, whether a citizen or not, was active in vast espionage ring determined to undermine the American war effort. The film was an attempt to justify Roosevelt's *Executive Order 9066* which in effect allowed the arrest and internment of almost everyone of Japanese descent living on the West Coast. The Office of War Information, the agency created to supervise American propaganda, deplored these hate movies, arguing "We are fighting a system not a race….." While the OWI manual for studios advised filmmakers to avoid portraying the Japanese as "little buck-toothed and treacherous". However, as Koppes and Black (1987:250) argue in their detailed study of film propaganda,

> In a country steeped in racist stereotypes, and dogged by a history of virulent anti-Japanese prejudice, the temptation to cast the Japanese in racial terms was overwhelming, In trying to soften racist imagery in the movies, OWI was fighting not only Hollywood's racism, but a perverse national reflex.[1]

The guidelines established by the OWI for war propaganda were generally ignored by filmmakers when it came to portrayals of the enemy, and the sinister, lisping, Jap with a penchant for torture, often most chillingly portrayed by the Chinese-born actor Richard Loo, remained a stock figure in Pacific-theatre war films until long after 1945.

Japanese treachery and cruelty was an easy target for patriotic filmmakers looking for a saleable format but it was much more difficult to explain to the public how America's armed forces had been so unprepared, or how easily a perceived racially inferior enemy had inflicted humiliating defeat after humiliating defeat on All-American boys. It was especially difficult to deal with the rapid fall of the Philippines – the major military base in the Pacific and virtually the personal fiefdom of publicity-hungry military-supremo Douglas MacArthur, America's most famous general. MacArthur was a significant and powerful figure in the American military and the long-time commander-in-Chief of the Philippines. Ignoring numerous warnings of Japanese intentions he, like most American commanders, was wrong-footed when the Japanese did invade the islands. So sudden and ferocious was the Japanese attack the Americans quickly became apathetic and continually gave ground to the Japanese until they were trapped on the Bataan Peninsula. At that time, MacArthur, his wife and his press secretary left for Australia, to prepare for the retaking of the islands, it was claimed. His last words to the defenders, "I shall return", were much-quoted in the press, as a mark of his conviction of eventual victory. His troops, those left behind on Bataan and the few who escaped took a different view of the gallant general when they sang,

> Oh you've heard of Doug MacArthur, the Hero of Bataan
> And how he's going to save us from the Empire of Japan
> Well now he's in a Brisbane bar putting up his feet
> While the guys he left behind are up the fucking creek!

---

[1] See also Donald, http//imagesjournal.com.

Of course, no hint of criticism about MacArthur's behaviour appeared in the media.

Wake Island **(1942)**

The first serious combat film about the war in the Pacific, *Wake Island* directed by John Farrow, was released in September 1942. This major production from Paramount told the story of the 400 or so men of the Marine garrison on Wake – a military outpost and Pan –American Airways refueling station for their China Clipper flying boats. The island, over 2000 miles from Pearl Harbour, and over 3000 miles from San Francisco, held out against vastly superior Japanese forces for several weeks until finally forced to surrender. The film shows how in 1940 the Americans, believing that the Japanese are sincere in their desire to find a peaceful solution to the crisis in the Pacific, avoid reinforcing Wake lest it antagonise the Japanese. Only slowly do they improve the defences; their error is naïveté in believing Japanese government statements. The film plays to the 'last stand' theme in American history. A written prologue informs the audience that,

> America and Americans have long been used to victory but the great names of her military history – Valley Forge – Custer's Last Stand – the Lost Battalion – represent the dark hours. There, small groups of men fought savagely to the death because in dying they gave eternal life to the ideas for which they died.
> Such a group was Marine Fighting Squadron 211, and the Wake Detachment of the First Defense Battalion.....the garrison at Wake Island.

The film shows how this small unit, defending a tiny atoll and without hope of reinforcement, successfully held off a Japanese invasion force for over two weeks, until without air cover, and desperately short of food, ammunition and medical supplies, the handful of survivors are forced to surrender. At the finale a voiceover tells us,

> These Marines fought a great fight. They wrote history. But this is not the end. There are other fighting leathernecks, other fighting Americans, 140 million of them, who's blood and sweat and fury will exact a just and terrible vengeance......

Wake Island was the first of the heroic 'last stand' sub-genre of combat movies that reconstructed the dark days of the first year of the war: a cycle that endured throughout the war and ended with John Ford's elegiac saga of the Navy's motor torpedo boat squadrons in the Philippines – *They Were Expendable* in 1945.

The Wake garrison, fight for something worth dying for and their deaths establish a moral superiority over the enemy. Their sacrifice is a wake- up call for all those Americans who stood idly by and allowed militarism and barbarism to flourish through the 1930s. The film was enthusiastically received by the public and critics alike. "....a film which should surely bring a surge of pride to every patriot's breast..." wrote the *New York Times*. While *Newsweek* said it was "Hollywood's first intelligent, honest, and completely successful attempt to dramatize the deeds of an American force on the fighting front" (Morella & Epstein, 1973:77). Yet despite such a reception, Wake Island was little more than a tribute to the bravery and determination of the Marines; and while it certainly avoided the clichéd viciousness of the 'Beast' movies, it did not completely live up to the propaganda functions required by the Office of War Information guidelines. The fall of Wake Island, then, was a powerful rallying cry, America's own 'Dunkirk' moment, perhaps, and which inspired an even more significant Pacific theatre combat movie, *Bataan*, the following year, which, as Jeanine Basinger has pointed out, laid the foundations of the US World War Two combat movie which was remarkably in-line with the OWI's propaganda requirements (Basinger, 1986).

The OWI Manual for Hollywood had suggested that one of the key propaganda elements of feature films should be to demonstrate the democratic way, "films should show democracy at work, avoid racial stereotypes, and show loyal aliens supporting the land of their adoption" (Koppes and Black, 1987:67). Clearly this was difficult to achieve in the combat film but one solution was to focus on the composition of the combat group – the platoon, company, squadron, naval crew or whatever, brought together for the purpose of waging war in the defence of democratic principles and made up of individuals from diverse racial and religious backgrounds, working together in harmony to defeat totalitarianism. *Bataan*, which began production towards the end of 1942, was an early example of a combat film that attempted to show this democratic way in action.

The Japanese invasion of the Philippine Islands began on 10th December. Japanese troops landed in the north of Luzon and began to push the American and Philippino garrison southwards. Despite the fact that the islands were the major American military base for the Pacific region, little thought had been given to their defence. A significant factor was the superiority of Japanese air and naval forces that severely restricted American actions. General MacArthur seemed incapable of coordinating a cohesive defensive strategy and simply responded to enemy offensives by pulling back his forces to new defensive positions. By the first week in January, the survivors were forced to withdraw to the Bataan peninsula and the fortress of Corregidor. Morale among the survivors hit rock bottom when MacArthur and his entourage left for Australia – the media made few references to his escape other than to explain that he had gone to Australia to coordinate Allied defence. It did, however, continually emphasise his famous and very public promise to the Philippino people, 'I shall return'. His troops, of course, put another interpretation on his departure that showed little respect for 'Dug Out' Doug, the 'Hero of Bataan'.

Bataan (1943)

MGMs film *Bataan* is set in the last chaotic days of the Japanese advance. A rag-tag group of thirteen survivors from various units are formed into a rear-guard to defend a bridge against the advancing Japanese to enable other units to escape to Australia. The film is clearly an imaginative re-working of the story of the Spartans last stand at Thermopylae. As the film's dedication makes clear,

> When Japan struck our desperate need was time – time to marshal new armies. Ninety-six priceless days were bought for us – with their lives – by the defenders of Bataan, the Philippine Army …fighting shoulder-to-shoulder with the Americans. To those immortal dead, who heroically stayed the wave of barbaric conquest, this picture is reverently dedicated.

Here death serves a specific purpose – delaying the Japanese advance. The group is commanded by the West-Pointer Captain Lassiter, but he really plays a minor part, the leading figure is clearly the hard-nosed professional soldier Sergeant Bill Dane, who organises the group and assignments. But it is the composition of the group that gives the film its interest and which establishes the formula for the combat movies that would come later, and which serves as a metaphor for a democracy at war. When we meet the group it is no surprise that it includes two Irish-Americans, a Filipino, a Hispanic-American from California (played by Desi Arnez), a Polish-American, a New York Jew, a middle-class college graduate, a mid-western farm boy and, quite unrealistically, a Black-American.

Dane provides firm leadership, experience and compassion and sets an example for the unit. Individual conflicts within the group are resolved by the nature of the mission: the need to sacrifice themselves so that others might live. As Dane tells the men, "Maybe it don't seem to do much good to fight here but we figure the men who died here may have done more than anyone to save the world. It don't matter much where a man dies as long as he dies for freedom". And one by one they die for freedom, shot down by unseen snipers trying to dislodge the band of heroes from their lonely position. Finally only Dane is left. As the Japanese advance, he shouts defiantly, "Come and get it suckers, we're still here - we'll always be here" – a somewhat less elegant but equally powerful variation on 'here we lie obedient to our word'. And as the smoke of battle obscures the last American standing the narrator tells us,

So fought the heroes of Bataan. Their sacrifice made possible our victories in the Coral Sea, at Midway, in the Bismarck Sea, on New Guinea and Guadalcanal. Their spirit will lead us back to Bataan.

Bataan was enormously popular with audiences, offering the first serious, and very brutal, account of the fall of the Philippines. Critics found much to praise in the film and despite some complaints from racist filmgoers, the inclusion of a Black American in the group was generally welcomed. Roy Wilkens of the National Association for the Advancement of Coloured People commended MGM for their achievement claiming that it shows "how superfluous racial and religious problems are when common danger is faced". However, despite his integration into the group, Kenneth Spencer still plays a stereotypical Black character, much given to singing spirituals and calling upon 'De Lawd' in times of stress. The film tells us that he has been serving with the Engineers, but in reality, because of the military's segregation policy, 'coloured' soldiers were only allowed to serve in service battalions until much later in the war. Nevertheless, much of the audience, especially those in the northern states, would have probably been unaware of such policies. His inclusion, however, makes for powerful propaganda and makes *Bataan*, and the combat films that followed a perfect metaphor for a democracy at war.

Dane is initially worried that these men aren't soldiers, "Do you see a soldier among them" he asks Feingold. But they soon step up to the mark and take their responsibilities seriously. They are volunteers, committed to a highly dangerous mission from which there is little chance of survival. At one point Dane, in conversation with his friend Feingold, the New Yorker, doubts their commitment to stick with the mission, but the older more experienced man tells him, "Those kids signed up for this unit just like you and me ..... but I don't think they'll put their tail between their legs and run any more than you will..... They are committed, they know exactly what's at stake and they know that countless other lives depend upon their actions". The group is a microcosm of American society with representatives of many of the major ethnic groups – Spanish, Irish, Polish, Jewish and Black Americans. Personal animosities are resolved or put aside as each man is forced to depend upon the other and accept that without that support their lives will become forfeit and the mission will fail. Social class and economic background mean little here – the college graduate Private Hardy, and even the air force lieutenant, happily defer to the working class Dane's obvious greater experience. This meritocratic ethos is reinforced by Dane, the experienced professional soldier, gradually rising to command. Even before Captain Lassiter is killed there is a clear understanding that he lacks experience and is subordinate to Dane who knows far more about soldiering: "Tell me if I give any stupid orders" he tells the sergeant, and so, in this exemplary democratic unit, it is Sergeant Dane who provides the leadership. The original script called for a fourteenth member of the unit, Private Edward Evening Star who, as the name implies was a full-blood Native American of the Sioux Tribe. According to Janine Basinger, the character was dropped because it linked *Bataan* too closely with the western and because the characterisation was weak (Basinger, 1986:46). The democratic, multi-ethnic nature of the combat group in *Bataan* provide the model for almost all later army films and not only for the remainder of WW11 but through Korea, Vietnam and Iraq as well.

Team Players: *Air Force* (1943)

The nature of the military unit in the army combat film has often earned attention from the historian but far less attention has been devoted an examination of the air war film and how they may have reflected the same democratic principles. This is almost certainly due to the more elitist nature of air forces. Certainly the pre-war public perception of the airmen, created in no small part by the air forces themselves, was of carefully selected and highly trained physical and intellectual elite. Aircrew, the men at the cutting edge of the war in the air, were usually officers, middle-class and often, university educated. Thus, when war came it was essential that the air force was seen to be just as democratised as any other branch of the armed forces, and perhaps more so in the light of the pre-war recruitment policy of the US Army Air Force which had refused to take Hispanics or Blacks. The popularity of flying movies between the wars had seen the dominance of the 'maverick' pilot – the 'lone eagle', the idiosyncratic ace determined to win through whatever the cost to others. Now, at the beginning of a total war aviation movies had to adopt role models more fitted to the concept of a democracy at war. Thus the 'organisation' man, the team player was adopted; and nowhere was this concept more appropriate than among the bomber crew, which in itself provided a useful object lesson for the nation.

Directed by Howard Hawks, the Air Corps were supportive and offered considerable help. According to Hawks' somewhat confused recollections, it was possible that the idea for the film actually came from General 'Hap' Arnold, the Air Corps Chief of Staff (McBride, 1982:90). Written by the talented Dudley Nicholls, the script for *Air Force* was based on an imaginative composite of the individual experiences of bomber crews from the early days of the war in the Pacific. General Arnold helpfully arranged the interviews for Nicholls and provided combat footage so that the writer could get 'the feel' of the air war. When it came to casting, Hawks decided that in order to achieve a realistic documentary quality, he would use relatively unknown actors. Only John Garfield had 'star' status but he had specifically requested a part in the movie. Filmed in Hollywood with some location work in Florida, *Air Force* was released in March 1943.

The film tells of the experiences of the crew of the 'Mary Ann', a B17 Flying Fortress over the first few days of the war. Sent to reinforce the garrison of

Honolulu on 6 December 1941, the aircraft is actually in the air when they pick up the news of the attack on Pearl Harbour. Diverted to an emergency airstrip on Maui, they begin to understand the full extent of Japanese infamy on 7 December when they are attacked on the airstrip by supposedly loyal Japanese immigrants. Ordered to the Philippines they finally arrive at an air base in Manila. On their first bombing mission the *Mary Ann* is damaged and the aircraft commander, Captain Quincannon, is killed. They are ordered to destroy their machine to prevent it falling into the hands of the enemy, but attempt to repair it themselves. As Japanese troops begin to overrun the airfield, they finally finish the repairs and take off for Australia. Near the Australian coast, they spot a Japanese invasion fleet and manage to radio its location to Allied Command. They wait for the bombing force to arrive, and the destruction of the enemy fleet provides the climax of the film. The *Mary Ann* just manages to reach safety and crash lands on an Australian beach. In a final coda we see the surviving members of the crew still serving together with another squadron, and preparing to take off for the first bombing mission against Tokyo.

Certainly, as Bosley Crowther pointed out in his review, the film is 'far-fetched' and over-crowded with incident, but a great "morale-boosting picture."[2] Throughout the film the American armed forces are hard-pressed by a ferocious and merciless enemy; short of equipment, repairing their aircraft with hand-made parts made of scraps, the airmen take whatever is thrown at them and not once do they question their belief in an eventual American victory. The film ends at some point in the future with that victory finally in sight as American bombers take off to begin the onslaught against the Japanese homeland. However, it is in the constant repetition of the democratic nature of American society, as seen through the microcosm of the crew of the *Mary Ann* that is really at the propaganda heart of *Air Force*.

The film opens with a prologue from the 'Gettysburg Address', Abraham Lincoln's great reaffirmation of the basic democratic principles upon which the Constitution of the United States had been built. This reinforces the cast listing which contains no character names, simply the function of the crewman – 'Captain', John Ridgely; 'Navigator', Charles Drake; Gunner, John Garfield, and so on. When we do learn their names it comes as no surprise that we have the same ethnic and religious mix common from other combat films. 'Quincannon' – the Irish-American pilot; 'Xavier Williams' the co-pilot with Hispanic origins; 'Hauser', the navigator of German descent, and 'Weinberg', the Jewish New Yorker - 'Winocki, another gunner, could even be of Native –

---

[2] *New York Times*, 4 February 1943.

American stock. The veteran crew chief, 'Sergeant White' (WASP?) acts as a firm but benevolent father figure and it is his common sense and belief in the 'American way', that provides much of the cohesive force that holds the crew together, performing the same function as Sergeant Dane in *Bataan*.

What is emphasised throughout the movies is the importance of teamwork – a constant repetition of the basic fact that every man in the crew must perform his particularly role to the best of his ability for the bomber to operate effectively. Just before they take off for the flight to Honolulu, the mother of one of the younger members of the crew ask the captain to look after her son. "He'll be looking after me; that's how the crew of a bomber functions", the pilot tells her. The importance of team work is further explored during the long flight when Winocki, the gunner, burning with resentment because he was washed out of pilot training, tells the other gunners he's going to get out of the Air Corps as soon as he can. Blinded by the glamour of being a pilot, he refuses to accept how important everyone's role is. His barely-suppressed anger and resentment earns him a rebuke from Quincannon,

> It takes all of us to make this ship function. We all belong to this airplane. Every man has to rely on every other man to do the right thing at the right time. You play football, Winocki, you know how one man can gum up the whole works. You got to play ball with us and play the game!

When Winocki finds out that both the navigator and bombardier also failed flying school he begins to see reason. Later when he hears about Pearl Harbour and the treachery of the Japanese he becomes determined to play his part to make the Mary Ann an effective war machine. The subsequent adventures of the bomber highlight the special skills of each member of the crew.

The pilot who skillfully flies the *Mary Ann* and brings her safely down on the most primitive of jungle airstrips; the navigator who plots the course that takes the bomber over thousands of miles of trackless ocean; the gunners who defend her against attack and the crew chief who keeps her flying, constantly improvising spare parts and ways to maintain efficiency, all are essential to the continued success of the bomber. As the crew provides a study in democratic collaboration to pursue the war, the part played by the aircraft should not be overlooked. The *Mary Ann*, a Boeing B17 'Flying Fortress', is another member of the team – the best fighting machine that American technology can provide. Despite rough landings and battle damage, the bomber continues to function, to carry the crew on their mission and back to safety. Little wonder, then, that the crew ascribe almost human characteristics to the ship – a mark of their affection and dependence. Film scholar Robin Wood (1981:95) has noted the crew of the *Mary Ann*,

> Appears an ideal democracy in microcosm: the atmosphere is one of voluntary service, of discipline freely accepted; a perfect balance is achieved

between individual fulfilment and responsibility of each member to the whole. The crew enact the values they are fighting for.

The perfection of the democratized bomber crew/infantry unit/naval team fighting together for victory was repeated in a host of air force films in 1943 like *Rear Gunner, Aerial Gunner* and *Bombardier* and in documentary films like William Wyler's *Memphis Belle*. The sentiment was transferred to numerous army and marine movies like *Guadalcanal Diary,* and in 1945 to naval films like *Fighting Lady* and *They Were Expendable*, a standard format through which to demonstrate how America's wars are for freedom, justice and democracy. However, perhaps the most original variation was Zoltan Korda's 1943 production *Sahara* with Humphrey Bogart. This located Bogart's tank crew in North Africa. The sole survivors of a battle with the Afrika Korps, they make for the Allied lines. Along the way they pick up an Australian, a Free Frenchman, Several Englishmen, a Canadian and a Sudanese Rifleman, along with a rather pathetic Italian prisoner and a viciously arrogant Nazi Pilot. The tank became a microcosm of the United Nations fighting its way through hostile territory. A ridiculously improbable story, as *Time Magazine* pointed out, yet one that was splendidly entertaining and perfectly suited to the mood of the times (Morella and Epstein, 1973:156).

The group, the combat unit, is now the standard format for American war films and has been since the formula was established in 1943. Cinematic combat groups have fought and re-fought the Second World War, through Korea War and even those wars that might be considered morally dubious such as Vietnam, Iraq and beyond. In these later wars, however, there was considerably less emphasis on the 'democratic' way.

Conclusion

Feature films were perhaps the single most important channel for the dissemination of American propaganda throughout the Second World War, and much of that propaganda focused on the democratic nature of American society - a timely reminder of the need for national unity in order to wage total war. Films like *Bataan* took the hyphen out of American identity, albeit temporarily, and taught valuable lessons about the nature of democracy and willing collaboration. Yet the irony is that almost within months of the end of the Second World War, the Cold War ushered in a period of fear, repression and censorship in which America almost completely forgot the meaning of democracy and a free society.

References

Basinger, J. (1986). *The World War 11 Combat Movie: Anatomy of a Genre*. USA. New York: Columbia University Press.

Donald, R. R. 'Savages, Swines & Buffoons: Hollywood's Selected Stereotypical Characterizations of the Japanese, Germans and Italians in Films Produced During WW11', *Images: A Journal of Film and Popular Culture*, http//imagesjournal.com.

Koppes, C. R. and Black, G. (1987). *Hollywood Goes to War*. USA. New York, Free Press.

Furhammer, L. and Isaksson, F. (1971). *Politics and Film*. USA. New York: Praeger Publishers.

McBride, J. (ed.) (1982). *Hawks on Hawks*. USA. Berkeley: University of California.

Morella, J. and Epstein, E. (1973). *The Films of World War 11*. USA. Secaucus NJ: Citadel Press.

Wood, R. (1981). *Howard Hawks*. UK. London: British Film Institute.

Chapter 2

Mrs. Miniver (1942): Moral Identity and Creation of the Other

Christopher Hart
University of Chester, UK

Introduction

This chapter is about a fictional English woman called Mrs. Miniver. *Mrs. Miniver* (1942), is one of the most popular World War II films and is often labelled as a 'why we fight'; but this is too general a label. Mrs. Miniver is a film about moral values and is far from a simplistic piece of propaganda. On release, in June, 1942, the film exceeded all expectations, grossing $5,358,000 in North America (the highest for any MGM film at the time). In Britain, it was named the top box office attraction of 1942[1]. Some 555 of the 592 film critics polled by American magazine *Film Daily* named it the best film of 1942. Nominated for 12 Academy Awards in 1942, *Mrs. Miniver* won 6, including 'Outstanding Motion Picture', 'Best Director' and 'Best Screen Play'. But for what possible reasons was, and still is, *Mrs. Miniver* both popular and significant?

William Wyler's War

Mrs. Miniver was directed by William Wyler; European born from a Jewish family. According to Wyler, *Mrs. Miniver* had a clear purpose; to show the isolationists[2] that the people of Britain were not in any war but were fighting for

---

[1] 'Mrs. Miniver,' Excellent Picture of England at War, Opens at the Music Hall June 5, 1942 *The New York Times;* Tribute to Human Courage: 'Mrs. Miniver' Expresses the Inspiring Strength and Dignity of Ordinary Civilians Under Total War, June 14, 1942 *The New York Times;* "Mrs. Miniver": The Family in War-Time, July 8, 1942 *The Times (London);* "Mrs. Miniver" Sets a Record, August 9, 1942 *The New York Times;* Academy Award for 'Mrs. Miniver': Best Film of 1942, March 6, 1943 *The Times* (London).
[2] Ceplair and Englund (1979-1983) report on the hearing held by Congress beginning in the Autumn of 1941 to investigate the claim Hollywood was pushing for the USA to get involved the

freedom and humanity (Herman, 1995:235). The film was to play on a number of interrelated concepts that are typically American. That concept is not 'we're in this together' or the message 'this is the reason we are fighting'. *Mrs. Miniver* is not a 'why we are fighting' film. After the Japanese attack on Pearl Harbor on the 7th December, 1941, Americans knew why they were in the war. *Mrs. Miniver*, was made prior to this attack. It's aim was to tell its American audience 'we have a decision to make' and that decision is about morality and the fate of humanity and all that is wrapped up in such a concept.

Wyler was utterly opposed to Nazism, the Nazis and those who gave implicit support to them. This may have, and probably did, come from his visit, his honeymoon, to Europe in 1935. He had been asked by Carl Laemmle[3] to enquire about the situation of his relatives in Germany. Laemmle devoted most of his efforts and money trying to save people from the Nazi murder camps. Wyler did not have the resources and money some others had in Hollywood. Nevertheless, he was active in petitioning the State Department for visas to allow those in danger, many his relatives, to travel to America. This was no easy matter. The State Department insisted that immigrants should have a financial sponsor and Wyler was not a wealthy man. In July 1941, America closed its border to German-Jewish refugees; leaving many who had been delayed by American bureaucracy to their fate; to end their lives in the death camps[4].

In the summer of 1941 Wyler accepted Sidney Franklin's (an MGM producer) offer to direct *Mrs. Miniver*. The simplicity of Struther's original vignettes[5] of a normal British family provided the ideal material to tell America it had a decision to make. In themselves Struther's short stories (letters) were not about the war but about people and their relationships; how they went about daily life and the things that concerned them. Struther's characters were, however, believable, likable and interesting. As vignettes the tales of *Mrs. Miniver* provide a window into the lives of her family, friends and neighbours. This was an ideal frame of reference to provide an insight into what was happening in Britain to normal people, just like normal Americans.

European war on the side of the British. There was, of course, some truth to this claim. This investigation was later derided as a "sorry example of Congressional dimwittedness." Also see, Moser, 2001; Birdwell, 1999; Casty, 2009.

[3] Carl Laemmle founded Universal Studios. One had to pay for permission to leave Germany and also had to pay when coming to the United States. It is known that Carl Laemmle paid those dues for hundreds of people, not only from Laupheim, is hometown, but from the whole of Wuerttemberg.

[4] Some of this can be attributed to anti-Semitism. Senators Nye and Clark mentioned, during the Congressional investigation, the Jewish background to the filmmakers in Hollywood (Bidwell, 1999:161).

[5] Jan Struther, 1937-39, Court Pages of *The Times*.

The narrative: an overview

Mrs. Miniver is divided into, preface, normal life, class differences and love, war is declared, meeting evil, bombing and destruction, the flower show and death of innocence, and the vicar's speech. The story centres around the Miniver family; Kay Miniver, her husband Clem, children, Vin (at Oxford), Judy (is about 11 years old) and Toby (is about 7 years old). They live an upper middle-class lifestyle that is highly romanticised and Americanised. The story begins in the late summer of 1939.

The film opens with a preface that rolls up the frame:

This story of an average English middle-class family begins with the summer of 1939; when the sun shone down on a happy, careless people, who worked and played, reared their children and tended their gardens in that happy, easy-going England that was so soon to be fighting desperately for her way of life and life itself.

Normal life

Kay (Greer Garson) is seen in what is taken as London, she is shopping. She buys an expensive hat. On the train she meets her local vicar (Henry Wilcoxon). Their exchange goes as follows,

Kay :   I'm afraid I do like nice things. Things far beyond my means
          sometimes. Oh, pretty clothes... ...and good schools for the
          children, the car, the garden, you know.
Vicar :   Yes, I know.
Kay: Does it give you a lovely guilty feeling?
Vicar :   Lovely.
Kay: Oh, vicar!
Vicar :   Fellow sinners.
Vicar :   What will the village say?
Kay :   Oh, I think the village knows... you're a very understanding
          person. That's why you do so much good.

We then get the first indication that life is about to change for Kay and all others she knows. The dialogue continues,

Vicar :   Well, I hope I do. I hope I can when they need me.
Kay: You mean, you think there is trouble coming?

At the station (Balham[6]) she is met by the local stationmaster, Mr. Ballard (Henry Travers). He asks to show her his special rose that he wants to name after her – the 'Mrs. Miniver Rose'. He says, she is the nicest lady in town. Meanwhile, Clem Miniver (Walter Pidgeon) has bought a car - a Lagonda. Later that evening, back home in the 'Starlings' (the Minivers house) while being served dinner by a maid, both eventually confess to their extravagances. They agree that money is for enjoying. Next day they are to pick up their eldest son, Vin (Richard Ney), from the local railway station. He is coming home from Oxford University for the summer holidays.

Vin arrives and the family embraces. Vin is smoking a pipe, as is Clem. His mother comments on how he has changed and that he had shaved off his lovely moustache. He replies that he hasn't got time for the vanities of life with the world in such a serious state and on the verge of possible conflict.

Class differences and love

Vin is with his parents in the garden enjoying refreshments when Carol Beldon (Teresa Wright) arrives. She has gone to see Kay with a request. Carol is the granddaughter of Lady Beldon (May Whitty), the local aristocrat who lives at the Manor House. Carol asks Kay if she could persuade Mr. Ballard to withdraw his rose, the Miniver Rose, from the forthcoming flower show. She fears that if her grandmother lost it would upset her. Vin, full of the excitement of new ideas about social class, power and authority, makes a speech. He criticises Carol, claiming her request is typical of the ruling nobility to maintain their position and control over the people. Carol does not accept Vin's portrayal of her and her grandmother but, nevertheless, apologies to Kay asking her not to approach Mr. Ballard. Carol turns to Vin and tells him that if he feels so strongly about inequalities he needs to stop talking and do something about it, as she has each summer in the slums of the East End of London.

That evening there is a dance at the local boating club. Carol meets Kay and Clem who try to apologise for Vin's outburst earlier that day. Carol surprises them by saying she finds Vin rather nice. Not knowing this Vin sends Carol a note asking her to meet him outside. She meets him and sees through his pompous stance. Vin asks Carol if he can write to her - as the next day she is off to Scotland for the remaining part of the summer holiday. Carol agrees to Vin's request.

---

[6] Balham while being a real neighbourhood in South London is fictionalised in Mrs. Miniver. It is, we may suppose, somewhere in Kent.

War is declared

A few weeks have passed and we see the Minivers at church. In a pew of their own, Vin spots Lady Beldon and Carol. Carol has returned early from Scotland. As the service begins the vicar is brought a note. He brings the service to a halt to announce Britain has declared war on Germany. He suggests people go home and make preparations. As Kay ushers the two young children out of their pew Vin goes over to Carol and Lady Beldon.

That evening the Minivers are all having dinner. The maid's fiancé, called Horace, calls asking to see her. He has been called up to join his regiment. Clem invites Horace to have a drink. Horace makes a toast and Vin announces he is joining the R.A.F. Kay and Clem say nothing but look concerned. Vin decides to visit Lady Beldon and Carol. Kay and Clem agree Vin is very young to be a fighter.

At Lady Beldon's, Vin is met by Carol. He tells her how much he likes her, she replies, this is only the third time they have met. Carol and Vin kiss for the first time. Lady Beldon comes into the room asking who Vin is. She is pompous and opinionated. She makes a sharp comment about the stationmaster for submitting his rose for the Beldon Cup – the top prize in the local flower show. The air raid siren sounds. Vin takes control when Lady Beldon protests that the Germans wouldn't dare bomb her. He insists they make preparations and take shelter in case of an air raid. Lady Beldon does as Vin requests by summoning the butler to tell him to take the staff into the cellar for safety.

Some months later Vin surprises his father (who has joined the Home Guard). He has left university and joined the R.A.F. and with the training cut short, is now a pilot. He has been stationed at an airbase near to Balham. They are in the local boating club, at the bar, the patrons joke about Lord Haw Haw[7] (who was on the radio) and talk about what may have happened to a German pilot recently shot down in the area.

Later that evening the Minivers, with Carol, are having diner. Vin boasts of having passed his training in a short time. Prompted by Toby asking Vin if he is going to marry Carol, Vin proposes to her. Everyone is happy when she says yes to Vin. The happiness is cut short. Vin receives a phone call from his base; he is ordered to return at once.

---

[7] Lord Haw Haw was the nickname of announces who broadcast Nazi propaganda. The most infamous was William Joyce – American born, raised in Ireland with a British passport – who was hanged in 1946.

That evening Kay and Clem go to bed, when turning off the lights, they hear the sound of aeroplane engines. One of the aeroplanes seems to have a problem with its engine. Kay jumps up runs to the window and leans out looking into the sky for the aeroplanes. Clem follows her and both look up to see British fighter planes flying overhead. Kay announces Vin is one of them. She remembered that he had told her of another pilot who when flying over his mothers house would rev his engine. Vin was doing likewise and we see British fighter planes heading into the distance. Vin is going into battle; his mother and father wish him luck.

That same evening Clem receives a phone call asking him to go to the local pub. He goes and finds lots of other boat owners congregating around the bar. They are told to fill up their boats with fuel and motor down river. We see a few, then dozens and eventually hundreds of small motorboats congregating at the mouth of a river. A navy corvette appears and tells them their destination is Dunkirk and if anyone wants to turn back, now is the time. No one turns back.

Meeting evil

Very early next morning Kay stands in her garden overlooking the river. She sees and greets Mr. Ballard. There has been no news from Clem or about Vin. Mr. Ballard quotes from the bible and leaves to go fishing. Kay then notices the German airman under some bushes. He has a gun and forces her into the house. Holding the gun she is forced to bring food and milk. The German is clearly injured. Exhausted he collapses. Kay takes the gun and hides it, then calls the police. She tells them to come quickly and to bring a doctor. The police and doctor arrive as the pilot regains consciousness. As he is been taken away he turns to her stating that he may be finished but more like him will come and destroy them, as they had destroyed thousands of others across Europe. Kay slaps him across his face.

Shortly afterwards Clem and his battered boat arrive home. He asks her if she knows about Dunkirk. She says she does and he replies that he need not then tell her of the horror. Kay puts Clem to bed and then hears aeroplanes flying over Starlings; one is revving its engine; Kay looks out of the window and says, its Vin. Both the men in her life have been into battle and both are, for now, safe.

Lady Beldon visits Kay. Lady Beldon is intent on persuading her that Vin and Carol should not marry; she thinks they are too young. Lady Beldon does not want Carol hurt if anything happens to Vin. Kay shows respect but no deference to Lady Beldon. She asks Lady Beldon how old she was when she married, already knowing the answer. She was 16 years old. Her husband was killed in the First World War. Kay gets Lady Beldon to confess that she has no regrets marrying; admitting she knew her plea would be lost on someone as nice as Kay. Carol and Vin marry, honeymooning in Scotland.

Bombing and destruction

When Carol and Vin are on their honeymoon an air raid forces the Minivers into their bomb shelter that is in the garden. Clem stands outside the shelter surveying the night sky and Starlings. Back inside the shelter the children are asleep in bunks. Clem and Kay joke a little then hear planes above. While Kay knits Clem reminiscences about the book *Alice in Wonderland*, that Kay had been reading to the children.

Then, the climate of the setting changes. We hear the sound of bombing. The shelter shakes a little then a lot. Bombs are falling; the children are woken up, they start to cry and the family huddle together in fear. The shelter is shaken and its door opens a little from the explosions around it. The bombing intensifies; the children scream. The bombing ends. Toby says that they nearly got them that time. Clem looks out of the shelter to see their house badly damaged.

Vin and Carol return from honeymoon to Starlings. They are shocked by the extent of the damage. The house is still livable and Kay shows them to their room. Kay and Clem make light of the damage. In the room Kay has prepared for the newly weds Carol confides in Kay about how happy she is but knows she may lose Vin.

The flower show and death of innocence

At the flower show the entire village is gathered for the announcement of the winners. The last prize to be announced is the Beldon Cup for the best rose. Lady Beldon is told in secret she has won. Nonetheless, she announces that Mr. Ballard's rose is the winner. The audience cheers her with a rapturous applause. Then the air raid siren sounds and everyone leaves. Lady Beldon says people can use her cellar for shelter. Vin knows he will be needed back at his base that is very near to the village. Kay and Carol drive him there. Returning they can see fighter planes battling low above them. Stray rounds from the battle above them hit their car. Carol has been shot. Kay gets her back to Starlings where Carol dies. Later, Vin arrives home and goes to the room where Carol is.

The vicar's speech

The Minivers are at church, standing together with Vin. The vicar stands on a makeshift pulpit, as the church has been badly damaged; the roof is missing and struts hold up some of the walls. He makes a moving speech asking why this terrible thing has and was happening; why Mr. Ballard, the winner only an hour before was killed, why a choir boy was killed and why a young girl, married only a couple of weeks ago in this very church was killed.

The vicar then reads from the Ninety-First Psalm. Lady Beldon is alone in her pew. As the hymn starts Vin leaves his family and goes and stands with Lady Beldon. They hold the hymn book together and sing, 'Onward Christian Solders'. Above, through the open roof, we see British fighter planes in a 'v' formation. The film ends with a call for Americans to buy war bonds.

Analysis of forms in *Mrs. Miniver*

In the following sections the interaction and definitions that make up the scenes showing the events in the film will be explained. The aim, in the first instance, is to make visible for discussion the forms of sociation that Wyler used to construct his story. The second aim is to forward a series of propositions about what *Mrs. Miniver* is about and what is asks from its American audience.

Value exchange

Where does *Mrs. Miniver* get its value from and how? By value we mean the sense of empathy it engendered and in so doing the accolades it received? Value, then, is about what we are, what we stand for, what we cherish and wish to protect and save. These concepts attain visibility in the definition of the situation in which the British are seen as standing in resistance to the Nazis, even in the knowledge, and likelihood, of possible defeat. It may be seen as the only real choice in terms of means for preserving the values held by the British. By values we mean, moral values and the distinction the narrative makes between universalism of ethics and nihilism.

Kay is the personification of humanity; she performs the answers to the question of what kinds of ethics have we here? Clem, on the other hand, personifies the collective of which Kay enacts. Even before the declaration of war we witness the kind of person Kay is and what she values. In the opening scenes she converses with the vicar. She compliments him on the good he does. Her reason is to let him know he is appreciated.

Then, on alighting from the train and in a hurry to get home, she delays her journey to give time to Mr. Ballard, the stationmaster. She responds to his request for her time and listens to him with genuine interest. He explains why he wants to name a rose he has bred to be called the 'Miniver Rose'. It is because Kay has always shown him time and kindness when using the station; in her he has seen an essential goodness. Her morality is something Mr. Ballard recognises and respects. The pivotal scene, however, to exhibit the moral universalism is Kay's interaction with the injured German pilot.

The pilot is young and so is her son Vin. Both are pilots flying missions over hostile, enemy lands. This one is injured. Vin could find himself in a similar situation in occupied Europe. Kay is a mother. She does what she hopes and expects all mothers would do; she tries to care for the injured young man. While afraid of him, she sees a boy who is injured, in an enemy country and alone. He is scared. When he collapses and is momentarily unconscious she removes his pistol - as if a dangerous toy being held by a child. She not only calls the police but specifically makes is clear a doctor is needed.

Illustration 1 *Kay comforts the German pilot*
© Warner Bros. Entertainment Inc.

Kay :   Starlings. I've got that German flyer, the one who escaped. In the kitchen. Yes, I'm all right. Will you come to the back door? He's wounded. Bring a doctor. Thank you.

Kay :   I took your gun.

German :   You call police?

Kay :   Yes. It's much better. Let me help you. There, now. It's much better this way. Really, it is. You'll be wonderfully looked after in a hospital. You'll be safe there. The war won't last forever.

At this stage she does not see him as an enemy or as being right or wrong. He is, to Kay the mother, a young man in need of care and help. However, when he is being taken away Kay's attitude changes abruptly. The German does not reciprocate her compassion. In this scene he becomes the Nazi and all that they stand for and want to do.

German :   We will come. We will bomb your cities... ...like Barcelona... ...Warsaw... ...Narvik, Rotterdam. Rotterdam we destroy in two hours.

Kay :   And thousands killed. Innocent people.

German :   Not innocent! - They were against us!

Kay :   Women and children!

German :   Thirty thousand in two hours. And we will do the same thing here!

She no longer sees the injured son of another women but a Nazi. In response, Kay slaps him. She is disgusted with him, as if he is a juvenile misbehaving. The slap is a chastisement. It shows disappointment; Kay's disappointment in the pilot for not understanding. His behaviour is categorised as infantile; he does not seem to know what, from Kay's standpoint, is right or wrong[8]. His focus is on the external outcomes of his and his country's actions. Death and destruction of whomever, regardless of their involvement or innocence, is irrelevant to him. The pilot is, of course, not a child. He is a man. As such, his egocentric view of what is wrong is perplexing. This in itself would not really matter if it were not for his statement,

German :   Soon we finish it. I'm finished... ...but others come... ...like me. Thousands, many thousands. Better. All of this... ...you will see. You will see. We will come. We will bomb your cities...

This is the face and attitude of one solitary Nazi. He makes it clear he is but one among many thousands of others, just like him. Here in is the danger and the warning. Nazis are a totality without moral anchors. They show deference not to the common good but to the power of the Nazi collective. If they are like this pilot and have his juvenile morality then a dark age threatens not only Europe but also the world.

Norms as moral choices

Kay personifies the humanity of the British. In the scene with the Nazi pilot it is words that make the contrast; Kay values humanity while the Nazi values destruction and killing. Kay knows Clem and Vin will be fighting the Nazis. In the previous event Clem is called out in the middle of the night. He does not know why; he goes because it his duty to go. He answers the phone; Kay immediately thinks it is Vin. Clem tells her it is only the river patrol and he is to report to the clubhouse of the boating club. She gets up to ensure Clem has a drink and food to take with him.

Where Kay's encounter with the Nazi is based on words, Clem's personification of their shared morality is more visual. Clem and the others are informed they are to sail down river to Ramsgate. We see a line of small motorboats following each other. The river widens and we see more and more little boats passing down river through the countryside, passing villages with churches; this is the land, the places and culture that are threatened by

---

[8] The comments and observations made in this section have their origins in the works of Kohlberg (1981) and generally the philosophy of ethics.

destruction. Eventually Clem pulls to a stop, saying there are thousands of them, boats that is. A British warship appears and an announcement over a loud speaker is made.

> Attention, everyone. Attention, please. Switch off your engines.
> As you know, the British Expeditionary Force... is trapped between the enemy and the sea. Four hundred thousand men are crowded on the beaches... under bombardment from artillery and planes.
> Their only chance to escape annihilation rests with you.
> Your destination is Dunkirk.
> It's my duty to tell you that the effort is not without risk.
> You are asked to cross miles of open sea... many of you in small boats that are far from seaworthy.
> Shore guns and enemy aircraft are going to make it tough for you.
> Any of you who wish to withdraw may do so now.

The camera scans across the faces of the boats showing the faces of the men. All look resolute. Clem turns to his mate, Nobby and asks, "All right with you?" Nobby gives the affirmative.

The armada of small boats set off together. The British already know what happened at Dunkirk. Here we see the moral conscience of the men. They do not turn back but as one, go towards danger from the sea and the enemy. The Germans had defeated the armies of Europe. The British army (and others) is surrounded; they face annihilation on the beaches only 20 or so miles away.

Illustration 2 *The small boats going to Dunkirk*
© Warner Bros. Entertainment Inc.

There is a possibility that through collective action they can be saved.

The normative message here is not a meta-ethical statement; there is no recourse to discussion of the moral facts. The situation has, however, been described to the men in the small boats. They know the dangers they will face. But do they all go because they feel they 'ought' to? The notion of ought is problematic[9]. The notion of 'ought' is too simplistic; it has too many possibilities for being contradicted. For example, when Kay takes the pistol from the German pilot, what ought she have done? She ought to have seen him as the enemy. Initially she does not do this. She sees him as a human being, someone else's son in need of care. She calls for the police, as she would be expected to do so. But she also stipulates a doctor is needed. There is no ought in the stipulation; it is an act of her humanity. The men go because they, as individuals, see it as the civilised course of action[10]; the armies on the beaches of Dunkirk need help and the men in the little boats have the means to help them. The men are acting rationally; they know what they are doing and what might happen to them. Their decision is, regardless of this knowledge, to go. Here we might say that Kay's act of individual humanity is matched by the collective humanity displayed by the men.

The display of values we see in these two sets of events is achieved with a contrast structure. Kay's nurturing concerns are contrasted with the pilot's lack of conscience. This establishes the difference between Kay, as British, and the pilot, as German and Nazi. Clem faces danger (and possible death) but makes a decision to go to Dunkirk. The contrast here is the decision; to go and do something or not to go and allow others to[11]. This establishes the difference between those who will defend humanity and those who will not.

Americanisation and value sharing

Mrs. Miniver is a simple story. It has very little action; no great acts of heroism, violence or sex. As cinema - the visual story telling genre that abstracts, categorises and typifies - it is primarily for entertainment. Wyler and the writers artfully know their intended audience and that they demand to be entertained. Character types, situations and setting are drawn to resonate with that audience and they are provided with a good story. Simple it may be *Mrs. Miniver*, nevertheless, shows a lot of content, all of which is intentional. That content consists of degrees of interaction (or sociation) among geographically and culturally near individuals and groups – the people of Balham. But not near to Americans. It is only about (with the exception of the German pilot) the people of Balham, living in a small village in England. The different

---

[9] Phillippa Foot (2009) argues that people do not act morally because they feel they ought to. She argues they behave morally when motivated by other factors - that are inherently and naturally human.

[10] John Stuart Mill (1863) talks about morality and civilization. He argues that morality is a powerful principle of human nature and to reach potential requires nurturing.

[11] The message is this is about making decisions and, as the audience, we heard Carol say to Vin, "do you do anything about it? A bit of action is required now and then."

interactions communicate relationships between the characters; that in turn (not separately) make visible for recognition the concept bounding that interaction. For example, Kay, having taken the gun from the German pilot, calls the police and also asks for a doctor to be sent. Visible for understanding here, is the humanity she shows to the enemy. Humanity is a key concept in *Mrs. Miniver* that drives the meaning of most events in the narrative.

In viewing (or reality) the concepts - such as, kindness, mercy, compassion and sacrifice - are not indistinguishable from the content of interactions and relationships and nor are these concepts unrelated; they do not stand alone; they form a meta-concept which is the story and the meaning it is intended to convey to its intended audience. This, in part, may explain why *Mrs. Miniver* though popular in Britain, was more popular with Americans. The forms of interaction were

Illustration 3 *Starlings*
© Warner Bros. Entertainment Inc.

recognisable to both audiences as were the settings in which the characters performed sociation. But some concepts such as the home (Starlings) were utterly Americanised forms of sociation.

Starlings is an idealised version, not of a British house, but an imagined home, of a typical American middle-class family. It has the white picket fence with a gate[12]. It is on a wide lane. It is an American's idea of house and home. Starlings then, may be said to have sufficient features to render it universally recognisable, and able to be placed as 'like us', by the collective American consciousness[13]. The idea of the small town with the order given by white-picket-fenced houses is an enduring concept in the American popular

---

[12] Colonial Williamsburg style fence and house appears in numerous films, including, *A Family Affair* (1937), *The Philadelphia Story* (1940), *My Favorite Wife* (1940), *It's a Wonderful Life* (1946), and *Young at Heart* (1954). In the UK actual houses were a mix of red brick, pebbledash and half timbering with red clay tile roofs and tile-hung walls. Other features included leaded glass in iron casement windows set in wood, heavy oak doors with iron nails and fittings - all reminiscing from Jacobean and Tudor times. The wooden colonial style with different levels has never been a design common to the British suburbs.

[13] Orvell (2012:14) argues "Again and again we find the small town offered as a microcosm of America, yet an American in which conflicts are resolved, differences elided, a world that stands symbolically for order."

imagination. Miles Orvell (2012) makes a number of insightful observations about the small town and its place in American popular culture and imagination. The small town, for Orvell, is engrained in the American idea; standing for freedom, democracy, order and decency. It is no coincidence that *Mrs. Miniver* and everything that happens in the film (except Dunkirk) happens in a small town reminiscent of the imagined small town America.

The people of Balham are friendly, happy and show contentment. Differences exist, as between Kay and Lady Beldon and between the latter and Mr. Ballard. Nonetheless, they are respectful and courteous to one another. Kay never shows deference to Lady Beldon. Even Lady Beldon, the fierce matriarch, shows humanity when she awards the prize for the best rose to Mr. Ballard.

Starlings is an essential feature of the setting for the unfolding of the action. We initially see Starlings as the home of the Minivers. It is unassuming, neat and full of life. Clem comes home to be greeted by Judy and her piano teacher; Toby comes down the stairs with his cat; the maid goes about her business as Kay talks on the telephone. The children eat super, dressed in dressing gowns, followed by Kay and Clem sitting down to dinner. This is their lives; ordinary, normal and uneventful. But its neatness and boundary is compromised. When Vin returns with Carol from their honeymoon he is shocked to see the damage done by the bombings. The

Illustration 4 *Starlings' bomb damage*
© Warner Bros. Entertainment Inc.

homecoming to Starlings of the honeymooners opens with a shot looking through the smashed downstairs windows. Once inside Carol and Vin survey the complete destruction of the dining room. The same place, not so long ago, he proposed to Carol and all of them were happy. On going through the font door Clem begins talk and normalises the damage to Starlings.

Clem:	Well, here we are. Welcome home, such as it is.
Vin:	It's quite a mess.
Carol:	It must've been dreadful.
Kay:	Oh, it's not as bad as it looks. We just didn't have time to clear it all up.
Clem:	The dining room there got the worst of it. But I always did want to do that room over.
Kay:	The upstairs is quite all right.

Then the sound of a piano being played is heard. We see Judy playing and Toby waving as if conducting the music. Happiness returns to the Miniver home.

Starlings, then, provides a reference point and major concept for the American audience, allowing them to see their cultural concepts related to home and family within a familiar, if idealised, object: the picket-fenced house. This is the place where people, the Minivers, were safe. But that happiness has been invaded and their safety threatened.

Conflict and decisions

Can the decision to fight be objective or is it always subjective? Objectively, the British faced defeat and the degradation that would bring. The Nazi war machine had been spectacularly successful and utterly ruthless in taking over northern Europe. Land based and airborne blitzkrieg had overwhelmed and destroyed the fighting forces of several countries and devastated major cities. In his parting outburst to Kay, the German pilot had made it very clear what the British people could expect. The same message was heard in the pub when over the radio we hear Lord Haw Haw exclaiming,

> [Radio] attention, England.
> This is your English friend in Germany again.
> Now, listen carefully while there's yet time - time to avoid further useless bloodshed.
> ...it's now eight months since your government declared war - eight months of progressive disaster for the enemies of the German Reich.
> France has been utterly defeated as I told you she would be, if you remember, and her invincible armies completely crushed.
> I need hardly tell you that England comes next on the list.

To fight in the face of possible annihilation suggests a supra-individual claim has been made and generally accepted by the people of Balham; they represent the British stand and character.

Kay may be seen as the representative of this claim. Kay, in particular, acts to focus this sentiment. Kay's morality brings into relief the evil she, Clem, Vin and Carol are against and the morality they want to defend. It is not a call to fight or to say this is what we are fighting against (though this is present). The call is about saving humanity.

There is, of course, a hint of pessimism. Mr. Ballard is pessimistic about winning the best rose competition. The idea of the rose (the symbol of the English), social class and opposites dominates the initial scenes until the air raid shelter scene. Mr. Ballard wins the competition against the odds. The weight of custom and expectation were against him; yet, he wins. He wins because he dared to enter the rose into the competition. Others saw his rose and saw a better rose than that entered by Lady Beldon. But the judges, afraid of her, award her the first prize. The judges rather than be the cause of conflict, acquiesced to the assumed authority of Lady Beldon. The judges were weak in the face of the facts. Nevertheless, Lady Beldon sees what has happened and awards the first prize the Mr. Ballard.

Lady Beldon did the right thing at the right time. She need not have done. If she had not, no one would have known, except the deferential judges. In doing the right thing, she makes a decision that goes against her own interests. Her decision was an end in itself. She did not do it because she faced naming and shaming; there would have been no real consequences. The reaction from the audience was, however, rapturous support. They recognised her decision for what it was; an honest recognition of the fact that her rose was good but there was a better one. The outcome was that both were winners; Mr. Ballard won the prize for best rose and Lady Beldon the prize for honesty.

The flower show is, then, about moral behaviour. It is about doing the right thing. The Minivers and the people of Balham (AKA the British) resisted and in doing so intensified the conflict because, as individuals, they saw their position within the supra-personal goal of saving humanity; they are doing the right thing by taking a moral stance. This common basis meant resistance and the costs associated with it. Hence, the escalation of the conflict, the costs and increasing irreconcilability, intensity and stubborn collective will to fight. The vicar says in the closing scene,

> Well, we have buried our dead... ...but we shall not forget them. Instead, they will inspire us with an unbreakable determination... ...to free ourselves and those who come after us... ...from the tyranny and terror that threaten to strike us down.

The increasing intensity of the dynamics for the common people, suffering the death of the bell ringer (Mr. Ballard) and the young wife, is bitterly felt by the audience. For the Minivers and Lady Beldon they exhibit common experiences that we, the audience, can understand, and thus see they (and possibly we also) have a common stance that gives us membership to the cause. That cause looks grim but there is no hint of pessimism or doubt. Mr. Ballard's simplicity and modesty and Lady Beldon's moral decision shows us that right can win.

Time and decisions

Time and temporality are important properties of *Mrs. Miniver*. In the opening scenes we see Kay getting on a London bus. She hesitates,

Bus conductor :   All right, lady, on or off, please.
Kay :   Oh, yes.

The bus conductor, as he is taking payments for tickets, is asked by Kay to stop the bus,

Bus conductor :   Fares, please.
Kay :   I'm sorry, conductor. Would you mind stopping?
Bus conductor :   Leaving us already?

Kay has made a choice. She is seen rushing along a busy London street, passing shops and weaving in and out of the crowd. The accompanying sound track is of bells. She arrives at a milliner's shop. On entering, the shop assistant says,

Shop assistant :   Why, Mrs. Miniver.
Kay :   You know, I... Don't tell me it's gone.
Shop assistant :   Just a minute.
Kay :   Oh, I was so afraid you'd sold it.
Shop assistant :   No. We knew you'd come back.
Kay :   I know it's foolish and extravagant... ..but I've simply
                     got to have it. Yes, pack it up quickly, don't give me
                     time to think.

Kay has had the time to do something for herself. She knows what she has done is a selfish act but not one with real consequences. She discusses her purchase, with the vicar, in the next scene. Kay gets on a commuter train where she meets her local vicar. They talk about the frivolities of buying nice things. The lightheartedness of the initial interaction turns serious when Kay asks the vicar,

Kay : You mean, you think there is trouble coming?

The vicar replies, that it is here, pointing to imminent arrival of Lady Beldon. He has, however, already said that he hopes he can do good when the time comes. The sense of the near future is in the present. We do not know the specifics of who 'they' are but it can be inferred they are the villagers, his parish and members of the local Church. The village stands for place and people: the English. The vicar's fear for the future is mixed with doubt about his own bravery and role in what he sees as inevitable. His hope is that he can meet the challenge of doing good for others when the time comes.

Once the train reaches Balham we see the station-master, Mr. Ballard.

Mr. Ballard :   I was looking for you on the...
Kay :   I missed it by two minutes. Isn't that shameful?
Mr. Ballard :   Well, time and tide waits for no man.

Kay :	And trains neither.
Mr. Ballard :	Are you too late, ma'am, to spare me a moment?
	I got something to show you.
Kay :	Well, I...
Mr. Ballard :	It's something very special.

Although in a hurry, Kay stops. She hears Mr. Ballard's request and listens to him, showing understanding that he wants to show her something important to him; something special that he wants to share with her.

This is the 'rose scene'. Mr. Ballard shows Kay *the* rose. He explains why it is special and that it takes time, effort and breeding to produce something so special. With that Kay mistakenly thinks he is asking her to give a name to his rose. Mr. Ballard corrects her, "No, ma'am, I got a name for it..."

Mr. Ballard :	I want to call it the 'Mrs. Miniver'. If you'll pardon me,
	ma'am... ...I've watched you go in and out of town for years
	now... ...and you've always had time to stop and have a word
	with me... ...and I've always waited for you to come home...
	...and you remind me of the flower.

Two things are happening here. The first is the film is, in itself, asking the audience to take time and listen to what is being asked of them.

Do not ignore the message, but take the time to hear what is being said and what you will be asked to do. The second happening here is the simple and stated symbolism of Kay and the rose; and all that the rose stands for and what she stands for; beauty, honesty, and simplicity. A part of this is the link to morality and the British. The rose, as Mr. Ballard remarks, needs breeding, care and time to be so beautiful. Such a thing of beauty does not come from nothing nor is it created quickly. The British unlike the Nazis have a long history. Kay is British and embodies that history and what it stands for. This includes being civilised; this we see in her actions with Mr. Ballard.

Illustration 6 *The Miniver Rose*
© Warner Bros. Entertainment Inc.

Taking time is also shown to be about using the time one has. When Vin meets Carol for the first time the *use* of time is the message. Carol has come to see Kay to ask her to ask Mr. Ballard to withdraw his rose from the forthcoming flower competition.

Vin criticised Carol and her grandmother. His mother interjects, apologising for Vin's bad manners.

Vin :   Don't apologize for me. I mean everything I say.
Carol :   Well, I'm glad to hear it, but do you do anything about it?
Vin :   Do? Why, what do you mean?
Carol :   If you feel something is wrong, what are you doing about it? I've spent holidays the last few years doing settlement work in London slums.
Vin :   You wallow in luxury all the year...
Carol :   I don't wallow!
Vin :   And think a few weeks playing Lady Bountiful...
Clem :   Come, Vin.

Carol :   It's not much, perhaps... ...but it's the only thing I know. What have you been doing?
Vin : I?   Well...
Carol :   I see. Just talk. Well, that's all right. It's easier.
Vin :   Listen, I didn't say...

In a calm retort Carol delivers the crucial line,

Carol :   Oh, don't apologize. I know how comfortable it is to curl up with a book full of big words... ...and think you're going to solve the problems of the universe. But you're not, you know. A bit of action is required now and then.

Carol does not want an apology but to let Vin know talking will not solve the problems of the world. The inference here is, talking will not solve the problems of conflict with the Nazis. Action, whatever it may be, needs to be decided on and time is running out.

What the vicar feared has come and war is declared. Life for the Minivers and everyone in the village has changed. Vin announces he has joined the R.A.F. as a flyer. The narrative compresses time to take the viewer through the first months of the war and into the summer of 1940[14]. Just prior to Dunkirk Vin has achieved his 'wings' and is now a pilot while Clem has joined the Home Guard. Vin meets his father in the local pub, surprises him and declares that even though the training was cut short he still managed to attain the rank of pilot officer.

---

[14] Dunkirk was between 27th May to 4th June, 1940. Clem motors off to Dunkirk after Vin has been seen flying off into battle.

Clem and Vin go back to Starlings where they are met by Kay and Carol. Vin does not know which to kiss first. That evening, over dinner Vin is prompted by his much younger brother to ask Carol to marry him. Vin says he was going to wait until the time was right but this is now wartime. He asks and she agrees to be his wife. As congratulations are being made Vin receives a telephone call from his base. He is needed and must go. The scene takes us from joy and happiness to trepidation and fear. Vin may be going into battle. This may be the last time they see him. What time they may have with Vin becomes the dominant theme.

Lady Beldon protests the marriage on the basis of what might happen to Vin, nonetheless, Vin and Carol marry. Returning from their honeymoon, Kay has prepared a bedroom for the newlyweds. Kay and Carol are in the room. Kay turns to Carol pointing out the view from the window,

Kay :   Have you seen the view here? It's really beautiful.
Carol :   Oh, it is.
Kay :   You're happy?
Carol :   Of course.

But the reality of the situation comes to the fore. These are not normal times. This is the summer of 1940 and Britain is the last main country standing in opposition to the Nazis in Western Europe[15]. The *Battle of Britain*[16] is about to begin followed by the *Blitz* of London and other British cities and towns[17]. Vin is a pilot and his uncertain future is shared by his mother and wife. Their common love and concern for Vin is voiced.

Carol :   I've had a lifetime of happiness in these last two weeks.
Kay :   But, Carol, that's only the beginning.
Carol :   Kay, I'm not afraid to face the truth...
            ...I know that I may lose him. He's young and he loves life, but he
            may die. Let me say it. He may be killed any day, any hour. You
            must have faced that in your mind.
Kay :   Yes, I've faced it.
Carol :   Then you know that every moment is precious. We mustn't waste
            time in fear. You won't hate me for saying this, will you?

---

[15] In July Churchill broadcast, "We shall seek no terms. We shall tolerate no parley. We may show mercy. We shall ask none." Norway fell to the Nazis in September, Greece to the Italians in October.
[16] The Battle of Britain was between 10 July - 31 October, 1940.
[17] The Blitz was between 7 September 1940 – 31 May 1941.

Kay :   No, Carol.

Carol :   I will be very happy. Every moment that I have him. Every moment.

If I must lose him, there'll be time enough for tears. There'll be a lifetime for tears.

Vin is a pilot. The expectation is it will be the servicemen – such as Vin - who will be the first to be killed. It is, however, Carol, the civilian, wife and granddaughter, who is killed. Carol did not have time to cry for Vin. The message is, time is not to be taken for granted, by anyone.

Conclusions: The Decision

Mrs. Miniver is a film that aims to present the experiences of others in ways that the audience can both empathise and then sympathise with. It is a film that provides surrogate experience and knowledge to those in America who, as yet, lack the knowledge, or the will to seek out the knowledge, of the dangers to humanity posed by the Nazis and those nations that acquiesce to them. *Mrs. Miniver* is a morality tale. Although released in June, 1942 the film plays with temporality. The *Battle of Britain* and the *Blitz* have actually happened; but not in the film. Nevertheless, as a moral tale it aims to show what has happened to people 'like us' who have made a moral decision to fight evil.

This allows for the telling of a prophecy of a possible future for these people, the English[18], who have taken a stand, who face possible defeat. If they are defeated a new world order will be created based on intolerance, hatred and fear; the antithesis of humanity.

Technically *Mrs. Miniver* has a number of problems to overcome. Chief among these is to provide the means, through entertainment, for an ambivalent audience to empathise with the characters on screen. How, given the geographic, social, economic and political distance and differences between the audience and events in Europe can a film elicit a sufficient surrogacy of understanding to bring about a change in mass consciousness? An aspect of this problem is to create a unity of understanding that goes beyond the mere aggregation of individuals. The mode of understanding requires in itself to be familiar to the audience. The content of events and of experiences of those events by people 'like us' needs to be sufficiently anchored in kinds of imagined reality to engender reciprocal relationships of recognisability. That relationship is not one based on naive awareness of the experiences of others. It requires a moral reciprocity in which the masses share similar recognition about places and hence feeling about what they stand for. It is Starlings, the white-picket

---

[18] By which we mean the British.

fenced home of the Minivers and the small town community of Balham that achieves the recognition and categorisation that the British are people 'like us', valuing what we value.

But this does not answer the question why the British decided to stand and fight. After Dunkirk the British were the last resistance in the west to Nazism. They could have capitulated; made a treaty with Hitler and acquiesced like the Vichy French. But they had not. They had made a mass and popular decision to make a stand and fight no matter what[19]. Why, given the high probability of defeat and the horrors this would entail, had the British made this decision? This is the other objective of *Mrs. Miniver*; to tell why the British had made this incredible decision; were they brave, stubborn or stupid? What did the British see and know that we, in America did not see and know? Several scenes provide the answer: Kay's encounter with the Nazi and what he stood for; Clem's decision to go to Dunkirk to save the lives of beleaguered soldiers; Lady

Illustration 7 *The vicar's speech*
© Warner Bros. Entertainment Inc.

Beldon's decision to award the prize, for best rose, to Mr. Ballard and Carol marrying Vin knowing he may be killed. These are not normal acts but acts of bravery and making a claim for the higher morality.

Mrs. Miniver could be seen to be about normal people in abnormal times; facing an uncertain future. They live in a small village and have, until now, gone about their daily lives of raising children, attending flower shows and shopping. War has been forced on them; it has destroyed their homes and killed people they loved. Yet, they resist and express no doubts as to whether they should fight on. *Mrs. Miniver* is really about making a choice. That choice is for America and Americans. *Mrs. Miniver* shows people making decisions

---

[19] Obviously there were dissenting voices that looked to making a treaty with Hitler. See McDonough, F., Brown, R., and Smith, D. (2002).

based on a taken-for-granted morality. Dreadful things are happening all around them yet, they continue to show compassion, kindness and care. *Mrs. Miniver* is, then, about moral choices.

Wyler tries to show that meaningfulness comes from individuals being able to live their lives no matter how seemingly, at times, frivolous it may be. The purpose of life is given in the fact of living it. The people of Balham are shown living their lives free from threat and dogma. We see social distinctions between the characters but never deference or humility. They live out their morality. It is a fundamental way in which they relate to each other and make sense of the world in regard to themselves, others and the world at large. This is a strong morality; it is internalized as the end in itself. This is contrasted with the morality of the 'other'; the Nazi.

The German pilot is pivotal to the moral choice. For Wyler, he is not merely a German; he is a Nazi. He exhibits the moral opposite to Kay. Where she stands for the natural morality of humankind, he stands for the denial of her morality. He is cold, indifferent and merciless. He relishes the thought of destruction and bringing suffering to others. His moral choice is that of the Nazi. It brings with it the Nazi antithesis to Kay's natural morality.

This is Wyler's film and message. Although the United States is now in the war, on the side of the British, Wyler's message still has the power to resonate. He is showing the American audience that isolationism was wrong. That there was a choice to be made and as Americans in a free society have made the right choice, for the right reasons; they have not stood back and sided with those who deny the innate morality that characterises humanity but chosen to stand with *Mrs. Miniver*, and defend civilization.

The final scene formulates the claim.

> We in this quiet corner of England... ...have suffered the loss of friends very dear to us. Some close to this church. George West, choirboy. James Ballard, stationmaster and bell-ringer... ...and the proud winner, only an hour before his death... ...of the Beldon Cup for his beautiful Miniver rose.
> And our hearts go out in sympathy... ...for the two families who share the cruel loss of a young girl... ...who was married at this altar only two weeks ago.
> The homes of many of us have been destroyed... ...and the lives of young and old have been taken. There's scarcely a household that hasn't been struck to the heart.
> And why? Surely you must have asked yourselves this question. Why, in all conscience... ...should these be the ones to suffer? Children, old people... ...a young girl at the height of her loveliness. Why these? Are these our soldiers?
> Are these our fighters? Why should they be sacrificed? I shall tell you why.

Because this is not only a war of soldiers in uniform... ...it is a war of the people. Of all the people. And it must be fought not only on the battlefield...

...but in the cities and in the villages. In the factories and on the farms. In the home and in the heart... ...of every man, woman and child who loves freedom.

Well, we have buried our dead... ...but we shall not forget them. Instead, they will inspire us with an unbreakable determination... ...to free ourselves and those who come after us... ...from the tyranny and terror that threaten to strike us down.

This is the people's war. It is our war. We are the fighters. Fight it, then. Fight it with all that is in us. And may God defend the right.

References

Birdwell, M. E. (1999). *Celluloid Soldiers: Warner Bros.'s Campaign against Nazism*. USA, New York: New York University Press.

Casty, A. (2009). *Communism in Hollywood: The Moral Paradoxes of Testimony, Silence, and Betrayal*. USA, Maryland: Scarecrow Press.

Ceplair, L. and Englund, S. (1983). *The Inquisition in Hollywood: Politics in the Film Community, 1930-1960*. USA. Berkeley: University of California Press.

Foot, P. (2009). Morality as a System of Hypothetical Imperatives. In S. M. Cahn, and P. Markie, *Ethics: History, Theory, and Contemporary Issues*. USA, New York: Oxford University Press.

Herman, J. (1995). *A Talent for Trouble: The Life of Hollywood's Most Acclaimed Director, William Wyler*. USA, New York: G.P. Putnam's Sons.

Kohlberg, L. (1981). *Essays on Moral Development, Vol. I: The Philosophy of Moral Development*. USA, San Francisco, CA: Harper & Row.

McDonough, F., Brown, R., and Smith, D. (1998). *Neville Chamberlain, Appeasement, and the British Road to War*. UK, Manchester: Manchester University Press.

Mill, J. S. (1863). *Utilitarianism: Of the Ultimate Sanction of the Principle of Utility*. http://www.gutenberg.org/cache/epub/11224/pg11224.txt. Chapter 3.

Moser, J. E. (2001). Gigantic Engines of Propaganda: The 1941 Senate Investigation of Hollywood. *Historian*, Volume 63, Issue 4:731–752, June 2001.

Orvell, M. (2012). *The Death and Life of Main Street: Small Towns in American Memory, Space, and Community*. USA, Carolina: The University of North Carolina Press.

Struther, J. (1937-39). 'Mrs. Miniver'. First published on the Court Page of *The Times*, London, at intervals from 1937 to 1939. First published in book form by Chatto and Windus, London, UK. 1939. First American edition,

Harcourt Brace, New York, USA. 1940.

Wyler, W. (Director) (1942) *Mrs. Miniver* [Motion Picture]. United States: MGM: Warner Bros. Entertainment Inc.

Chapter 3

Women in *Dad's Army*

Phylomena H. Badsey
University of Wolverhampton, UK

Introduction

The popular BBC comedy television series *Dad's Army*, written and produced by Jimmy Perry and David Croft, was first broadcast between 1968 and 1977, comprising 80 episodes in nine series and three Christmas specials. It was the first British television situation comedy series made about the Second World War; set in a fictitious provincial town called Walmington-on-Sea on the south coast of Kent, and following the activities of the Home Guard's Number 1 Platoon, D Company, East Kent Regiment, whose task is to protect the seafront 'from Stone's Amusement Arcade to the Novelty Rock Emporium' against German invasion. All the principal characters are men, and the very title of the series suggest a masculine world, with no women's involvement either as important characters in the series or in the real Home Guard. In fact women appear or are referenced in all but four of the 80 episodes of Dad's Army, in many cases as significant characters, and some women's characters appear frequently throughout the series. Women also played an underappreciated role in the real Home Guard, but even more as part of the wider society that supported it.

Cultural artifact

Dad's Army has become an important cultural artefact and an icon in terms of the British nation's collective memory and nostalgia for the Home Front during the Second World War. Sold around the world, the series is still being repeated on BBC television over 35 years later. The original transmission of the series' last ever episode, 'Never Too Old' (Series 9, Episode 6), transmitted on 13th November 1977, was watched by an estimated 12,524,000 million people (McCann, 2002:213). An episode of *Dad's Army* is on constant stand-by to be broadcast by the BBC in case of technical failure preventing the transmission of a scheduled programme (McCann, 2002:222). The series has had both an enormous media footprint, and impact on the British collective visual memory of the Second World War and how the British Home Front reacted to the threat of invasion in May 1940. It was featured in an exhibition staged at the Imperial War Museum, London, in 1974 that ran for nine months, as part of a wider display about the Second World War. It has been adopted as a feature film (1971) a radio programme (1974), and a stage musical (1975-76), plus releases of recordings of the show and its associated war-time songs; all of which were enormously popular with the public. Also in the 1970s, a board-game of *Dad's Army* was manufactured, together with a comic strip, colouring and 'dot-to-dot' books, souvenir magazines and annuals. Amateur and professional theatre productions of *Dad's Army* are frequently staged, and the series even has its own appreciation society founded in 1993, with a worldwide membership, a web-site and discussion bulletin board, and merchandise for sale (McCann, 2002:272). A museum dedicated to *Dad's Army* has been created at Thetford, Norfolk, were much of the location filming was done, The Friends of the museum commissioned a full side bronze statue of Captain George Mainwaring which was unveiled in June 2010. The DVD collection of the series, released in 2007, has also sold well and attracted a new and younger viewing audience.

The actors and writers

Dad's Army was an ensemble production, with the seven principal characters all members of the Walmington-on-Sea Home Guard platoon: Captain George Mainwaring (Arthur Lowe), Sergeant Arthur Wilson (John Le Mesurier), Lance Corporal Jack Jones (Clive Dunn), Private Charles Godfrey (Arnold Ridley), Private Joe Walker (James Beck), Private James 'Jock' Frazer (John Laurie) and Private Frank Pike (Ian Lavender), frequently joined by Mr. William Hodges (Bill Pertwee), the Chief A.R.P. (Air Raid Precautions) Warden and local green-grocer, disliked by Captain Mainwaring and the platoon, with much being made of the hostility between them over the use of St. Aldhelm's Church Hall. Several of these characters developed catch-phrases that have entered popular British culture and the national vocabulary: Captain Mainwaring's 'Stupid boy'; Sergeant Wilson's 'Do you think that's wise?' Lance Corporal Jones's 'Don't Panic!' Private Frazer's 'We're domed I tell you, doomed', Private Godfrey's 'May I be excused?' and Mr. Hodges's 'put that light out!'

The *Dad's Army* cast was made up of very experienced actors. Richard Webber's book *Dad's Army: Walmington Goes To War – The Complete Scripts of Series 1-4* provides wonderful insights into the working relationships between the cast, some of whom had very distinguished film and theatre careers, and many of whom had previously worked together in repertory theatre (Webber, 2001). Almost all the principal actors had also served in the armed forces as officers and NCOs in either or both the First and Second World Wars, or in the real Home Guard or the A.R.P., the prominent exceptions being James Beck (who died during Series 6) and Ian Lavender, who was only 22 years old at the start of *Dad's Army* in 1968, when he first played the 17 year old ingenu, Private Frank Pike (Webber, 2008:30). The internal chronology of *Dad's Army* starts in May 1940 with the forming of the L.D.V. (Local Defence Volunteers), soon renamed the Home Guard, and continues to about September 1942, although over nine series actual dates become immaterial. Private Pike's character does age from 17 to 19 years old, but he remains the soppy, innocent young boy who fails to grasp what is going on around him, in either his public or private worlds.

Writers and producers Jimmy Perry and David Croft also had first-hand experience of the Second World War. Perry joined the Home Guard in the summer of 1940 in London, and he was called up in 1943, joining the Royal Artillery. He was posted to the Far East, but spent much of his time organising base concert parties (Pertwee, 1989:15).

Croft became an A.R.P. Warden in 1939, and in 1942 he also joined the Royal Artillery, serving in North Africa, India and Malaya, eventually reaching the rank of major and serving on the War Office staff under Field Marshal Montgomery in London by the war's end (Pertwee, 1989:13-20). Perry and Croft used their own service experiences for the *Dad's Army* series, together with elements of farce, pantomime and summer season sketch comedy shows in which they had acted or directed. They paid great attention to detail, using the correct period uniforms, vehicles and weapons, together with props such as cigarette packets and newspapers. For the female characters in the series, great efforts were made to ensure that period clothes and hairstyles were worn, and that the language used to discuss wartime food and recipes was accurate. Each episode also reflects the real events, experiences and social attitudes of the time in which it is set.

The series was exceptionally successful from its first broadcast, attracting mass audiences and winning many television awards (McCann, 2002:100). It was perceived by the general public at the time to be an accurate representation of the era, and has even been cited in the memoirs of Second World War veterans: Ken Adams's memoir of active service in the war, *Healing in Hell*, describes his early experiences of army life in Great Britain, in Norfolk between June and November 1940 as 'we were a younger version of Dad's Army' (Adams, 2011:8). The signature tune of the series provides an excellent example of the confusion between fact and fiction in the popular mind. Jimmy Croft in fact wrote the words and the tune 'Who do you think you are kidding Mr Hitler?' for *Dad's Army*, and had it recorded in October 1968 by Bud Flanagan, a massively popular singer and entertainer of the 1940s and 1950s (this was Flanagan's last professional engagement, three months before his death, for which he was paid £105) (Webber, 2008:24). The song was created as a deliberate pastiche of the songs of the Second World War era, and won the Ivor Novello Award in 1970 for best television signature tune (Webber, 1997:29). However many people believe the song was written and performed by Flanagan in the 1940s or claim to remember hearing it during the war; a significant example of the problems of the history of memory.

The Home Guard

For a comedy series, *Dad's Army* does accurately reflect the feeling of crisis and lack of planning, together with the shortages of uniforms, weapons, training and command structure in the hasty creation in May 1940 of the L.D.V. (nicknamed Look, Duck, Vanish at the time). The first episode of *Dad's Army*, 'The Man and The Hour', opens on Tuesday 14th May 1940, shown by a desk calendar in the office of Mr Mainwaring, the local bank manager, who will become Captain Mainwaring of the Walmington-on-Sea Home Guard. It was on this date that Anthony Eden, Secretary of State for War, made his famous BBC radio broadcast after the 9 p.m. news, in which he asked men aged 17 to 65 years who were British subjects to defend the United Kingdom against possible invasion by joining the just formed Local Defence Volunteers. Over 250,000 men registered in the first 24 hours, a considerable number of whom had served in the First World War but also including younger men waiting military call up and those in reserved occupations (Cullen, 2011:21). Their role was part-time, 48 hours per month and unpaid, although subsistence allowances were later introduced. Prime Minister Winston Churchill changed the name in July 1940 to the Home Guard.

If we want a real Walmington-on-Sea, it is Hythe in Kent, part of the area close to Dover called 'Hell Fire Corner' that was the expected point of landing for the expected German invasion codenamed Operation Sea Lion (Scott, 2011:xviii). In the case of conditions being right for an invasion, with favourable moon and tide for German aircraft to drop paratroops and for landing craft, the War Office would issue the codeword 'Cromwell', and an actual invasion was to be signalled by the mass ringing of church bells. The port of Dover was frequently under bombardment, and enemy raiders often targeted the surrounding countryside and smaller towns. Most of the civilians in this coastal region were evacuated, but a few remained including Colonel (retired) Rodney Foster formerly of the Indian Army, who had he retired to Hythe in 1932 with his wife Phyllis and daughter Daphne, aged 26. On 16th May 1940 he volunteered for the L.D.V., aged 57, along with Daphne, a fluent German speaker. Like Captain Mainwaring's fictitious Walmington-on-Sea platoon, most Home Guard units were formed around places of employment or strategic locations. Rodney Foster, became Lieutenant Foster in command of Number 3 Platoon, A (Hythe) Company, 8th (Cinque Ports) Battalion of the East Kent Regiment, tasked to protect a stretch of coastline. Against standing orders he kept a detailed diary of his experiences, which includes clear and well executed drawings. In January 1943 he resigned from the Home Guard and joined the A.R.P., which demanded considerably more of his time and energy.

The primary role of the L.D.V./Home Guard in 1940 was to observe and report information back to the Regular Army in case of German invasion, or assault by paratroops, 'observation and reporting of airborne attack, security against the Fifth Column and the defence of their own locations,' including critical buildings such as waterworks, as depicted in the *Dad's Army* episode 'The Lion has Phones' (Series 3, Episode 3) (Cullen, 2001:37). It was also presumed that the invaders would receive active support from an organised 'Fifth Column' of Nazi sympathisers. Suspected Nazi supporters included non-interned enemy aliens, Sir Oswald Mosley's British Union of Fascists (and associated 'Blackshirt' members), the Communist Party of Great Britain (since Stalin had signed a non-aggression pact with Hitler in August 1939) and the Irish Republican Army, which had launched a brief bombing campaign in Great Britain 1939-1940; and all these groups are referenced in the *Dad's Army* series. In 'Command Decision' (Series 1, Episode 3) the I.R.A. is named; 'The Enemy Within the Gates' (Series 1, Episode 4) a Polish officer is suspected of being a German paratrooper; 'The Showing Up of Lance Corporal Jones' (Series 1, Episode 5) the vicar the Reverend Timothy Farthing (Frank Williams) comes under suspicion as a Fifth Columnist because he listens to the Lord Haw-Haw German radio propaganda broadcasts; 'Man Hunt'(Series 3, Episode 12) a parachute is found and a man with a foreign accent is seen in the local area; 'Absent Friends' (Series 4, Episode 6) an IRA suspect is arrested with the platoon as escort; 'Two and a Half Feather' (Series 4, Episode 8) a waitress at a British Restaurant remarks about 'capitalist lackeys'.

Although such fears proved to be unfounded, the threat of a 'Fifth Column' remained a source of constant concern within both the general population and the political elite (Cullen, 2001:28-32). The problem of complacency among the local population, following the so-called 'Phoney War' of September 1939 to April 1940, was referenced in 'Wake Up Walmington' (Series 9, Episode 1), which depicted Number 1 Platoon disguised as enemy paratroopers or members of a 'Fifth Column' gathering military intelligence, to see how locals responded. This also references a more serious depiction of the threat of German invasion and a 'Fifth Column' made during the war itself, the feature film *Went The Day Well* (1942), based on a Graham Greene story, a propaganda thriller set in a rural corner on the south coast of England, in which on 23rd May 1942 a group of Royal Engineers who turn out to be German paratroops in disguise arrive at the village of Bramley End, where the local squire Oliver Wilsford (Lesley Banks), who is also a corporal in the Home Guard, is in fact a Nazi sympathiser. With his help, the Germans trick the local population into giving them accommodation and information about the village's defence plans. Their mission is to set up radio equipment for the German invasion due within the next 48 hours; however their real identity is soon revealed, causing them to change to Plan B, which includes the murder of all four of the village Home Guard. The Germans interrupt a wedding in the church and imprison the congregation, but the people of Bramley End choose to fight back, in the course of which the Vicar Mr Aston (C.V. France) is killed. What is of particular interest about this film made during the war is that, in contrast to *Dad's Army*, the women of Bramley End from all social classes play a very active role in attempting to alert the authorities to the danger, and take up arms to fight and kill the German troops in their midst and protect the nation. This aspect may have contributed to the film's very poor public reception at the time of its release in 1942, one review describing it as "fair average thick-ear fiction for the unsophisticated masses". (Sandhu, 2010). But the film critic Phillip French wrote that "As a 10 year old in 1943 I found immensely comforting its clever device of using flashback to suggest that the events took place several years before Britain emerged victorious from the Second World War" (French, 2012).

The Regular Army was at first very opposed to the creation of the Home Guard, and to their being supplied and trained in the use of weapons and in techniques of irregular warfare, because it was seriously feared that this might become a 'people's army' outside military control. In May 1940, Tom Wintringham (commander of the British battalion in the Republican XV International Brigade which fought against the Fascists in the Spanish Civil War 1936-1939) established Osterley Park in Middlesex as an unofficial training school in guerrilla tactics for Home Guard units, portrayed for comic effect in the *Dad's Army* episode 'The Battle School' (Series 3, Episode 3); the value of this training was acknowledged when Osterley Park was taken over by the Regular Army in September 1940; as the distinguished military historian Ian Beckett has written, "In June 1942, any guerrilla role for the Home Guard was officially ruled out" (Beckett, 2001:21). By 1941-42 as organisation, training and equipment improved, the Home Guard adopted more of a static defence role – the blocking of roads and patrolling key sites, such as water works, and the creation of military strongpoints with 'keeps' which had to be defended, for example at railway junctions and bridges. Between June 1941 and December 1944 the Home Guard's role expanded to area and civil defence, working closely with the A.R.P. Wardens, and in isolated areas Home Guard members had combined both these roles with their security role. *Dad's Army* does not reflect the later developments in the Home Guard from early 1943 onwards. As the threat of German invasion receded, the Home Guard became more of a training organisation for young men prior to their being called up for regular service, and practised static and mobile ambush tactics, or from 1944 more ambitious 'fox-hunting' expeditions to round up invaders. By this date the Home Guard had developed into an extremely efficient training organisation, feeding conscripts into the Regular Armed Forces and providing home defence and civilian aid, often working closely with the A.R.P., police and fire services. Many of the original L.D.V./Home Guard volunteers who were over-age (as depicted in *Dad's Army*) had stood down and left the organisation by this time. The ranks of the Home Guard were filled with younger men who were awaiting formal call-up, and with men of military age but in reserved occupations, certainly in the case of heavily industrial areas. There was also an active role for women in the Home Guard's ranks. In their studies of the Home Guard, both Stephen Cullen and David Carrol write at length about its evolving military professionalism of the Home Guard, including the role of women, but these are not aspects accurately reflected in *Dad's Army*. The Home Guard was formally stood down in November 1944, by which time it was a very different organisation from that depicted in the television series.

Bill Cotton, BBC Head of Light Entertainment in 1970 and Controller BBC1 in 1977, remarked that *"Dad's Army*, in my opinion, is a wonderful document of social history – it captures so much of the atmosphere of the Second World War. I am positive that in a hundred years time people will be watching it to get a feel of the period, probably in preference to the mass of factual material that will be available" (Pertwee, 1989:12). For any historians this statement is one of deep concern, but for those researching women's history and war it is a dangerous and outrageous statement, which detracts from the reality of the Second World War and their contribution to it. In the very first *Dad's Army* episode, 'The Man and the Hour,' we learn that Mrs. Mavis Pike (Janet Davis) is on the beach of Walmington-on-Sea, filling sandbags to help defend the town, as the seawater goes over her wellington boots. Mrs. Pike is a widow and housewife, the mother of Private Frank Pike and close friend of Sergeant Arthur Wilson, and an important figure throughout the run of *Dad's Army*. This involvement of women from the start of the threat of German invasion and the creation of the L.D.V. reflected the reality. Many women found the official reaction to their attempts to serve in the L.D.V./Home Guard to be hostile. Daphne Foster, the German-speaking daughter of Rodney Foster at Hythe, found that the police sergeant refused to register her, and many women all over Great Britain had similar experiences; instead she became heavily involved with the Girl Guides, and at the end of the war was part of the Guide International Service providing help in Europe for concentration camp survivors (Scott, 2011:43). Nevertheless the L.D.V/ Home Guard did recruit women from the start, and, though women never *officially* bore arms, Cabinet minutes of 10th July 1940 record: "it was urged that those [women] who wished to do so should be provided with uniforms and allowed to use arms" (Cullen, 2011:35). In London, on the River Thames, the Upper Thames Patrol Launch included women, and a photograph dated July 1940 held by the Imperial War Museum clearly shows a woman steering a motor launch, accompanied by two men, one of them armed with a shotgun (Carrol, 2002:87). In Devon, in August 1940, women were members of the Dartmoor Mounted Patrol which was part of the local L.D.V.; as locals they had the required knowledge and horse riding skills, and coming from a farming community this would probably include experience of handling weapons (Storey, 2009:6).

Women, war and *Dad's Army*

Objections to women being armed or even trained in firing weapons were very strong, following British cultural and gender stereotypes of 1940, although as the war progressed these views would be challenged. If an invasion and occupation of Great Britain had taken place, many women, whether members of the Home Guard or not, would have been active in resistance work (as discussed by Juliette Pattinson 2007). Whatever the War Office or local officials might decree, the L.V.D./Home Guard had in its ranks men of considerable military experience and innovation who were willing to consider new forms of warfare, and this included accepting women and training them to use weapons. This was done on an unofficial and individual basis by supportive former retired regular Army officers and NCOs who encouraged training in the use of firearms, and many L.V.D./Home Guard Units had female members trained in both armed and unarmed combat, Those units which contained former members of the International Brigades who had fought the Fascists in Spain 1936-1939 particularly welcomed women members as equals. In November 1941, an official announcement was published in the national press that forbade the practice, but it nevertheless continued, with care being taken that no record of such arrangements was kept (Summerfield and Peniston-Bird, 2007:66-67). In the House of Commons, Dr Edith Summerskill MP constantly asked questions in support of women having a full and active combat role in defending Great Britain, declaring on 18th December 1941 that, "I am not asking for women to be included solely as cooks and clerks in the Home Guard but in the same capacity as men, with equal rights and no privileges," meaning no special consideration (Summerfield and Peniston-Bird, 2007:64). Only now, as items such as private photographs, letters and diaries come to light, left among the possession of some elderly woman after her death, is this ignored or denied history of the Home Guard being recovered and acknowledged.

There were also cases of women taking the initiative for themselves, one of the strangest being Lady Helena Gleichen, who in March 1940 formed her own staff and tenants into the 'Much Marcle Watchers' (as their armbands were inscribed), who nightly patrolled her extensive estate on the Herefordshire border with Wales; she feared that this under populated area would be an ideal landing site for German parachute troops and requested weapons from the local battalion to support her patrol's efforts (Storey, 2009:5-6). More serious and lasting examples of armed women's organisations being created to support the Home Guard were a West London a group called the Amazon Defence Corps, which comprised of pre-war women rifle club members. A photograph shows the Watford Women's Defence Unit, who was unofficial members of the local Home Guard, receiving rifle training. The most widespread of these groups was the Women's Home Defence Corps (W.H.D.) that claimed a membership of 30,000 in April 1943, and undertook rifle training often supervised by their local Home Guard (Cullen, 2011:116). It is regrettable that very little hard evidence of women's active service in the Home Guard survives. Despite the existence of some photographs, it is certainly not part of our collective visual memory of the Home Guard as depicted in *Dad's Army*. The last *Dad's Army* episode 'Never Too Old' (Series 9, Episode 6) brought the series to an end in an apparently timeless bubble still in mid-1942. After the real Home Guard was stood down on 14th November 1944, King George VI made a radio broadcast on Sunday 3rd December 1944 in which he paid tribute to the women who had performed the traditional role of supporters for their husbands, saying "for most of you – and I must add for your wives too – your service in the Home Guard has not been easy" (Pertwee, 1989:144). But no mention was made of the women who had served in the Home Guard or in its associated organisations.

This point is further developed by the attention drawn in Stephen Cullen's book *In Search of the Real Dad's Army* to the women who served alongside special Home Guard volunteers in the Auxiliary Units, part of the clandestine 'stay-behind' organisation which would have been the combat element of a British resistance movement had a German occupation taken place. These women were trained in sabotage and assassination, radio communications, and escape and survival techniques (Cullen, 2011:118). More widely, because the greatest value of the Home Guard was their local knowledge, women were just as valuable as men in this role. Penny Summerfield and Corinna Peniston-Bird's seminal work on women in the Home Guard, *Contesting Home Defence*, does much to reveal women's active role in defending Great Britain, and in establishing the difference between historical fact and the popular television culture of which *Dad's Army* Series is an important part. It has been estimated that in the early years of the war 50,000 women were already serving in the Home Guard, in an unofficial capacity. In April 1943, after the changes to the Home Guard which came later than the period covered by *Dad's Army*, women were given a formal and official role, known as the Women's Home Guard Auxiliary (W.H.G.A.) But these women were nominated to undertake primarily clerical and communications duties, preference was given to those over the age of 45, and by March 1944 only 28,000 were registered (Cullen, 2011:55). Between 1941 and 1944 the Home Guard also took over the crewing of many anti-aircraft guns and coastal defence guns: it is estimated that 100,000 Royal Artillery gunners were released for overseas service by this decision (Storey, 2009:11). By August 1944, half of the anti-aircraft crews were Home Guard, and many of these had mixed sex crews (Cullen, 2011:55). At the time, having women in mixed sex anti-aircraft crews, whether Regular Army or Home Guard, was a source of controversy and frequent disapproval. Although these women officially had a non-combatant role as spotters, there is considerable anecdotal evidence that they also took part in loading and firing the guns.

Each episode of *Dad's Army* nevertheless reflects real events, experiences and social attitudes of the time in which it is set (Webber, 2001:39). The domestic home front of Walmington-on-Sea is best represented in scenes set in the butchers shop owned by Lance Corporal Jack Jones. In 'The Armoured Might of Lance Corporal Jones' (Series 3, Episode 1) we learn much about the complexity of meat rationing faced by women in the town, and the practical problems of family life in wartime. From 1968 to 1977 the women characters in *Dad's Army* slowly developed to become more visible and vocal, as Justices of the Peace, magistrates, committee members, and in uniform as members of the Women's Auxiliary Air Force (W.A.A.F.), the Land Army, and the Auxiliary Territorial Service (A.T.S.). Women as civilians appear as non-speaking extras in numerous episodes, but budget limits restricted the numbers, so that as David Croft remarked; "the streets of Walmington-on-Sea were always deserted" (Webber, 1997:29).

Other than Mrs. Pike, the main speaking women characters in the series include the fierce Mrs. Anthea Yateman (Olive Mercer) who appeared in nine episodes, the wife Mr. Maurice Yeatman, the Verger; or Miss Janet King (Caroline Dowdeswell), who appeared in five episodes as the secretary to George Mainwaring as manager of the Walmington-on-Sea branch of Swallows Bank, where Arthur Wilson also works as chief clerk and Frank Pike as the office boy (Webber, 1997:142;152). Women also appear doing jobs they have undertaken to support the war effort, such as the middle-class 'Clippie' or bus-conductress in 'Soldier's Farewell' (Series 5, Episode 3), the working class cooks and waitresses employed in the 'British Restaurant' (communal kitchens) in 'The Two And A Half Feathers' (Series 4, Episode 8), the railway guard in 'The Royal Train' (Series 6, Episode 3), or the farmer Mrs. Prentice (Brenda Cowling) in 'All is Safely Gathered In' (Series 5, Episode 8). Glamorous young women also appear through the series, including the line of girlfriends of Private Walker, and perhaps most famously Laura La Plaz (Barbara Windsor) in 'Shooting Pains' (Series 1, Episode 6), a music hall sharpshooter, whose help the platoon need to pass a shooting test. In 'Ring Dem Bells' (Series 8, Episode 1), an older woman is the most aggressive member of a crowd surrounding a group of suspected Nazi paratroopers (in fact 1 Platoon members dressed in German uniforms for a training film), attacking them with an umbrella.

As already mentioned, in *Dad's Army* women characters appear or are significantly referenced in all but four of the 80 episodes of the series, the exceptions being 'The Battle School' (Series 3, Episode 3), 'Room at the Bottom' (Series 3, Episode 6,), 'Don't Fence Me In' (Series 4, Episode 5), and 'The Desperate Drive of Corporal Jones' (Series 5, Episode 5). One episode in particular entitled 'Mum's Army' (Series 4, Episode 9) features women heavily. In a distortion of the real history of the involvement of women in the Home Guard, the story line is that the 'womenfolk' have asked to serve in the Home Guard to help defend the town. This is coupled with a romantic episode loosely based on the film *Brief Encounter* (1945), in which Captain Mainwaring has a romantic liaison with a Mrs. Fiona Gray (Carmen Silvera) that ends at the railway station, since she is returning to London because their relationship has become common gossip in the Walmingham-on-Sea (Webber, 2001:382).

Jimmy Perry remarked of this episode, "After the first read-through of 'Mum's Army', which Arthur initially didn't like, he remarked for all to hear: "If I'd read this script before I came to rehearsal I would have refused to do it". By Thursday he was saying: "This script – sheer genius" (Webber, 2001:12). But just as *Dad's Army* as a comedy series draws on a set of national and class stereotypes for its men characters, such as the dour Scottish undertaker Jock Fraser, the windbag Welsh photojournalist Private Cheeseman (Talfryn Thomas), the working class Cockney Spiv Joe Walker, and the effete upper-class Englishman Arthur Wilson, so its women characters are also largely stereotypes.

The writers also at first drew on stereotypes for the series' three main female characters: Mrs. Mavis Pike, Mrs. Marcia Mildred Fox (Pamela Cundel), and Captain Mainwaring's wife Mrs. Elizabeth Mainwaring, are based on the traditional comic composition of the Witches Coven as the mother, the virgin and the hag. However, over time each evolved into a fully rounded individual.

Over the nine series, there is much ambiguity and speculation in the series about Mrs. Pike's past and present relationship with Arthur Wilson, and the paternity of her son Frank. The complexity of this relationship and the social norms of 1940 is best expressed in 'Sergeant Wilson's Little Secret' (Series 2, Episode 4) first transmitted in March 1969, in which Sergeant Wilson mistakenly believes that Mrs. Pike is pregnant, and discusses this with Captain Mainwaring, also his boss as the bank. Like all the first two series of *Dad's Army*, the episode was made in black and white, and for that reason it has never been repeated on television (the first colour transmission was for Series 3 in September 1969). However, it is one of the three episodes that still survive from Series 2, and is available in the DVD box set. The other episodes of Series 2 (although not Series 1) are missing presumed wiped, and although copies of the scripts are available, they do not always reflect what was broadcast, since the episodes were recorded live in the studio and Arthur Lowe as Captain Mainwaring often improvised (Perry and Croft, 1998). The BBC received many letters of complaint following the transmission of 'Sergeant Wilson's Little Secret', "claiming it was immoral, lewd and a bad example to young people" (Perry and Croft, 1998:108).

As social attitudes changed slightly in the course of *Dad's Army*, the series explored the complexity of Mrs. Pike's relationship with Sergeant Wilson further. We learn in 'Getting the Bird' (Series 5, episode 4) transmitted in November 1972, that Arthur Wilson is in fact married but separated, and has a daughter referenced as the Wren in the credits (Seretta Wilson], something which he has kept secret from everyone, in particular Mrs. Pike. His daughter is now a member of the Women's Royal Naval Service (W.R.N.S.) and is visiting her father before been posted on active service.

Their conversation is overheard by Private Frazer, who is both the platoon and town gossip, followed by this exchange between them:

Wilson: Her mother left me when she was a baby – I've seen very little of her, really, though I did manage to send her to a good school.
Frazer: She does you credit.
Wilson: Yes, it was worth it, I think. Still it's all in the past. I didn't really want anyone to know.
Frazer: I'm an old blabbermouth, but I really promise you that nobody will ever learn anything of this from me.
Wilson: Thank you, Frazer – that's very kind of you.
There is every expectation that Frazer will keep his word, observing the social conventions of the time.

In the later episode 'The Making of Private Pike' (Series 9, Episode 2) transmitted in October 1977, Frank Pike innocently appears to break the sexual code of the time. A.R.P. Chief Warden Hodges has his attractive niece Sylvia (Jean Gilpin) staying with him on home leave from the A.T.S.; she is attracted to Private Pike and arranges to go on a date with him later that evening, for which they 'borrow' the Home Guard staff car. But Pike, who has had a very sheltered upbringing and is very naive, is not responsive to Sylvia's sexual advances. The car runs out of petrol and they have to push it nine miles back home from the cinema at nearby Eastgate, meaning they have been out together the whole night. Mrs. Pike's reaction is distress over Frank's absence, while Hodges's reaction as Sylvia's uncle is that they must get married; he is also concerned that this might be reported in the local newspaper. Silvia's response reflects the attitude of 1977:

Sylva: Are you out of your mind! I'm not marrying a soppy boy like him.

The episode ends with Sergeant Wilson having an avuncular talk with Private Pike, in which Wilson says that "Our sort of society has a rather rigid framework and if we don't stay within it, people point the finger at us". Over the entire series of *Dad's Army*, Mrs. Pike's character is always very assertive and independent. She puts out incendiary bombs and clears jammed rifles, as well as being very protective towards her son Frank.[1] Bill Pertwee, writes about the character of Mrs. Pike, "Janet looked like a pretty housewife, someone you would want to come home to, which was exactly what she was intended to be when she was cast as Mrs. Pike, mother of Frank Pike, and in a very discreet way the comforter of Sergeant Wilson" (Pertwee, 1989:77). In 'High Finance' (Series 8, Episode 5), we learn that Hodges has tried to extort implied sexual favours from Mrs. Pike in lieu of £50 back rent, a considerable sum of money in 1940. What is of interest in this episode is that Mrs. Pike refuses to be a victim of the situation or accede to Mr. Hodges's demands, and

---

[1] Perry and Croft *Dad's Army The Lost Scripts*, Series 2, episode 12 *Under Fire* (missing presumed wiped) and Series 3, episode 4 *The Bullet is Not For Firing* broadcast September/December 1969.

within the internal logic of the series she attempts to resolve the issue herself, by seeking a loan. As the denouement scene unfolds the rest of the characters around the table also find Hodges's behaviour unacceptable, with Captain Mainwaring who has always regarded Hodges as both 'common' and 'a mere tradesman' supporting Sergeant Wilson when he hits Hodges. The character of Mrs. Pike is a constant thread that links all 80 episodes, appearing in 30 of them. She represents the world of Walmington-on-Sea, quite literally the 'mother' that the platoon seeks to protect (Webber, 1997:77).

Mrs. Marcia Mildred Fox appeared in 13 episodes. She is married at the start of *Dad's Army* but is soon windowed, and starts a long platonic relationship with Lance Corporal Jones, with members of the platoon discovering them together in the cinema or having tea at the Marigold Tearooms (Webber, 1997:133). We also learn that Jones has admired her for 17 years, and his marriage to her is the subject of the series' final episode 'Never Too Old' (Series 9, Episode 6). While Mrs. Fox is regarded as 'flashy' by Captain Mainwaring, he does comment favourably on their proposed marriage, remarking;

Mainwaring: After all they are both the same class.
Wilson: Do you really think class matters?
Mainwaring: No question, no question about it at all. Its families that make the trouble, I had to contend with all sorts of snobbish rubbish when I married Elisabeth.

This class consciousness is reflected in 'War Dance' (Series 3, Episode 9), in which Private Pike wishes to marry Violet Gibbons (unaccredited), a member of the A.T.S. who is the daughter of Captain Mainwaring's former cleaner and at one time worked in the local fish shop. Pike has kept this relationship a secret from his mother, who would be required to give her consent to the marriage, but is considering announcing his engagement. Both as Pike's commanding officer and as his manager at Swallows Bank, Mainwaring is vigorously opposed to the engagement, citing social differences that would damage Pike's promotional chances and status at the bank (Webber, 1997:242). In contrast, unsullied by the war Mrs. Fox seeks happiness and future joy in the years to come, as Mrs. Jones - the bride - she represents the virgin in the series.

The invisible female character is Elizabeth, Captain Mainwaring's wife, who never appears on screen or is ever heard. She is 'shown' once in the series, as a prominent downward bulge in the upper bunk of the Anderson shelter where Mainwaring attempts to sleep on the lower bunk in 'A Soldier's Farewell' (Series 5, Episode 4). This establishes her as a lady of large proportions, drawing on the comic music-hall convention of a short husband being bullied by his over-large wife. All that the audience knows about her comes from the reaction of the other characters to her. The impression created is that she dominates George Mainwaring as her husband, who is downtrodden and unhappy but refuses to admit this in public. He also has a position to maintain in the town, both as bank manager and as captain of the Home Guard platoon, and to be seen to be unhappily married would reflect badly on his social and professional standing. We learn that he never felt at ease with his wife's parents, and nor did they ever accept that his middle-class employment in the bank was equal to his wife's family social connections; he makes repeated references in the series to being grammar school educated, and is resentful of Wilson as a public school boy. This comes into particular focus in 'The Honourable' (Series 6, Episode 5) when Wilson inherits a courtesy title and his aristocratic background becomes public knowledge in the town.

Elizabeth Mainwaring we learn is a vegetarian who likes cats, has a shy and jealous nature, and led a very sheltered life before her marriage. We view their relationship and home life through Captain Mainwaring's reactions either when speaking to her on his office telephone, or in comments to others. We learn in 'The Big Parade' (Series 4, Episode 1) that she has not been to the cinema since *The Jazz Singer* the first successful 'talkie' in 1927. In 'If the Cap Fits' (Series 5, Episode 6), we discover that Captain Mainwaring learned to play the bagpipes while on his honeymoon with Elizabeth, because there was very little else to do on a lonely Scottish island. In Absent Friends (Series 4, Episode 6) we learn they have a cat called Empress, and Mainwaring describes the state of his marriage to the platoon;

> Mainwarring: As a result of a misunderstanding between Corporal Jones and myself... certain rumours are circulating round the town regarding Mrs. Mainwaring's condition. They are quite untrue. Mrs. Mainwaring and I have never been blessed in that manner, although in all other respects our marriage has been a most happy one – in fact-quite blissful.
> *Phone Rings.*
> Wilson: Er... the phone is ringing, sir – shall I answer it?
> Mainwaring: No. (*Sadly*) It's probably for me.

Mrs. Mainwaring is the hag, the frightful woman who bullies and orders her husband about, but she is actually the most interesting female character in the *Dad's Army* series. She is frightened but does not evacuate from the invasion area, she remains in her home to support her husband, whom she chose to marry over her family's objections. Mrs. Mainwaring refuses to play the expected part of the bank manager's wife in local provincial society, but in 'The Godiva Affair' (Series 7, Episode 4) she rides through the town wearing only 'fleshings' or a body-stocking as Lady Godiva, much to her husband's shock and horror (he faints on seeing her), causing an exchange between Privates Jones and Frazer;

> Jones: Poor Mr Mainwaring, he'll never get over the shock.
> Frazer: No and neither will the horse.

Over the nine series, Mrs. Mainwaring's character provides the viewing audience with the blank space onto which they can project their own changing opinions about women, and perhaps marriage, both during the Second World War and between the years 1968 to 1977 a time of massive social change.

Conclusions

The representation of women in *Dad's Army* is important, together with class and national identity that must be considered in any discourse analysis or understanding of the television series as a cultural artefact or icon of the Second World War, but it must never be regarded as an accurate historical record. The issue of the confusion of historical fact and fiction created in the general public's mind by a successful BBC television comedy has already attracted the attention of historians over the First World War, with the BBC television series *BlackAdder Goes Forth*, first broadcast in 1989, a light comedy about British troops' experience of trench warfare on the Western Front 1914-1918. Many distinguished military historians have contributed to what has become known as the 'Two Western Fronts' debate about the representation of the First World War in the wider cultural memory in this way (Badsey, 2001:113-125). I would suggest in studying the Second World War, we should learn from this experience. The BBC television series *Dad's Army* has excellent production values, is well acted and celebrates and honours the Home Guard with humour and respect, its massive popularity has now produced its own mythology and cultural history. Considerable scholarly analysis and research has been undertaken on cultural memory, nostalgia and the meaning of war in popular British films and television, Michael Paris writes, "Perhaps because it was the nation's last great achievement on the world stage before relegation to the second division, 1939-45 has become, for the British people, a never - ending story told and retold to remind ourselves of a glorious past, in a far less glorious and depressing present" (Paris, 2000:221). While Jeffrey Richards writes of *Dad's Army*, "Not only is there a society; it has shared memories and shared values. It has an ideal of national identity rooted in tradition, community, tolerance and good nature" (Richards, 1997:366). What it is not is an accurate reflection of the reality of the British Home Front experience of women who served in L.D.V./Home Guard, even if the television series it is often referenced in texts by men as mirroring their own experiences in May 1940. It should not be considered as an historical documentary or as a source for primary research on the Second World War. However *Dad's Army* it is a valuable source for assessing British popular culture and society in the 20th century and its attitudes to class, gender, identity and race and should be watched and enjoyed (it is a comedy show) by audiences in the 21st century on that basis.

References

Books:

Adams, K. and Adams, M. (eds.) (2011). *Healing in Hell - The Memoirs of a Far Eastern POW Medic.* UK.   South Yorkshire: Pen & Sword,

Beckett, I. (2001). *Modern Insurgencies and Counter-Insurgencies: Guerrillas and their Opponents since 1750.* UK. London: Routledge.

Carrol, D. (2002). *Dad's Army: The Home Guard 1940-44.* UK. Gloucestershire: Sutton Publishing.

Coultass, C. (1989). *Images for Battle: British Film and the Second World War 1939-1945.* UK. London: Associated University Press.

Cullen, Stephen. M. (2011). *In Search of the Real Dad's Army - The Home Guard and the Defence of the United   Kingdom 1940-1944.* UK. South Yorkshire: Pen and Sword.

Longman, N. (1974). *The Real Dad's Army.* UK. London: Arrow.

McCann, G. (2002). *Dad's Army - The Story of a Classic Television Show.* UK. London: Fourth Estate.

Paris, M. (2000). *Warrior Nation Images of War in British Popular Culture 1850-2000.* UK. London: Reaktion Books.

Perry, J. and Croft, D. 1998). *Dad's Army - The Lost Episodes.* UK. London: Virgin.

Pertwee, B. (1989). *Dad's Army: The Making of a Television Legend.* UK. London: David & Charles.

Richards, J. (1997). *Films and British National Identity From Dickens to Dad's Army.* UK. Manchester: Manchester University Press.

Scott. R. (ed.) (2011). *The Real Dad's Army – The War Diaries of Col. Rodney Foster.* UK. London: Viking.

Storey, N. (2009). *The Home Guard.* UK. Oxford: Shire Publications.

Summerfield, P. and Peniston-Bird, C, (2007) *Contesting Home Defence – Men, Women and the Home Guard in the Second World War.* UK. Manchester: Manchester University Press.

Webber, R. (ed.) (2001). *Dad's Army: Walmington Goes To War – The Complete Scripts of Series 1-4.* UK. London: Orion Books.

Webber, R. (1997). *Dad's Army: A Celebration.* UK. London: Virgin Books.

Webber, R. (2008). *Dad's Army: The Best Scenes, Jokes and One-Liners.* UK. London: Harper Collins.

Film Reviews:

French, P. 'Went the Day Well', *The Observer*, 11th July 2010, accessed on-line 2nd May 2012.

Sandhu, S. 'Went the Day Well?' *The Daily Telegraph*, 8th July 2010, accessed on-line 2nd May 2012.

Chapter 4

The German Service of the BBC during the Second World War: Attitudes towards Satire as a Weapon of War

Kristina Meier
Freie Universität Berlin, Germany

Introduction

Historians have been poring over Joseph Goebbels and his reputedly efficient propaganda apparatus ever since the Second World War. In particular, the Nazi manipulation of radio as a medium to gain and maintain power is well researched. But few people have explored the leading opponent of Goebbels' propaganda machine - the German Service of the BBC. Fewer still have acknowledged that the BBC's radio transmissions to Germany entailed not only news and comment but also drew upon an unusual and unprecedented method of British psychological warfare - satire - as a form of counterpropaganda. Hitherto the combination of radio and satire as part of a propaganda effort had never been exploited.

These pioneering satire feature programmes - *Frau Wernicke, Der Gefreite Adolf Hirnschal* and *Kurt und Willi* - were written by German exiles under the close supervision of British authorities. From mid-1940 until the end of the war these three programmes were transmitted weekly or fortnightly and their significance as a mirror of British propaganda strategies has long been overlooked. So what did the authors of these programmes, the BBC officials and the relevant governmental institutions hope, to achieve with "satire as a weapon of war" (Lucas, 1978:452, own translation). And was there a consensus about how it should be applied and whether it was an effective strategy at all?

This chapter will analyse the different attitudes towards the BBC's unexpected and revolutionary take on propaganda, drawing extensively on documents from the BBC Written Archives Centre (WAC) as well as The National Archives (TNA). A brief introduction to the satirical programmes and their historical context will be followed by more specific examples of the approach to satire and the heated debate this inspired within the BBC. The paper concludes with a brief discourse on satire as a morally appropriate measure for the fight against Nazism. Was it acceptable "to laugh amid the hell's noise of the war machinery" (Lucas, 1978:455, own translation), as one of the programme's authors phrased it?

Making Public Opinion

The prelude to what came to be referred to as the "war of words" (Briggs, 1970:3) took place at the height of the Sudeten crisis on September 27th 1938 when Neville Chamberlain had his speech translated in German and transmitted on BBC shortwave radio. The British Prime Minister warned of the apparent danger of war and expressed his wish for peace. It was the first attempt by the British government to directly communicate with the Germans and bypass Nazi censorship. It was also the moment when the German Service of the BBC was born.

The purpose of this broadcasting station was to break the monopoly on news, which the Nazis had installed through their homogenising of the German media - part of the *Gleichschaltung* that was designed to streamline citizens into the National Socialist ideology and affected all areas of their lives.[1] The exceptional role this new medium could play in the indoctrination of an entire nation was something Goebbels had pointed out as early as March 1933 when he spoke to the heads of German radio stations: "With this instrument you are making public opinion. If you do it well we shall win the people over" (quoted in Bramsted, 1965:63). In August of that year he declared that radio had the potential to be of "truly revolutionary significance" (quoted in Bramsted, 1965:63). Although Nazi propaganda was directed mostly at its own people it also had some influence on an international scale. During the Berlin Olympics of 1936 the German Propaganda Ministry built up an extensive foreign language broadcasting system, clearly recognising the potential of radio much earlier than most other countries. By contrast the British foreign radio service was slow to develop.

Even after Chamberlain's first translated broadcast in 1938 the BBC's entry into counterpropaganda was pedestrian and hindered by several factors including institutional power quarrels, inexperienced staff and, most of all, by concerns that transmissions to Germany may be understood as a direct provocation and hinder the fragile settlement that was reached with Hitler in the Munich Agreement. Charles Cruickshank summarised the imbalanced

---

[1] The tight control of Goebbels' Propaganda Ministry resulted in a totalitarian media system whereby independent media ceased to exist and the flow of news was strictly controlled.

situation in his book *The Fourth Arm - Psychological Warfare 1938-45*: "The Nazis might pour out oceans of anti-British propaganda without a murmur of protest from Westminster, but the merest threat of a droplet in reply had to be defended to the Führer" (Cruickshank, 1981:10). So when war broke out the German Service was still in its infancy and lacked staff, equipment and a routine to approach the daily task of counterpropaganda in an adequate and comprehensive way. Furthermore, the propaganda apparatus that was supposed to back the transmissions was equally underdeveloped and unprepared for the task that lay before it, as the author Ellic Howe, who came to be involved in propaganda later in the war, states: "If Dr Goebbels had been given even an inkling of the confusion which prevailed in the British 'Propaganda Ministry' he would have experienced a delicious sense of *Schadenfreude*" (Howe, 1982:43).[2]

For the German audience it was now forbidden to listen to foreign stations such as the German Service of the BBC. Those caught committing the criminal offence of tuning in to the 'wrong' station were jailed; the highest charge for spreading news from enemy broadcasts was the death penalty.[3] Germans brave enough to disregard the law had to beware of eavesdroppers and ill-meaning neighbours and so would listen under blankets or in dimly lit backrooms. In any case the sound of foreign stations was distorted because the authorities heavily jammed the transmissions. Nevertheless, as explained by a BBC document which set out its propaganda strategy, the German Service continued with programmes aimed "at stimulating doubts among the confident and at encouraging defeatism and irritation with the regime in the apathetic" (TNA FO, 898/183:25.02.1940).

Initially the German Service consisted almost exclusively of news bulletins. This sparked some internal criticism for being too bland or academic (TNA FO, 898/7:12.03.1940). Expansion was only gradual; talks and comments were integrated and the content adjusted to target different groups such as soldiers, workers or women. But the idea of a vivid and captivating production - let alone a mentally stimulating form of satire, which delivered its critical message in a subtle manner – seemed inconceivable. The satirist's technique of taking

---

[2] The development of the British Propaganda apparatus cannot be afforded any room here. Particularly until autumn 1941 – when the Political Warfare Executive (PWE) was established – it was constantly in transition.

[3] A Decree on Exceptional Radio Measures (*Die Verordnung über außerordentliche Rundfunkmaßnahmen*) that took effect on September 1st 1939 made listening to enemy stations a crime. The official reason for the law was given as follows: "In a modern war the opponent doesn't only fight with military weapons but also by means that should influence the soul of the people [...] One of these means is the wireless. Every word that the enemy transmits across is naturally dishonest." (quoted in Brinitzer, 1969:61, own translation).

aspects of reality and blowing them out of proportion, his polarisation of opinion and his stylistic play with ambiguity and loaded remarks opposed the beliefs of the Planning and Broadcasting Committee. This committee was formed of BBC representatives and members of the Electra House (E.H.) - the institution responsible for propaganda to enemy countries. It regarded the German Service principally as a station that should "consist of straight news" (TNA FO, 898/8:15.04.1940).

This plain approach is reflected in another recommendation of the Committee in April 1940, which points out to the German staff of the BBC that the production of the women's broadcast needs special handling:

> It should be noted that these broadcasts were addressed to women. The announcers should therefore speak very slowly, distinctly and simply. It was well known that women listeners were liable to mis-understand anything complicated (TNA FO, 898/8:04.04.1940).

The committee's attitude reveals not only a questionable assessment of its female listeners but also a simple-mindedness that failed to grasp the potential of diversity and complexity that radio had to offer and how it could be utilised for purposes of propaganda.

A first major exception was made on April 1st 1940 when a Hitler parody was transmitted.[4] The Planning and Broadcasting Committee only permitted this after it reassured itself that this was not part of a fundamental change to the overall tone of the German Service. It was, after all, only an April fools' joke. Humour remained contrary to the general policy: "It was recognised that such an item would, in itself, be contrary to Department E.H.'s policy but that in this instance, it might be put over as a joke" (TNA FO, 898/7:29.03.1940).

Only months later the policy had changed fundamentally. That the Committee turned to a more light-hearted approach was all the more extraordinary at a time when the French had just capitulated, when the situation for Britain almost could not have been worse and when Germany's propaganda machine was at full blast with the victory trumpets of German radio blowing louder than ever before.

Yet it was in July 1940, when Britain was isolated, fighting a seemingly impregnable enemy and contemplating the threat of invasion, that the first

---

[4] The Hitler parody *Der Führer spricht* was initially performed at the London based Austrian exile theatre *Laterndl* by Martin Miller. This small theatre, which followed the Viennese tradition of the *Kleinkunstbühne* and focused on political cabaret, was a meeting point for Austrian and other German-speaking exiles (Dove, 2000:209). Contrary to the intent of the Planning and Broadcasting Committee, Miller's Hitler parody was the first of many that were to follow.

character feature was introduced into the women's programme: *Frau Wernicke*. With breath-taking speed – thus ignoring previous instructions to "speak very slowly, distinctly and simply" – this fictional middle-aged woman yatters away in Berlin jargon. The listener comes to know Frau Wernicke as a tough yet spirited, chatty Berlin housewife complaining about injustices, rationing and the contradictions of everyday life in wartime, through it all displaying a robust common sense. The subversive effect intended by the author derives from the juxtaposition of her pseudo-naïve enthusiasm and the life she describes as well as from the contrasts created by her seemingly innocent games of question and answer.

The programme is a monologue but Frau Wernicke speaks as if she is having a conversation with a companion, paraphrasing her friend's concerns and questions and answering them herself, often in full-blown rants. Indeed the style of delivery is so convincing that the listener almost pictures the friend as present. It is impossible to translate Frau Wernicke's Berlin dialect and her breathless, voluble style directly into English. The reader has to imagine a woman who would ask her friend why she is so upset and then immediately launch into an answer herself:

Do you have no understanding for the exceptional luck that we can be there when the whole world is healed by the German spirit? [...] and yet still as a German mother [...] you are doing nothing else but whining and whimpering as if it is nothing but lies and deceptions. And why? Only because your husband had to close his business and because your boy is now with the *Wehrmacht* and has had enough of it and because your girl, Elsbeth, has to do a second mandatory year of state labour and because – as you put it – you don't have a family life anymore and you are not happy – only because of such frills and furbelows (WAC M:22.03.1941).[5]

The disastrous effects of war to family life are thus summarised by Frau Wernicke, using the word "only" as an ironic reference to the grave realities that anyone would be upset about. In another episode, her 'friend', Frau Spindler, is worried about her son's destiny on the western front. Frau Wernicke sees this very differently: "He is right at the front when things start to move towards

---

[5] The translation serves only to give a rough idea of the nature of Frau Wernicke's monologue. The original German script reads: "ham Se denn jar keen Jefiehl für det unjeheure Jlück, det wa dabei sein dürfen, wie d janze Welt am deutschen Wesen jenest [...] und trotz alledem, Sie, ne deutsche Frau un Mutta, [...] Sie dun nischt wie quängeln und quarren, wie wenn det alles nischt wäre wie Lug und Trug – und warum? Bloss, weil der Mann hat seene Murksbude zumachen müssen, und weil der Junge in de Wehrmacht is und de Nase pläng hat, und weil det Mächen, de Elsbeth, noch'n zweetes Flichtjahr abreissen muss, und weil Se – wie Se sajen – keen Familjenleben mehr ham und nicht glücklich sin – mit ee'm Wort allet wejen sone Lappalje un Kinkerlitzchen."

England."[6] And moreover, she argues, if he dies he would die a hero's death and display "real vigour [...] when he lets himself be shot for the Führer".[7] She hereby plays on the absurdities of Nazi propaganda and the alleged merits of the *Heldentod* - the hero's death. It is a stark satirical ploy, which makes clear that the reverse must be true: that the death of a son can never be consoled by a *Heldentod*. Her frank and drastic way of arguing is clearly intended to create fear among Germans of the consequences of war and raise some fundamental questions: "What do we do with a fatherland that has sacrificed all its sons? Spindler, you can't ask those tricky questions."[8] By refusing to give an answer the question lingers and the listener is encouraged to think about where this war is heading.

The *Frau Wernicke* series was written by Bruno Adler, an art historian and author who had been lecturing at the Bauhaus and published highly regarded biographies of Matthias Claudius and of Adalbert Stifter before he fled to England in 1936. The voice behind *Frau Wernicke* is the exiled actress Annemarie Hase, who was quite well known in Germany and became a member of Bertolt Brecht's Ensemble after the war. *Frau Wernicke* was the BBC's satirical trailblazer and it was the first time when "propaganda aims of the British government were cloaked in literary garments" (Taylor, 1999:43), as the historian Jennifer Taylor describes it.

The formation of the Feature Department under Walter Rilla and the arrival of Hugh Greene - later head of the German Service - in the autumn of 1940 initiated a more extensive change in tone. A human touch became more important. Songs and dramatised items were increasingly included and the BBC's attempt to fight Hitler with laughter was further expanded by launching two more satire programmes in December 1940.

Die Briefe des Gefreiten Adolf Hirnschal an seine Frau in Zwieselsdorf - to give the programme its full German title - consisted of fictitious letters written by a German corporal on the front line to his wife back home. The protagonist reads the letters to his fighting comrade before they are posted.[9] Adolf Hirnschal frequently states glowing admiration for the "beloved Führer" and sounds whole-heartedly dedicated to the cause. Yet because of his wildly exaggerated outbursts in most inappropriate situations you suspect that his devotion isn't thoroughbred but rather a self-protective way of exposing the

---

[6] "der is doch jleich vornedran, wenn et losjeht jejen Engelland" (WAC M:22.03.1941).

[7] "richtje Lebenskraft zeicht sich, wenn er sich jern for sein Führer arschiessen lässt" (WAC M:22.03.1941).

[8] "Wat wa mit n Vaterland anfangen, wenn wa alle Söhne jeopfert haben? Spindler sone tickschen Frajen dürfen Se nich stellen." (WAC M:22.03.1941).

[9] The *Hirnschal* letters were read by the comedian and actor Fritz Schrecker, who had emigrated from Vienna in 1938 (Trapp, 1999:847).

shallowness and mendacity of Nazi claims. Hiding behind Hitler quotes and Nazi propaganda, he takes it ad absurdum. An inundation of anecdotes, comparisons, dreams and allegories allows the listener to come to only one conclusion: this war is cruel and unnecessary and while normal people suffer and fight, immoral and corrupt leaders benefit. Discrediting the National Socialist leaders, and Hitler in particular, was a *leitmotif* of the programme.

In his first letter after war is declared on Russia, Hirnschal writes from the eastern front. He is telling his wife, in direct speech, how he welcomed the news from his lieutenant that they are being transferred to the Russian border:

> I jump up in joy and say: 'Mr. Lieutenant, kindly asking for permission to express that I am tremendously pleased that we are now fraternising with the Russians. Did not our beloved Führer already say in 1939 that our friendship with the Russians is irrevocable and irreversible' (Lucas, 1945:39, own translation).[10]

Without being openly critical, Hirnschal contrasts Hitler's earlier statement with his current action, all under the cover of absolute loyalty. Hirnschal goes on to say that two weeks later a grenade hit their base. The lieutenant was trapped and badly injured and while they wait for help Hirnschal calms him down and encourages him to think of nice things. Again, as so often, Hirnschal recalls his own words in direct speech:

> Mr. Lieutenant could be thinking of the German women who are now full of excitement, sitting in front of the speakers to hear about our heroic stories. Mr. Lieutenant could be thinking of his dear mum who is now perhaps sitting in the cellar and the English aircraft bombs are hitting around her. How nice is it to know your family is in safety while we defend the holy German earth near Ternopil (Lucas, 1945:39, own translation).[11]

---

[10] The original German script reads: "Herr Leutnant, bitte melden zu dürfen, das freut mich riesig, daß wir uns jetzt mit den Russen verbrüdern. Hat nicht unser geliebter Führer schon 1939 gesagt, unsere Freundschaft mit den Russen ist endgültig und unabänderlich." This appears in a book published by Robert Lucas in 1945, which provides the transcripts of 50 *Hirnschal* letters (Lucas 1945).

[11] "[D]enken Herr Leutnant an die deutschen Frauen, die wo jetzt voll Spannung vor den Lautsprechern sitzen, um von unseren Heldentaten zu hören. Denken Herr Leutnant zum Beispiel an die liebe Frau Mutter vin Herrn Leutnant, die wo vielleicht gerade im Keller sitzt, und die englischen Fliegerbomben schlagen rings um sie ein. Wie schön ist es, seine Familie so in Sicherheit zu wissen, während wir hier bei Tarnopol die heilige deutsche Erde verteidigen." (Lucas, 1945:41)

The author of this programme was the Austrian Robert Lucas, who could rely on previous experience with politically motivated satire. He had been writing for a socialist cabaret in Vienna before he fled the country. Political cabaret meant, in his words, to "put the laughter into the service of propaganda and enlightenment" (quoted in Müller, 2004:70, own translation).

The third satire programme was *Kurt und Willi*. This was written by Bruno Adler - author of *Frau Wernicke* - in cooperation with the Scottish poet Norman Cameron. It is a dialogue between two friends – Kurt Krüger and Willi Schimanksi, the former being a schoolmaster, the latter an official in the German Propaganda Ministry.[12] While discussing the events of the war over a beer in a bar near Potsdamer Platz in Berlin, Kurt assumes the role of the naïve 'average' German, a loyal patriot who believes in whatever is announced by the national media. Willi - through his work in the Propaganda Ministry - has a better insight. He is a cynical, immoral opportunist leaking to his friend the latest subterfuges and tricks he and his colleagues in the Ministry have devised. The character of Willi is in fact serving the British propaganda cause, becoming what Taylor calls the "propagandists' propagandist" (Taylor, 2007:18).

Kurt und Willi exists as a vehicle for intelligence information that would have been difficult to convey to the Germans via characters like Frau Wernicke or Adolf Hirnschal. Kurt turns to his friend whenever he finds things inexplicable. Wondering why winter collections for the eastern front were instigated so late, he remarks sarcastically to Willi: "December is a fine time to start thinking about that." To this Willi lets Kurt in on a little secret:

> Well, strictly between ourselves, Kurt, the Führer assured the OKW [Supreme Command of the Armed Forces] that the campaign would be over by the winter - so the OKW assumed that we needed winter equipment only for a garrison force of a million men. And now? Now there are five million to provide for – it's not easy my boy! (WAC M:03.12.1941).[13]

Like *Frau Wernicke* and *Der Gefreite Adolf Hirnschal*, the *Kurt und Willi* programmes were short features, rarely exceeding seven minutes. Each episode could be understood in isolation but the characters unfold through time. This allows the listener to develop a bond with the protagonists much like occurs with modern-day soap operas.

These three programmes ran for almost the entire period of the war, which makes them the most consistent example of anti-Nazi satire targeted at

---

[12] *Kurt und Willi* was initially read out by whomever was in the studio but from 1941 Peter Ihle und Fritz Wendhausen became the permanent voices of those two characters.

[13] This quote has been taken from the English translation of this episode that was undertaken for censorship reasons and has survived - with a handful of other English scripts – in the Written Archives Centre of the BBC.

Germans and compelling evidence of the changing strategies of British counterpropaganda.[14] Inevitably this subject raises the instinctive question: did these programmes have any effect? Was satire a weapon that converted Germans to the British viewpoint and lower their morale to keep this war going? It would be true to say that detailed analysis of the satirical programmes has been absent since the war. But it is equally true that, where there have been attempts to recall their significance, there has been a tendency to exaggerate the effect they had upon their target audience.

In 1969 Hugh Greene, head of the German Service during the war and later Director General of the BBC, proclaimed: "Satire played its part [...] and it is worth remembering that ridicule is an effective weapon against dictatorships" (Greene 1969:25). And his former propaganda boss, who headed the German Section of the Political Warfare Executive (PWE) that was founded in 1941, sees it the same way: "Entertainment is a valuable narcotic for dulling the sensibilities of a propaganda-conscious mind. A subversive thought can be instilled even into a Nazi mind, under the cover of laughter" (Crossman, 1971:343). Journalist Tom Hickman, in his account of the BBC's wartime history (published by the BBC), claims "laughter was as much a munition of war as shells and aircraft engines" (Hickman, 1995:47). This conviction is repeated in a radio transmission that was produced for the 40th anniversary of the German Service: "Amongst news and commentaries, satire and humour were above all the sharpest weapons of the BBC to which the beastly stern Nazi-regime had no real answer" (Krämer & Saaler, 25.09.1978:17'27, own translation). And a staff member of the German Service, Carl Brinitzer, summarised in his memoirs the alleged accomplishment of satire and parody even more enthusiastically. "We experienced", he wrote, "that there can be hardly a more efficient weapon against dictators in existence than the weapon of ridiculousness" (Brinitzer, 1969:121, own translation).

These testimonies trumpet the satire programmes as a psychological masterstroke of war. However the impact of those broadcasts is empirically immeasurable. We can't even estimate how many Germans were listening. The BBC believes that towards the end of the war between ten and fifteen million listeners would tune into the German Service (vgl. BBC, 1988:10).[15] But

---

[14] *Frau Wernicke* was broadcast - with the exception of a three-month break in early 1941 - from July 1940 to January 1944. *Kurt und Willi* and *Adolf Hirnschal* both ran from December 1940 until the end of the war.

[15] Evidently in Germany there was no empirical evaluation undertaken since listening to 'enemy stations' was forbidden. Britain by contrast, used the *Mass Observation* and a study - *Hamburg Broadcast Propaganda: The Extent and Effect of its Impact on the British Public during mid-Winter 1939/40* (Briggs, 1970:148) - to evaluate the success of the enemy's English broadcasts. At the end of the war the Americans started a listening survey in western Germany. But since this is only a fragment, and one possibly distorted by the interviewee's desire to demonstrate a pro-Ally attitude, the validity of the data is limited (Diller, 1998).

whether indeed millions of Germans closed their curtains to secretly, in Frau Wernicke's words, "inhale the English with the duvet over the head and the radio close by" (WAC M:12.09.1942) is a matter of pure speculation.[16] Furthermore, to judge from the many files of the Written Archives Centre of the BBC and The National Archives, the post-war celebration of the satire programmes was exaggerated perhaps as a means to develop a congruent and consistent historical narrative. A more accurate reflection of the German Service at this time would point to the quarrels and doubts that were common between both the staff of the German Service and the governmental propagandists with whom they were inextricably tied. To illustrate this, let us now look more closely at how satire came to be born in the German Service and how it worked in practice.

A Shot in the Dark

"All right, we might as well give it a try" (Lucas, 1978:452). These were the rather uninspiring words of Robert Lucas's supervisors that, according to the author, accompanied his first *Hirnschal* script in the autumn of 1940. Lucas explained that they were giving *Hirnschal* a try because, frankly, there was not much to lose or, as Hugh Greene put it, "if we lose the war, we would all be shot anyway" (cited in BBC, 1988:3, own translation).

This suggests that the German Service ventured into the experiment of using satire as a weapon of war partly out of desperation, rather than as a result of someone's brainchild or a calculated strategy. It was a sudden step into the unknown triggered by the anxious mood and multiple changes within Britain at the time. The very real threat of imminent invasion caused a reaction bordering on the hysterical; witness the mass internment of 27,000 (almost 40%) German-speaking exiles after the capitulation of France (Joos, 2009:59). The switch from the 'dull' phoney war (and bland radio production) to the emotional upheaval of real war seems to be closely linked to the German Service's adoption of satire, itself part of a broader transition designed to influence German listeners using emotive content. It may have also partly been caused by the governmental change from Chamberlain to the more polemic, charismatic Winston Churchill in May 1940. Structural changes within the propaganda departments were also undertaken and that too may have affected the tone of the messages to Germany.

The first months of war had been characterised by a static and conservative approach. Now the BBC entered a period of experimental broadcasts that

---

[16] In the German original script it reads: "det englisch inhalieren mit de Decke iebern Kopp und n Radio" (WAC M:12.09.1942).

70

included entertainment. It is impossible to know to what degree each of the aforementioned factors influenced the BBC's growing taste for entertaining content but the first signs of a general change in attitude were visible in spring 1940 when the Electra House Adviser on Germany encouraged more lucid, amusing programmes, arguing that "good bait catches fine fish" (TNA FO 898/3:31.05.1940, own translation).

The pilot broadcast - *Frau Wernicke on politics* - on July 17th 1940 went down very well with the Planning Committee: "Very much in favour of getting some more talks from Frau Wernecke [sic]" (WAC E2/344:19.07.1940). The trial continued with the second episode, *Frau Wernicke on the war*, which was similarly popular with the committee: "Very favourable comments were made on the last Frau Wernicke broadcast" (WAC E2/344:30.07.1940).

But the praise did not amount to a consensus. In particular, there was disagreement whether *Frau Wernicke* was pitched in an effective way: "Monsignor Vance felt that the Frau Wernicke conversations lacked all propaganda value and he doubted whether it was worth continuing to put them over" (TNA FO 898/8:10.08.1940). But only a couple of days later Frederick A. Voigt, the Adviser on Germany to the Department for Enemy Propaganda, "stated the case for including items of entertainment value in the German programmes with particular reference to Frau Wernicke's conversations. No discussion took place, but there was no dissension" (TNA FO 898/8:17.08.1940). The debate was closed for the time being.

These early broadcasts of *Frau Wernicke*, which pioneered the use of radio satire, are almost completely ignored by researchers, probably by the lack of surviving manuscripts up until March 1941. Yet the focus of the early series can be roughly gleaned from the invoices of Annemarie Hase, the voice behind Frau Wernicke, which reveal the titles of many episodes – *Frau Wernicke in the air raid shelter*, *Frau Wernicke queues up*, *Frau Wernicke's housekeeping worries*, *Frau Wernicke and the merry widow*. Furthermore Bruno Adler and his BBC supervisor, Christina Gibson, discuss some of these episodes in a rare and extensive correspondence in the late summer and autumn of 1940. These primary sources are valuable because they describe in detail the daily production process and reveal the interaction and tension between a German exile and his supervisor. This demanding and delicate relationship - with Adler seeking independence and artistic freedom and Gibson exerting the interests of the Electra House (and thus the British government) - has been hitherto masked by history. The Adler-Gibson letters also provide evidence of how carefully the content of the series was orchestrated for purposes of propaganda.

Though he was the author of *Frau Wernicke,* Adler's influence on propaganda content remained marginal. The policy of the programme, the message and even the subject was usually determined by Gibson, who in turn was representing the wishes of the Electra House. Adler was also sent direct instructions on propaganda by the Electra House: "It was agreed that C.H.Q.

[Country Headquarters in Woburn Abbey, where the E.H. was based since the outbreak of war] should provide a directive for the next *Frau Wernicke* talk, in which Frau Wernicke would be once again in a Berlin air raid shelter" (TNA FO, 898/8:01.10.1940).

Adler would have to alter the script if it did not meet the approval of Gibson or of the Planning and Broadcasting Committee (many of whom were members of the Electra House). This process of control was a challenging and irritating experience for Adler. "I am certainly quite prepared to alter this script for next Sunday's relay," he wrote to Gibson in August 1940, "if you consider it desirable. I feel it is rather hard to adapt myself completely to all suggestions given" (WAC Adler: 28.08.1940). Adler's tone is always polite but between the lines there is a whiff of frustration about what the Electra House considers "desirable". A glance at Gibson's letters sheds light on the production process and the commanding role she played in it:

> Would you be kind enough to let me know as soon as you decide on the subject of Frau Wernicke's talk for next week? It will then be possible for me to tell you whether in principle the subject would be suitable. One suggestion I have had is Frau Wernicke talking about the invasion of England - that she doesn't know when it will come off but she does know that it will be the end of her son (or Frau Spindler's?) (WAC Adler:09.08.1940).

Adler agreed on the subject matter; *Frau Wernicke on an Historic Occasion* was about the fictional invasion of England by Germany (WAC Adler:11.08.1942).[17] A similar theme characterises the pair's subsequent correspondence. Gibson is always courteous but she is firm too. Her comments may be phrased as suggestions but they act more as guidelines, if not orders. Here is another of her quasi-diktats to Adler, offering precious insight into the specific demands:

> Here are some suggestions, which may be of use to you for next week's edition of *Frau Wernicke*. It would seem that her natural subject of conversation in the shelter would be air raids, and that as she must at any rate keep up an appearance of being a good Nazi in such surroundings, she

---

[17] The content of this programme is revealed through a letter written from Gibson to Adler dated August 11th 1942: "Do you remember in 1940 on either August 15th or September 15th - and alas, I cannot remember which, and all our records have been
bombed, - Frau Wernicke gave a talk on the day when Hitler should have made his triumphal entry into London? I remember it as being a particularly good one and I wondered whether, as this Saturday is August 15th, it might not be worth while [sic] looking up that script if you can possibly find a copy in the country and simply repeating it" (WAC Adler:11.08.1942).

might appear to be a woman who accepts as true all the most fantastic German statements ("London in flames", "Most English cities destroyed", "No English ship can pass through the Channel", etc. etc.). At the same time, she should tell of the damage done by the RAF in Germany, perhaps using the technique of remarks such as: "I know the English have blown half the Krupp works [German steel factory] to pieces, but what does it matter? London is destroyed already." This sort of remark could be repeated and would give an opportunity to mention in detail much of the damage that has been done by the RAF. [...] Frau Wernicke should appear to be convinced that the war will be over very shortly [...] I enclose some details of British air raids on Germany so that you may be able to quote a few actual places (WAC Adler:30.08.1940).

The fact that Gibson encloses material about the damage done by the RAF shows that the subject has in fact already been decided upon. Further remarks such as "I now offer you a few suggestions for you to ignore" (WAC Adler:04.11.1940) are either a subtle effort to exert pressure or else pure irony. Gibson must have been aware that Adler, as an 'enemy alien', was not in a position to oppose her - for financial reasons as much as for the sceptical mood that prevailed within the BBC towards German-speaking exiles.

The British propaganda establishment was certainly concerned about the involvement of German-speaking exiles in such delicate matters. Their knowledge was needed but they were also a risk, as the *Memorandum on Psychological Approach to Problems of Propaganda* points out: "They may really be enemy agents and they may be blinded with prejudice" (TNA FO, 898/181:n.d). It wasn't only for the threat of treachery that control was so tight. The BBC did not want the German Service to sound like a station that was run by disaffected German exiles. Thus "everything possible was being done to eradicate the 'émigré' tone from the German broadcasts" (TNA FO, 898/8:20.04.1940). The point of the BBC's 'white' propaganda transmissions - as opposed to 'black' propaganda, which concealed its source, was to give Germans the official British perspective. Leonard Miall, the BBC's former European Talks Editor, underlined this point when reflecting on the German Service in 1988: "In talking to Germany about what we were doing, or thinking or hoping, it became important to emphasise this really meant 'we the British' rather than 'we the Refugee Germans'" (BBC, 1988:99). Quite clearly, Bruno Adler and Robert Lucas had little chance of incorporating their own political views into their satire programmes.

Discussions about the art of satire itself are almost completely absent in the exchanges between supervisor and author. This demonstrates that satire was merely a means to an end for the BBC and for the propaganda officials. It was not the medium but the message that was important. For Adler, however, the *way* in which this message was conveyed was crucial:

> If Frau Wernicke is supposed to air Nazi ideas, she can only do this by pretending it, as she is no Nazi at heart. Her only way to criticise Nazism [sic.] is to provoke opposition by irony and exaggeration and putting insidious questions. Usually at the end of her conversations she gets so truly passionate that she has to give away where she really stands (WAC Adler:28.08.1940)

Restricted in the choice of subject and governed by British propaganda policy, Adler worked instead on lending *Frau Wernicke* its satirical twist. His adherence to the instructions of Christina Gibson paid off. In the autumn of 1940 the Planning and Broadcasting Committee minutes describe him as a "persona grata at Broadcasting House" (TNA FO, 898/8:03.10.1940) and suggest that he should live and work at Country Headquarters. It was Gibson who approached Adler with the proposal of directly working for the Electra House. Adler, she claims, was "extremely pleased with the idea" (WAC Adler:04.10.1940). With Adler's integration into the Electra House, letters that describe the working process cease to exist but we can reasonably assume that his work continued to be heavily monitored.

We can also suppose that Robert Lucas was supervised in a similar way to Adler. Whereas the latter was a freelancer for the BBC, Lucas was employed directly by the German Service. This may explain why there is no written correspondence between Lucas and his supervisors among the files of the BBC's Written Archives. His experience of writing a wartime satirical series for the German Service is related to us via his own post-war reflections.

The author's confidence in the programmes suffered in particular because he did not know who, if anyone, was listening. "It was paralysing to speak into the dark without any echo" (Lucas, 1978:453, own translation), he relates in a brief essay written in 1978. He made reference to this uncertainty when speaking shortly after the war: "You hear no applause, no objection [...] from which to see whether you have hit the right tone" (Lucas 19.07.1947:3'14 min, own translation). He goes on to say that they had "no idea whether there would be at least 50 people in Germany listening to us" (Lucas, 19.07.1947:3'35, own translation). Later in his life Lucas openly refers to the fragile existence of the satire programmes: "[I]n the first two years of the war we felt very vulnerable and insecure" (DLA Lucas, 1983:37).

The only feedback Lucas or Adler received was that of the propaganda authorities. Both must have known that without any evidence of impact, satire as a means of propaganda was open to criticism. A government paper entitled *Proposals regarding Propaganda to the Enemy*, written in the summer of 1941, questions the benefits of this sort of programme: "We think that there is comparatively little scope for 'features', i.e. drama, music, dialogue, monologues. When they are included, they must be of very excellent quality, achieving a degree of artistry or satire that compels attention" (TNA FO,

898/182:17.06.1941).

It was only later in the war that intelligence reports allowed for hope that the satire programmes had been heard and welcomed by Germans. In a letter to the financial department, Leonard Miall, the BBC's European Talks Editor, refers to the intelligence reports, praises the propaganda value of *Frau Wernicke* and fights for a pay rise for the actress Annemarie Hase. Although it is very unlikely that either Hase or Bruno Adler read the letter it nevertheless is evidence of at least some support:

> Frau Wernicke is one of the very best of the regular features of our German Service and evidence from inside Germany shows us that her propaganda value is enormous. Hence Miss Hase is, for us, an extremely valuable person. Her voice is so rich and distinctive that we don't wish to allow her to be used in any other capacity except as Frau Wernicke. She is a refugee actress with no other means of support and therefore her weekly income is only £3.13.6 which is not very much these days. [...] I would not make a request of this sort were it not in fact that Frau Wernicke is a propaganda weapon of enormous value to us (WAC Hase:29.09.1942).[18]

Miall clearly believed in satire as a weapon of propaganda even though proof of its effectiveness did not exist. However, on top of the intelligence suggesting that there was a German audience out there, the first letters from listeners started to come in at the beginning of 1943. Robert Lucas remembers these first thrilling signs of an audience. He quotes a note from an anonymous *Wehrmacht* officer that appeared to have been sent via Switzerland: "With a little group of staff operation officers I listened as often as possible to Hirnschal. The last letter about Stalingrad (8.2.1943) was simply great and completely accurate" (quoted in Lucas, 1978:454, own translation).

But these responses were exceptions. Lucas continued to experience the sensation of "speak[ing] into the dark" right up until the Allied invasion of Germany. "The dark only lifted when the allied troops in the fifth year of war advanced onto German soil. That is when it was shown that we did not speak to an empty theatre" (Lucas, 19.07.1947:19'58, own translation).

Lucas published a selection of the *Hirnschal* letters shortly after the war (Lucas, 1945) and its success was interpreted as another indication of the popularity of the BBC's satire programmes.[19] But we should be wary of exaggerating their contemporary significance. Certainly no one had expected

---

[18] Miall's passionate plea was successful and Hase had her weekly salary raised from £4 to £5.50 (WAC Hase:04.10.1942).
[19] There were several editions of the *Hirnschal* letters and the latest was published in 2007. Uwe Naumann, the scholar of anti-fascist satire, published transcripts of the *Frau Wernicke* programmes in 1990 (Naumann, 1990).

these features to have a literary afterlife. The manuscripts have survived more by chance than through careful preservation. As former BBC staff member Carl Brinitzer points out in his memoirs: "We had other things to do in war than archiving manuscripts and keeping them for posterity" (Brinitzer, 1969:16, own translation). Undoubtedly these feature programmes are distinctive for their character but their importance within the daily routines of the German Service seems to have been inflated since the war. In fact the nature of the work was more mundane - they were journalistic productions designed to break the Nazi hold on German minds. In no way were they considered on a par with the BBC newsreels (Hickman, 1995:105). Indeed sometimes the satire programmes had to be curtailed in favour of news bulletins or they were cancelled at the last minute to make room for breaking news (Dove, 2003:64).

Only after the war did the myth of satire as an effective psychological tool take hold and the doubts about its worth became traded for beaming confidence. Lucas said in a 1947 radio broadcast: "We believe that we can today say that our experiment to use humour as a weapon of war succeeded fully" (Lucas, 19.07.1947:20'16, own translation). It seems there is a temptation to idealise the morally sound, democratic spirit of the times - especially in light of victory - and frame the satire programmes within that context, to portray them as the fruits of a united cast of characters who were sharp to the benefits of satire. It should be resisted for it comes at the expense of historical accuracy.

In January 1944 *Frau Wernicke* was taken off air. Multiple publications refer to an eye operation of Annemarie Hase (Naumann, 1990:173, Taylor, 1999:49). A letter from Christina Gibson to Hase shows this to be incorrect:

> I write to tell you that the decision has been made to take the Frau Wernicke programme off the air. [...] I expect you know that it has had a longer run than any other feature in our programmes, but it is now generally felt by those in charge of policy and programme direction that it should not be continued any longer (WAC Hase:21.01.1944).

For Hase this was quite a blow. Her response is touching and reveals that playing Frau Wernicke was much more than a simple job to her:

> I can't deny that your decision to take the Wernicke-Programme off the air was a great disappointment to me, not so much in economical as in ideological [sic.] respect. I have always looked at my work at the B.B.C. as a responsible task [...] as a contribution – if only a small one – to the allied cause and a means of conveying genuine true and democratic spirit to some of my fellow countrymen (WAC Hase:24.01.1944).

The realities of the BBC's attitude to *Frau Wernicke* and the use of satire as a weapon do not sit comfortably with the rose-tinted accounts that have appeared since the war. Debate about the merits of the satire programmes never ceased while they were being produced. In August 1944 the BBC Director of European Broadcast, Noel Newsome, wrote to the Head of the German Service about a broadcast of *Kurt und Willi*:

> If this was funny and entertaining it could only have served the lamentable purpose of easing the tension in Germany, just as, for instance, wisecracks about 'doodle bugs' reduce tension here about robot bombs [...] If *Kurt und Willi* were not really funny the feature was a waste of precious time in any case.
>
> On their home radio the Germans [...] should not get jokes, when they tune in to London.
>
> I consider that to continue in this phase established features such as, *Kurt und Willi*, Hirnschal, etc., popular for their entertainment value and quite out of tune with the electrical atmosphere which must prevail in the Reich, is completely false psychology.
>
> I am convinced that we must at once recast our entire German schedule (WAC E1/758/2:08.08.1944).

Newsome's criticisms are based largely on the "false psychology" of using satire as a weapon of war – which it fails to aid the Allied cause. But is there not also a hint of the deeper moral question in Newsome's condemnation? Does he struggle to see the funny side of Kurt und Willi because it is "out of tune" with the horrors of war? He says that Germans should not be listening to jokes on the BBC – because it is inappropriate? Is it wrong, to return to the words of Lucas, "to laugh amid the hell's noise of the war machinery"?

The final section of this chapter will look at the moral issues that arise when satire takes Nazism as its subject, before we end with a consideration of the question which remains relevant today: what can political satire achieve?

Laughing at Horror

Sceptics such as the philosopher Theodor Adorno have insisted that antifascist satire, by its very nature, is wholly inappropriate. It fails to neither grasp nor depict reality and, worse still, it ignores or trivialises the gravity of National Socialism through ridicule and laughter (Adorno, 1990:418). But, for the two authors of the satire programmes, this misses the point. Robert Lucas and Bruno Adler had chosen to escape from the gruesome reality into accentuated unrealism in order to awaken Germans to the horrors and absurdities around them. Here is Adler's assessment of his satire programmes in 1962:

> My dialogues [...] were backed by certain matters of fact, insofar they

contained something documentative – but they extend beyond that by being like a caricature [...] an accentuated parody, leaving aside, what in the current context is dispensable and overemphasizing what helps the cause. (Adler quoted in Wittek, 1962:233, own translation)

Adler argued that those who thought he wanted to simply amuse did not understand his satire (DLA Adler:31.12.1962). Indeed, it is disturbing issues and sincere emotions that often lie at the heart of satire. Meaningless, trivial matters cannot form the constitutive element of satire. Lucas utilised the method of shock consciously for his *Hirnschal* letters: "It was a humour that bordered on the areas of horror. Joke and lunacy could hardly be distinguished anymore" (Lucas, 19.07.1947:10'20, own translation). He too opposed the idea that his satire programme was an amusement tool:

If you find those letters amusing than please remember that they were meant dead serious. They should cause laughter that was supposed to kill. They weren't written to amuse but to help to destroy a criminal system whose pure existence made it impossible for any human being in any place of the world to laugh jauntily (Lucas, 19.07.1947:15'42, own translation).

The authors did not take their task light-heartedly and their programmes were not intended to be taken light-heartedly either. They did not wish simply to humiliate their opponent: "Satire is only allowed where you can sense that behind the attack certain real values are being defended [...] where the opponent isn't simply ridiculed [...] but attacked in his moral centre" (DLA Adler:31.12.1962, own translation).

What *Frau Wernicke, Kurt und Willi* and the *Hirnschal* letters illustrate is that satire itself is not degrading. What is degrading is the inhumane, murderous reality of National Socialism. For Bruno Adler and Robert Lucas, the idea of satire as a morally unacceptable method was wide of the mark. Lucas explained what satire was to him in a radio programme after the war:

It seemed to me very important [...] in the battle for the souls of the German population – and that is what it was about in those years – to use the weapon of humour and [...] the acidic effect that satire can have (Pilger, n.d.:37'47min.).

When war ended numerous letters reached the BBC expressing gratitude for the satire programmes. However it is difficult to know how many were from Germans who were desperate to conceal their Nazi past and wrote these letters to portray themselves as silent resisters who listened to the BBC. One such letter, sent to Robert Lucas in November 1945, shows the difficulty in establishing what kind of feelings and changes the programmes provoked within its audience:

> You cannot know how much the serious and cathartic cheeriness of your *Hirnschal* brought light to hundreds of thousands, indeed, millions during all those years of hell. Every *Hirnschal* evening a giant corona would congregate around the radio in my small house. And none of us remained without comfort or relief. God shall bless you for this! (quoted in Naumann, 2003:93, own translation).

High praise indeed, although a "cathartic cheeriness" that, like a valve releasing pressure, brought relief to the listener and may have eased the subversive tension was probably not quite what Lucas, the BBC or the Electra House had in mind.

But did not the laughter at least remind people of being human? And was it not an achievement to have conveyed a sense of hope to listeners that they are not alone? This brings us to the fundamental question of political satire: When is it successful? If it is well produced? If it has a big audience? If it incites subversive acts or disobedience?

But one cannot reduce the significance of satire to such concrete black and white terms. It seems to have been neither a failure nor an ingenious weapon of war. Satire will rarely achieve anything so tangible. It serves mainly as a device to awaken sentiment. Anti-fascist satire could only be a further medium to exploit existing scepticism and encourage critical thought. If it also provided pleasure and comfort to the listener then we are talking about psychological components that have a greater significance that cannot be measured by a cold calculation of cost and benefit.

But perhaps it was not only about the recipient. The existential value of these broadcasts for the authors themselves should not be underestimated. While other exiled artists were isolated and desperate (many of them – Walter Benjamin, Stefan Zweig or Kurt Tucholsky – committed suicide) Adler, Lucas and even Hase had the opportunity to play an active role and express themselves, at least to a degree.

Lucas and Adler could not stop the National Socialist machine with satire and it is unclear how many German souls – if any – they won over. But the vagaries of the impact they were having should not obscure the fact that German exiled artists were carrying the fight against Hitler and for the German people. Lucas was simply "glad that, in a humble way, we would play our part in fighting Hitler." (DLA Lucas, 1983:37)

His and Adler's desire to write critical satire of Nazism came from the hope for a different, democratic Germany. That alone should silence all questions of the programmes' *raison d'être*. Drawing attention to the human values endangered by the Nazi regime was a duty that intellectuals had to take on regardless of the impact they may or may not have. As Adler declares, "whose profession it is to write, could not lock himself into the ivory tower of the aesthetes and scholars, when in the world around him, namely the German world, insanity and ignominies were part of the daily (dis)order" (DLA Adler:20.03.1968, own translation).

Conclusion

It was never in doubt that Britain had to fight Nazism on the airwaves. But the way in which to fight was not so clear. The attempts to depict the BBC's satire programme as a result of a united group effort, with the German-speaking exiles at its centre, are part of a post-war myth. The governmental control of the authors was strict and the debates among the involved parties about the purpose of the programmes and the merits of satire never ceased. In any case, why conceal the inconsistencies and conflicts within the BBC when their very existence does at least reflect a more liberal atmosphere, which wasn't silenced and 'homogenised' by a totalitarian authority.

"To laugh amid the hell's noise of the war machinery and the hysterical screaming of Nazi-Propaganda" was a unique, bold and innovative approach. It was a direct challenge to German propaganda, which had suppressed almost all humane thinking. Understanding satire and giving in to the impulse of laughter was contrary to the rigid, grim nature of Nazism. Satire may have had a limited input as a "weapon of war" but that it existed at all in this capacity was a show of faith in the intellect and, above all, humanity of the would-be German audience. And that in itself is a considerable legacy.

References

Adorno, Theodor, W. (1990). Engagement. In Rolf Tiedemann (Ed.), *Noten zur Literatur. Gesammelte Schriften* (Vol. 11:409-430). Germany.
Frankfurt am Main: Suhrkamp.
Bramsted, Ernest, K. (1965). *Goebbels and National Socialist Propaganda 1925-1945*. USA. Michigan State: Michigan State University Press.
British Broadcasting Corporation (1988). *'Hier ist England' - 'Live aus London'. Das deutsche Programm der British Broadcasting Corporation 1938-88*. UK.
London: BBC External Service.
Briggs, A. (1970). *The History of Broadcasting in the United Kingdom. The war of words*. UK. Oxford: Oxford University Press.
Brinitzer, C. (1969). *Hier spricht London. Von einem der dabei war*. Germany.
Hamburg: Hoffmann und Campe.
Crossman, R. (1971). Supplementary Essay. In Daniel Lerner (Ed.), *Psychological Warfare against Nazi-Germany - The Sykewar Campaign, D-Day to VE-Day*. USA. Cambridge, Massachusetts: MIT Press. (Pp.323-346)

Cruickshank, C. (1981). *The Fourth Arm - Psychological Warfare 1938-45*. UK. Oxford: Oxford University Press.

Diller, A. (1998). Haben Sie Auslandssender gehört? Eine amerikanische Hörerbefragung am Ende des Zweiten Weltkrieges, *Rundfunk und Geschichte*. 24 (1):54-62.

Dove, R. (2000). Theatre of War: The Austrian Exile Theatre Laterndl. In Anthony Grenville (Ed.), *German-speaking Exiles in Great Britain. The Yearbook of the Research Centre for German and Austrian Studies* (Pp.209-230). Amsterdam: Rodopi.

Dove, R. (2003). 'It tickles my Viennes humour': Feature Programmes in the BBC Austrian Service, 1943-1945. In Charmian Brinson & Richard Dove (Ed.), *Die Stimme der Wahrheit - German-Language Broadcasting by the BBC. The Yearbook of the Research Centre for German and Austrian Studies* (Vol. 5:57-71). Amsterdam: Rodopi.

Greene, Sir Hugh Carleton (1969). *The Third Floor Front*. UK. London: Bodley Head.

Hickman, T. (1995). *What did you do in the war, Auntie? The BBC at War 1939-45*. UK. London: BBC Books.

Howe, E. (1982). *The Black Game. British Subversive Operations Against the Germans During the Second World War*. UK. London. Queen Anne Press.

Joos, J. (2009). Britische Verlage und die deutsche Opposition gegen den Nationalsozialismus in Großbritannien. In Edita Koch and Henrike Walter (Eds.), *Exil. Forschung, Erkenntnisse, Ergebnisse* (Vol.29,2:58–82). Germany. Frankfurt am Main: Exil Verlag.

Lucas, R. (1945). *Adolf Hirnschal. Die Briefe des Gefreiten Adolf Hirnschal an seine Frau in Zwieselsdorf.* Germany. Zürich: Europa-Verlag.

Lucas, R. (1978). Über den Gefreiten Hirnschal und seine Briefe. *Literatur und Kritik*, 128:452-455.

Müller, C. (2004). Zwischen Tradition und Innovation: Zum sozialdemokratischen Politischen Kabarett im Wien der Zwischenkriegszeit. In Oswald Panagl & Robert Kriechbaumer (Eds.), *Stachel wider den Zeitgeist. Kabarett, Flüsterwitze und Subversives* Wien: Böhlau. (Pp.59-78).

Naumann, U. (1990). Frau Wernicke im Ätherkrieg. Nachwort. In Uwe Naumann (Ed.), *Bruno Adler. Frau Wernicke. Kommentare einer Volksjenossin'.* Mannheim: Persona Verlag. (Pp.157-173).

Naumann, U. (2003). Im Ätherkrieg. Die satirischen Sendungen der BBC im Zweiten Weltkrieg. In Joanne McNally & Peter Sprengel (Eds.), *Hundert Jahre Kabarett. Zur Inszenierung gesellschaftlicher Identität zwischen Protest und Propaganda.* Würzburg: Könighausen & Neumann. (Pp.87-95).

Taylor, J. (1999). The 'Endsieg' as Ever-Receding Goal. In Ian Wallace (Ed.), *German-speaking Exiles in Great Britain. Yearbook of the Research Centre for German and Austrian Exile Studies* (Vol. 1:43-57). Amsterdam: Rodopi.

Taylor, J. (2007). The propagandists' propagandist. Bruno Adler's 'Kurt und

Willi' dialogues as expression of British propaganda objectives. In Charmian
Brinson, Richard Dove & Jennifer Taylor (Eds.), *'Immortal Austria'? Austrians in
Exile in Britain. Yearbook of the Research Centre for German and Austrian Exile
Studies* (Vol. 8:19-31). Amsterdam: Rodopi.

Trapp, F. (Ed.) (1999). Fritz Schrecker. In Frithjof Trapp, Bärbel Schrader,
Dieter Wenk & Ingrid Maaß (Eds.), *Handbuch des deutschsprachigen Exiltheaters
1933-1945* (Vol. 2,2:847-848). München: K.G.Saur.

Wittek, B. (1962). *Der britische Ätherkrieg gegen das Dritte Reich. Die deutschsprachigen
Kriegssendungen der British Broadcasting Corporation.* Münster: C.J. Fahle.

Recordings

Krämer, G. & Saaler, P. (1978, September 25). *Hier spricht London - 40 Jahre
BBC in deutscher Sprache* (49min.) [Radio Broadcast]. German Service, British
Broadcasting Corporation.

Lucas, R. (1947, July 19th) In *Gespräch mit einem Mitarbeiter des deutschsprachigen
Dienstes der BBC während des 2. Weltkrieges über "Humor als Kriegswaffe"*
(22'37min.) [Radio Broadcast]. Schweizer Rundfunk.

Pilger, K. (n.d.) *Radiosatiren für das Reich - Der "Ätherkrieg" von BBC London
gegen Nazideutschland* (43'53min.) [Radio Broadcast]. Deutschlandsender.

Written Archives Centre of the BBC in Caversham (WAC)

WAC M	Feature manuscripts of the German Service (1940–1945)
WAC E1/758/2	Programme Arrangements File 1b (1942-1949)
WAC E2/344	German Planning Committee Minutes (1940-942)
WAC Adler	Personal File Bruno Adler
WAC Hase	Personal File Annemarie Hase

The National Archives in Kew Gardens (TNA)

TNA FO 898/3	E.H. and SO1; Propaganda Policy & Aims (1939-1940)
TNA FO 898/7	Planning and Broadcasting Committee Notes (1939-1940)
TNA FO 898/8	Planning and Broadcasting Committee Notes (1940-1941)
TNA FO 898/181	P.W.E. Propaganda Policy Plans (1941)
TNA FO 898/182	BBC German Propaganda/ Working Plans for Programmes (1941-1943)

TNA FO 898/183   General Directives for Propaganda to Germany
                        (1941-1944)

Deutsches Literaturarchiv Marbach (DLA)

Bruno Adler (1968, March 20th) *Der uneigentliche Deutsche.* [Radio Script].
Bruno Adler and Austin Harrison (1962, December 31) *The Two
    Comrades. Harrison and Adler.* [Radio Script] BBC German Soviet Zone
    Programme.
Lucas, Robert (1983). *The German Service of the BBC.* [paper for PEN
    Symposium Report, London] (Pp.35 - 41).

Chapter 5

Magnet of debate
Vrij Nederland, a Dutch weekly at the centre of post-war discussions about the Second World War[1]

Chris van der Heijden
University of Applied Sciences, The Netherlands

Introduction

In May 1965 the Dutch weekly *Vrij Nederland* extensively interviewed a number of students of an Amsterdam high school about World War Two and its aftermath in the Netherlands. The title of the interview – "Do I draw the conclusion that we almost didn't learn anything" – reflects the opinion of the interviewees that nothing had changed for the better since the war. Their elders thought, so the students said, that they had liberated Europe from the Nazis. That was untrue. The Allied forces and a small group of Dutch resistance fighters liberated them: they were liberated. The majority of the Dutch had done nothing but wait and see. It was one of the reasons why they, according to the interviewees, were also responsible for what had happened.

---

[1] The text of this article is a very short and concentrated version of what has been published in a book about the aftermath of the Second World War in the Netherlands, titled Dat nooit meer. De nasleep van de Tweede Wereldoorlog in Nederland [Never again. The Aftermath of the Second World War in the Netherlands] (Amsterdam, 2011). All the references are to be found in that text.

By supporting Colijn's [Dutch Prime Minister before the war] politics of neutrality, they were guilty of the death of twenty million Russians, six million Jews and more than fifty million others.

With hindsight both May 1965 and this article do have a special position in the Dutch aftermath of the Second World War. So does *Vrij Nederland*, although this was already apparent immediately after the war. The magazine was founded at the beginning of the war and is typical for the Dutch resistance: they fought by words instead of by arms.

Intellectual Resistance

While in Belgium and France, approximately one per cent of the population took up arms, this percentage was much lower in the Netherlands: some 25,000 on a population of 9 million, which is only 0.27 per cent, just a quarter of the percentage in the other countries. On the other hand, the intellectual resistance in the Netherlands was comparatively much more important: it consisted of more than a thousand illegal books, some 90 illegal publishing houses and an illegal press of thousands of small newspapers, magazines and handwritten notes.

Only a number of these were really important and reached high circulation figures. Probably the most successful of these was *Vrij Nederland*. That is one of the reasons why its editor in chief, Henk van Randwijk, spoke in public on Dam Square in the centre of Amsterdam in May 1945. It was his finest hour and the finest hour of his magazine. "They" (in parentheses) had won the war. The future should be theirs. The country should change and the resistance, accordingly, should lead the way. The war had generated a new way of thinking and acting. So Van Randwijk and *Vrij Nederland* thought.

They were mistaken however. Almost immediately after the liberation, things started to change dramatically. The restoration of the country took much longer than predicted. Collaborators were not as rigorously punished as many, mostly former resistance fighters, wanted. In the meantime, the same resistance fighters did not receive the honour they thought was rightfully theirs. Many people longed for a change but it never came. So the first post-war elections meant a return to the pre-war situation and showed that the war had just been an interlude.

Shadows of the War

In the first months after the liberation much was written and said about what had happened during the war and what this meant for the future. Then people fell silent, the more because nobody wanted to listen. People did not want to remember any longer, they wanted to go ahead with their lives. And to make things worse, immediately after the war the Netherlands entered into a conflict with its former colony, nowadays Indonesia. Most Dutch people supported the government's decision to invade the country and restore order by force.

Not so *Vrij Nederland* and Henk van Randwijk. The Dutch invasion of Indonesia reminded them of the Germans and their occupational forces. That is why on the day the Dutch government decided to invade Dutch India, Van Randwijk wrote an angry and nowadays famous article in which he reminded the Dutch public of their thoughts during the war. "Because I'm a Dutchman" was the title of it. Van Randwijk argued that the Dutch treatment of the Indonesian people should be resisted like the Dutch themselves had resisted the Germans. There was something more important than national pride, he wrote, something more important than self-interest: ethics, morals, and the acceptance of the other as equal. That was what the war was fought for; that was why the Nazis had to be defeated. Because they had a way of thinking that was brutal, barbarian, unacceptable. And now, just two years after the war, the Dutch showed the same mentality. According to Van Randwijk and *Vrij Nederland*, it was disgusting.

But Van Randwijk's way of thinking was not that of the Dutch majority. Therefore his article had important consequences both for the man himself and for his magazine. *Vrij Nederland* had already lost a big part of its readership after the war, because readers were no longer interested in resistance journalism. After Van Randwijk's critical article the remaining readers also left. Statistics tell the story. While *Vrij Nederland* printed more than 100,000 copies in May 1945, in 1947 there were 32,000 left and in 1955 just 19,000. But not only the public gave up on the magazine, van Randwijk did too. Disappointed he went to Indonesia to help the young country to build its own democracy. In the meantime just like everybody else, he spoke less and less about the war. The same happened in *Vrij Nederland*. During the fifties the war was not an important subject of discussion. People only talked about it out of obligation. The war was a shadow, inevitable and inescapable but preferably forgotten.

All this changed in the beginning of the 1960s. From that decade onwards the shadow became a mirror. The change showed itself both in *Vrij Nederland* and in Henk van Randwijk's biography. Somewhere in 1958, 1959 and surely in 1960 the war in the Netherlands and elsewhere started to attract attention again. The reasons for this renewed interest are not easy to find. The international popularity of Anne Frank, the renewed interest in Israel, symbolised by the enormous success of Leon Uris' novel *Exodus* but most of all the excitation around Eichmann are some of the factors of the ubiquitous revival of interest in the recent past. In the Netherlands this revival was particularly strong because of one man: Loe de Jong. in May 1960 he started *De Bezetting* (the Occupation), a television series that turned him into the most important Dutch historian of the Second World War. It consisted of 26 parts and was televised over five years, ending in May 1965. Its tone and content were in concordance with De Jong's wartime experience (during the war he had worked in London for the free Dutch radio), which means that the perspective of the series was that of the allied forces and the Dutch resistance. The end of the first programme is a case in point: it shows some Dutch men rowing a boat to England and the image of one of the most important Dutch war monuments, the *Dokwerker*. During the war it was a symbol of those who stood up against the Germans.

But Loe de Jong was not the only one to give an overview of Dutch war history in the period 1960-1965. So did Henk van Randwijk: at the end of the year 1960 he began a long series of articles about the war in the leading liberal newspaper *Het Algemeen Handelsblad* under his resistance name. His perspective was similar to de Jong's, in that it suggested that war history has to be dominated, just as the war itself had been, by the antithesis between (good) resistance and (bad) collaboration. This vision of Dutch war history was the more important (and welcome) because, according to Van Randwijk and to a lesser extent Loe de Jong, the Dutch had been on the good side during the war. Of course some people had collaborated. But the majority did what they had to do and "resisted", if not actively, in any case passively. The same idea dominated *Vrij Nederland*, which had another former resistance fighter as its editor in chief from 1955 onwards.

And then, just as the story of the war seemed to be fixed and clear, things suddenly seemed to change. In April 1965 Jacques Presser, a Dutch Jewish historian who had lost his wife and many friends during the war, published a book that was translated into English as *Ashes in the Wind*. It had an enormous impact. As far as I know never before in Dutch history a book was received as this one. Critics were almost too shy to criticize it; they just cited it and made extracts. The first print of 11,000 copies was sold in a day or two. The same happened to the second, third and fourth editions. All newspapers and magazine wrote long articles about the book. The author appeared on television, radio and everywhere else. And every time he repeated what he had also said in his book: more or less the same as the younger generation said in the interview that appeared two weeks later in *Vrij Nederland*. Of course, nobody doubted that the Nazis were guilty of murdering the Jews. But, according to Presser, the bystanders were also guilty. He even went so far as to inculpate himself. "Even I haven't been much more than a weak human being during the war," he wrote, "trying to save my own life." But when Presser, a Jew who had to hide to avoid being killed, was guilty, how much more guilty were the others. Presser was very clear about that:

> They didn't know; they didn't want to know; they didn't need to know. It all went so smoothly, so clean... Everybody had his own problems. Therefore it was easy to comfort yourself. How often the writer of this book didn't hear it after the war. You mustn't forget what we had to suffer. He didn't forget it. He still doesn't.

Presser's attack on his own generation fell the more on fertile ground because in the same time things started to change dramatically in the Netherlands. Probably the most important reason for the vehemence of this change is that the Netherlands, until that moment, had been a very conservative country. As said, just after the war the left wing resistance press tried to force a breakthrough. It didn't come about. Now it did. And it was mostly a younger generation that made, thereby using all the arguments it could find. One of those concerned the war. They used that not only because the older generation against whom they rebelled understood it but also because the subject of war at that historical point in time – the middle of the sixties - was much discussed anyway. Not only by De Jong, Van Randwijk and Presser but also because of contemporary reasons: the war in Vietnam, for example. In March 1965 the Americans stationed troops in the country and almost immediately international protests started. In the Netherlands, the war-excitement had still another reason. On 6 May 1965, one day after the traditional War Remembrance Day and at the same moment De Jong completed his television series, Van Randwijk his newspaper series and everybody was talking about Presser's book, it became known that the Dutch Crown Princess had started a relationship with a German who had fought in the war. That was the straw that seemed to break the camel's back. Protests followed everywhere.

The general tendency was simple: things had to change radically. If they did not, it was assumed that past events would be repeated. That is what Jacques Presser wrote about in his book on the Shoah and Ed Hoornik, one of the veterans of Dutch literature, in *Vrij Nederland*. He was editor in chief of the most important cultural Dutch magazine, a poet, writer and the centre of an Amsterdam group of young, upcoming intellectuals. During the war Hoornik had been in Dachau. Until 1965 he had only spoken indirectly about his experiences. But then, again in May 1965, he published an article in *Vrij Nederland* with the title *Voor altijd Dachau*, "Dachau forever". In this article he wrote about his first post-war visit to the concentration camp where he had been interned. It was a strange journey, simultaneously sad and happy. Sad it was because it reminded him of a past he preferred to forget. But it was also happy because the confrontation helped him to understand his own pains and sorrows. That is why the supreme moment of his journey came when he found the gutter in Dachau through which the blood of the beaten and the executed flew, according to his memory. It made him happy because now he knew his memories were not the invention of a sick mind. They were true. He was not sick. He was a victim. And worse: nobody bothered.

It was in *Vrij Nederland* that all these lines of thought and all these persons from the mid sixties onwards came together and formed the story of the war that is typical for that of the Netherlands. To repeat it systematically and in the order of appearance in this article:

The younger generation was critical about the wartime experiences of their elders. With hindsight, it is easy to see that their criticism was quite unrelated to the war itself. They used the war for their political views. Just like the resistance fighters during the war had fought the Germans, they fought their elders. The parallel was just too good not to be used.

Then there were those from the older generation who really had fought the Germans. During the 1950s they had been relatively silent about the war because nobody wanted to listen. When this changed at the beginning of the 1960s, they started to talk and repeated what they had said during and shortly after the war. Generally, their view was the opposite of that of the younger generation. In any case they thought, just as they had done during the war, in terms of black and white, collaboration and resistance. In their opinion, the Dutch had been on the good side.

The members of the older generation who had been victims during the war, Jews like Jacques Presser or former concentration camp prisoners like Eduard Hoornik thought differently. But until the mid 1960s their silence had been even stronger. But when they started to speak they were even more critical than the young about Dutch behaviour during and after the war. Who had assisted them? Who after the war had shown interest in their wants? Nobody. They thought it was unforgivable.

In the second half of the sixties and the beginning of the seventies these three tendencies or perspectives on the Second World War fought for supremacy in *Vrij Nederland*. In the beginning the hierarchy was clear. The perspectives of Loe de Jong (who also wrote weekly commentaries for the magazine) and Henk van Randwijk (who had returned to the magazine after years of absence) dominated the discourse, especially because the editor in chief of the magazine was from the same generation as they were and had the same wartime experiences. But slowly, slowly they lost ground, because there was a fourth group or perspective that came to play an important role. Although I have not mentioned it explicitly yet, they were probably decisive to the future of the Dutch war image. In any case they were decisive to the image of the war that dominated *Vrij Nederland* in the period 1970-1980. This fourth group consisted of relatively young journalists who started work for the magazine in the sixties. Most of them were older than the young people who took to the streets for a political change and who, in general, were university and high school students, between seventeen and twenty-five years old. The new generation of *Vrij Nederland* journalists was older, born before the war and at least twenty-five but mostly between thirty and forty years old in 1965. They had experienced the war as children and started to dominate the journalistic field in the 1960s and 1970s when they were at their prime. They agreed with the young, not with the old, and with the third group, those who had suffered during the war, people like Jacques Presser and Ed. Hoornik. This was quite logical since they had also suffered, if not physically then at least mentally.

All these tendencies collided around 1970 when Loe de Jong published the first tome of his grand series of books about the Netherlands in the Second World War. It was critically reviewed in *Vrij Nederland* by one of those younger journalists. Loe de Jong left the magazine because of this review and dedicated himself completely to his historical work. At more or less the same moment the Weinreb affair started in the Netherlands: a rather complicated case about a Jew who had saved a lot of people during the war apparently for money or so the rumours had it. The affair lasted for years. Generally, the younger generation and *Vrij Nederland* supported Weinreb while the mainstream media and people such as Loe de Jong opposed him. They disliked Weinreb even more because he strived for societal changes, behaved like an old hippie and advocated insubordination. At last Weinreb was unmasked as an imposter in a large study executed by the institute of Second World War Studies of which Loe de Jong was the director. This study was published in 1976, at the end of the radicalism of the sixties. It was a victory for Loe de Jong and his perspective on the war. This victory became even stronger because in the meantime De Jong published his enormous war history: book after book after book, a total of 30 tomes, 16,000 pages or 26 kilo. Nobody knew as much about the war as he did. Nobody could compete with him. Nobody was supported as he was by a complete institute and a staff of tens of collaborators.

So from the mid 1970s until the last decade of the twentieth century, World War Two in the Netherlands was more or less Loe de Jong's war. In the process De Jong did change his perspective on the war. His books differed from his television series. For instance he showed more interest in the victims than he had done before. It was one more reason for the reception of his work as definite, at last even by *Vrij Nederland*. The year 1985, when De Jong's work was almost finished, was dominated by his enormous influence. Literally hundreds of books, articles, documentaries and interviews were published that reflected his view one way or another. De Jong's television series had been dominated by the idea of a good Dutch population fighting a bad enemy. The books contained a more general idea of good and bad. Bad in any case was everybody or everything that inflicted harm on innocent people, Jews, children, Roma and Sinti, disabled, homosexuals and the many that survived but suffered bombardments, hunger and persecution. As a consequence *Vrij Nederland* published dozens of articles in the seventies and eighties in which individual victims told their story. The question of guilt was rarely answered because it seemed evident: the Nazis and their accomplices were guilty. It is true that professionals criticized this perspective and pleaded for a more balanced view. But their influence was small. It is also true that the critical perspective of the two younger generations and the war victims lived on. But it was of secondary importance. It could not compete with that of Loe de Jong. It just slumbered in the background.

A Question of Generations

In the mid-1990s these slumbering tendencies suddenly became dominant. Again the change is easier to observe than to explain. In any case, in or around the year 1995 the embarrassing perspective on the war that had seen an upsurge in the 1960s became popular. It could have been a question of generations: those who had been 20 in 1965 now were 50 and powerful. It could be a consequence of historical dynamics: since the end of the 1980s more and more awkward stories about the war have become known. One of those is the simple fact that in the Netherlands a bigger percentage of Jews had died during the war than anywhere else in the Western world. These stories invigorated themselves and created a different, more critical atmosphere. This atmosphere was enhanced by actuality, in the first place by what happened in the summer of 1995 in Srebrenica, former Yugoslavia, where Dutch soldiers had to protect a Bosnian population against the Serbs. They did not or could not, in any case for the first time since World War Two genocide was committed on European soil - under Dutch eyes.

Also embarrassing were the stories of Swiss behaviour during the war. Shortly after they became known, it was discovered that Dutch banks, lawyers and bureaucrats had behaved in more or less the same way. And then, to name but one example out of many, there was new research by a younger generation of historians. This research showed things to be more complicated and less lofty than they had been seen until then. The consequences were enormous and caused a complete turnover of the dominant image of the Netherlands during the war.

In 2001 I published a book in which I contend that most of the Dutchmen had indeed just tried to live on during the war. Not everybody agreed, far from it, but everybody did agree that the image of good and bad, resistance and collaboration was too simple and too narrow a perspective. At the same time, most people also agreed that the victims' perspective had been too narrow. The result has been chaos. The war, or to put I more precisely the image of the war of Loe de Jong and the old *Vrij Nederland*, has had his time. That is certain. But it is still unclear which image or images are taking its place. In the meantime confusion reigns. This confusion was perfectly expressed by Henk Hofland, one of those who took the lead in the public and journalistic debate at the end of the 1960s and the beginning of the 1970s. He was born in 1927 and experienced the war as a young boy. He and his generation have always identified themselves with the war. Hofland and his friends were critical of the older generation, critical also of Loe de Jong's image of the war. But they agreed with him about the clear differences between good and bad, black and white. But from the mid 1990s onwards this clearness became disturbed. The confusing outcome is shown in an article about Henk Hofland published in one of the first editions of *Vrij Nederland* of this year. The cover shows the portrait of an older man, melancholically looking into the lens. "The war is over", the headline says, and a strapline: "the here and now of H.J.A. Hofland". About this here and now the article is clear. It is confusing. About the background of that confusion the article is also clear: the present lacks a compass. Even about the former compass there is no doubt: "the legacy of the war lost his validity" and no other value has taken its place yet.

References

Ester, Hans en Wam de Moor, (1994). *Een halve eeuw geleden. De verwerking van de Tweede Wereldoorlog in de literatuur.* Amsterdam. Amsterdam University Press.

Ginkel, Rob van: Rondom de stilte, (2011). *Herdenkingscultuur in Nederland.* UK. London: Springer.

Heijden, Chris van der, (2011). *Dat nooit meer. De nasleep van de Tweede Werel doorlog in Nederland.* Amsterdam. Contact.

Heijden, Chris van der, (2001). *Grijs verleden. Nederland en de Tweede Wereldoorlog.* Amsterdam.

Jong, L. De, (1969-1991). *Het Koninkrijk der Nederlanden.* In de Tweede Wereldoorlog, 14 dln. Amsterdam. Den Haag.

Keizer, Madelon de en Marije Plomp (ed.), (2010) Een open zenuw. Hoe wijons de Tweede Wereldoorlog herinneren. Amsterdam. Springer.

Mulder, G. en P. Koedijk, (1988): *H.M. van Randwijk.* Een biografie. Amsterdam. Van Gurcum. Amsterdam. Amsterdam University Press.

Schram, D.H. en C. Geljon (1990). *Overal sporen.* De verwerking van de Tweede Wereldoorlog in literatuur en kunst. Amsterdam

Vree, Frank van (1995). *In de schaduw van Auschwitz.* Herinneringen, beelden, geschiedenis. USA. Michigan. Michigan University Press.

Chapter 6

All in this Together? Manchester and its Newspapers in the Aftermath of the Christmas Blitz 1940

Guy Hodgson
University of Chester, UK

Introduction

In August 2011 the Prime Minister David Cameron used the wartime narrative of his predecessor, Winston Churchill, in a speech entitled "We're all in this together," a call for resolution and patience about the UK's economic problems. It was a theme he returned to at the Conservative Party Conference two months later, prompting James Kirkup, of the *Daily Telegraph*, to write:

> I don't think you have to be a historian to get the impression that Mr Cameron would like you to think about British bulldogs, Sir Winston Churchill and the war... Mr Cameron is pitching himself as the man to lead us into the battle to come. Quietly, he's recasting himself, changing his role from sunshine kid to economic war leader (Kirkup, 2011).

The expression "we're all in this together" is a lasting legacy of the Second World War and stemmed from the notion that the conflict removed the social barriers of the 1930s.[1] Food was rationed, privilege was removed and if your name was on one of the hundreds of tons of bombs dropped by the *Luftwaffe* then it did not matter if that name was double-barrelled or if it was prefixed by a title. It is an idyll of equality that has been questioned by historians, Calder (1991) and Gardiner (2010) among them. Ponting (1990:138) wrote:

---

[1] The expression 'we're all in this together' came originally from the US, where it became a common war cry in the Second World War before spreading to Britain.

One of the central myths of 1940, cultivated at the time and embellished since, was that Britain was galvanised by crisis to change old ways of working, and became united as never before, with a strong bond of equality of sacrifice... The reality was very different.

This chapter will examine the veracity of the unity of purpose, one of the myths deriving from the Blitz, and show that people had a more nuanced experience between 1939 and 1945. It will look at the social conditions in Britain in the Second World War, the support for the war, the anti-German and Italian backlash and the psychological consequences of the aerial bombardment. It will explore the relatively neglected area of the north of England in the Second World War, with Manchester as its focus. There has been much research into London's Blitz – a search of the British Library catalogue using the key words "Manchester Blitz" in December 2012 revealed two, largely pictorial, books, an article and a journal, while "London Blitz" produced 187, 35 and three respectively – but relatively little about cities elsewhere in the UK (http://www.bl.uk). By most criteria this is justified in that London suffered nearly half the British deaths caused by the *Luftwaffe*'s bombing, 29,890 to 30,705 (O'Brien, 1955:677), but the narrative of the chirpy East Ender has become pervasive, so that other, provincial, tales have been overwhelmed). In a book that asserts a distinctive northern English cultural identity, the broadcaster Stuart Maconie noted that South Shields, in the north east of England, suffered 200 air raids in the Second World War and 156 people were killed:

> One direct hit on the marketplace killed more than 40 people sheltering in tunnels below the square. These are statistics to remember next time you watch a programme about the Blitz. It will be about London as always and feature Piccadilly Circus in flames and cheery Cockneys making their way to Tube stations. If you trusted the London media you could be forgiven for thinking that the south won the war single-handed and that northern England was as quiet as Switzerland. It wasn't, as the people in South Shields will testify (Maconie, 2007:303).

The chapter uses Manchester's Blitz in December 1940, when nearly 1,000 people died, as the starting point to monitor unity in the weeks that followed at a time when the sense of togetherness was given its most severe test. It will do so by examining contemporary accounts in the Home Intelligence and Mass Observation archives and by monitoring the city's newspapers to see if the highly censored editions of wartime Britain reflected the tensions brought by severe bombing by the *Luftwaffe*. It will look at the reporting of crime, the incidences of which rose significantly between 1939 and 1945, and at readers' letters to examine whether discordant voices were given a platform.

The Social Divide

Britain entered the war in 1939 with considerable social problems. Unemployment had disfigured a generation, a scar on the country that even re-armament from 1938 could not cure quickly. In January 1940 1.3m people were unemployed, a year later 653,000 were still out of work and the figure did not drop to below 200,000 until June 1941. The surplus workforce did not soothe industrial relations and even in 1941, with Britain near its lowest ebb, more than a million days were lost to strikes. This rose to 3.7m in 1944, a figure not matched again until 1955 (Butler and Sloman, 1974:341). Inflation also took a toll on household incomes, average prices rising 19 per cent in 1940 compared to an 11 per cent increase in salaries (Ponting, 1990:138). The consequence was deep deprivation in some of the poorer areas, MP Russell Thomson reporting to Parliament in 1942 that 25 per cent of children in Merseyside were living below the poverty line. Research at Christ's Hospital, a public school in Sussex, revealed that its pupils were 2.4 inches taller at the age of 13 than comparable boys at elementary schools. The benefit of a good diet became even more pronounced at 17 when the difference in height was 3.8 inches (*Hansard*, HC Deb, 30 June 1942, vol 381, cols 38-182).

Rationing of food should have brought equality. Joan Styan (2004), a housewife in London, recalled:

> The rich were hit the same as the poor and, whatever we wanted, we had to queue for... The standard phrase from the customer to the shop assistant was: "Is there anything under the counter?" We were only allowed 2 ounces of butter each week so we often had bread and dripping or condensed milk on our bread. The hardships seemed endless.

Mrs Styan's belief that the rich were also suffering was not true. Harold Nicolson, a junior minister at the Ministry of Information, spent much of his time eating in the clubs of St James's, London. On one occasion he had to eat in the refectory of the ministry's headquarters, recording in his diary: "It is absolutely foul... It is run on the cafeteria system and we have got to queue up with trays with the messenger boys" (Nicolson, October 21, 1940, cited in Ponting, 1990:141). His more normal eating habits had been revealed a month earlier: "Dine with Guy Burgess at the Reform and have the best cooked grouse that I have ever eaten" (Nicolson, 1970:109). Hastings (2011:342), citing the novelist Anthony Powell, wrote: "Privileged Britons remained privileged indeed. 'The extraordinary thing about the war was that people who really didn't want to be involved in it were not'."

Other evidence countered the myth of togetherness. Affluent parents sent 17,000 children abroad in the six months after June 1940 (Ponting, 1990:148); in the army former public schoolboys were 14 times more likely to be officers, the navy reserved half of its officer cadet places for public schoolboys and the officer class of the RAF were awarded the Distinguished Flying Cross and first class rail travel while sergeant pilots, predominantly from the lower classes, received only the Distinguished Flying Medal and a third class railway carriage (Hylton, 2001, p. 58). Until November 1940 work at the Foreign Office did not start until 11am, while at the Ministry of Economic Warfare a memo had to be sent out insisting staff were at their desks by 10am (Ponting, 1990:141).

Knightley wrote that The Blitz was not the great social leveller: "The protection a Londoner got from German bombs depended on how much money he had" (Knightley, 2002:261). An American journalist Ralph Ingersoll recalled visiting a shelter on the Isle of Dogs to find just six buckets acting as toilets for 8,000 people. These overflowed on to the floor where people were sleeping. "The whole experience shocked so that it numbed," he wrote, before driving to the Dorchester Hotel in the West End where guests were housed in individual and comfortable beds in an underground area that had been the hotel's Turkish baths. There he noticed that one berth had a note pinned to its curtain reading "Reserved for Lord Halifax", the Foreign Secretary (Longmate, 1981:78). By the end of September 1940 an estimated 177,000 Londoners were sheltering in 80 tube stations (Hylton, 2001:88). An even more notorious shelter was The Tilbury in Stepney, railway vaults and storage sheds in the Liverpool Street Station goods yard, which the *Daily Herald* journalist Ritchie Calder (1941:39) described as "the most unhygienic place I have ever seen". He added:

> Sanitation barely existed. The only provision was for a handful of workmen usually employed there. The result was that roadways were ankle deep in filth which was trodden into blankets on which people were to sleep. Great stacks of London's margarine were stored there. Hundreds of cartons were hopelessly fouled every night (Calder, 1941:41).

Life in The Tilbury was so appalling, the inhabitants became a tourist attraction for "people 'up West' to gawp at the hellish conditions their fellow Londoners were suffering a few miles away" (Gardiner, 2010:74).

Us and Them

While the British public largely supported the war – an opinion poll conducted by the British Institute of Public Opinion in October 1939 found that 89 per cent favoured fighting "until Hitlerism goes" (cited in Watson, 1980) – the reaction was not uniform. Home Intelligence reported there was little national unity at the start of the war (Mass Observation. SxMOA1/1/6/2/3, FR 568) and Calder listed several groups who, initially at least, had grave misgivings about the conflict. These included members of the far left and right, Irish republicans, and miners, who still harboured grievances against Churchill dating back to the General Strike (Calder, 1991, pp. 65-89). There was also the peace movement. More than 120,000 Britons joined the Peace Pledge Union within a year of its launch in 1936 and a Cheshire diarist (Shipway, 1941) surveying Manchester's bomb damage for Mass Observation felt aggrieved enough about the government's efforts to preserve peace to write in January 1941: "I must say that all this destruction of cities is no more than England deserves for its wanton destruction of the League of Nations." The government put pressure on the BBC and Fleet Street to ensure their voices remained virtually unheard, however, Bingham noting that Vera Brittain, who advocated a pacifist stance even during the war, found it difficult to find space in newspapers to promote her views. "She was perceived to be challenging the 'national interest'," he wrote (Bingham, 2004:208). A reader's letter from G. A. Sutherland (1941) in the *Manchester Guardian* was an indicator of a national mood of intolerance. It read:

> By its action in protecting the public from the pernicious singing of the Orpheus Choir under the direction of the pacifist Sir Hugh Robertson the BBC has earned the plaudits of all prudent patriots. It therefore came as a great shock to read in the *Radio Times* that a lifelong pacifist Sir Arthur Eddington was actually being allowed to disseminate his insidious astronomical theories in a talk with the significant title "Other Worlds". Should not the person responsible for subjecting the nation to so grave a risk be immediately removed from office?

There is little sign there of latitude or forgiveness, but, ironically, the message pushed by Fleet Street was of fighting for freedoms that included speech. The letter above notwithstanding, Calder pointed out there is a mass of evidence suggesting tolerance predominated in Britain in 1940 and that the persecution of foreigners and scares about traitors were halted before too much damage was done. But he added: "There is also ample evidence, familiar and unfamiliar, to indicate widespread fear and paranoia bordering on panic" (Calder, 1991, pp. 109-13). Motorists were killed or wounded by trigger-happy Local Defence Volunteers; Germans, some of them Jews who had fled their native country to escape Hitler's persecution, were interned; and Italian shops were ransacked and 4,000 Italians were arrested, many of whom were sent to a makeshift prison camp in Warth Mills, a wrecked and rat-infested cotton mill in Bury, Lancashire, nine miles north of Manchester. The only light, Hylton (2001) stated, came through a glass roof, many panes of which were broken, and 500 half-starved men shared 18 cold-water taps and filthy toilets. The Red Cross complained, as did the Ministry of Information's Sir Walter Monckton, who wrote: "The two men who succeeded in committing suicide had already been in Hitler's concentration camps. Against these, they held out but this camp had broken their spirit" (Hylton, 2001:15).

Others were deported to the Isle of Man where they were housed two to a bed at Onchan. Hylton (2001:15) wrote that a survey of the internees gave an indication of the threat they posed: "Of the 1491 inmates, 121 were artists or men of letters, 113 scientists or teachers, 68 lawyers and 67 engineers; 1230 were Jewish: 148 were married to British women, and no fewer than 1,080 of them had attempted to sign up in the British armed forces, to fight the Germans." This mass imprisonment occurred despite assurances in March 1940 from the Home Secretary Sir John Anderson, who had told Parliament (*Hansard*, HC Deb, 1 March 1940, vol. 35, cols 410-11): "There would be no justification for a policy under which all aliens of German and Austrian nationality were treated alike, without regard to the fact that the majority of them are refugees from Nazi oppression and are bitterly opposed to the present regime in Germany."

To compound this treatment, on 1 July 1940 more than a thousand of these prisoners set sail from Liverpool for Canadian internment on the Arandora Star and 600 perished when they were torpedoed by a U Boat off the north-west of Ireland the following day. The dead, according to Calder (1991), included a well-known German socialist opponent of Hitler and the secretary of the Italian League of the Rights of Man. None of this rests easily of with the myth of quiet bravery under the bomb and Fleet Street compounded this crime by continuing to attack the internees. According to the *Daily Express* ("Germans Torpedo Germans," 1940):

> Soldiers and sailors…told of panic among the aliens when they realised the ship was sinking. All condemned the cowardice of the Germans, who fought madly to get into the boats. "The Germans were fighting the Italians to escape, they were great hulking brutes," said one soldier. "They punched and kicked their way past the Italians. We had to restrain them forcibly… But the Italians were just as bad. The whole mob thought of their own skins first. The scramble for the boats was sickening."

A subsequent investigation proved this account to be wholly false and this, coupled with similar excesses by the press, eventually changed the national mood and the proportion of the public in favour of internment fell from 55 per cent in July 1940 to 30 per cent in August (Hylton, 2001).

If the public's antagonism to British-based Germans and Italians moderated, there is evidence that anti-Semitism was more ingrained. Hylton (2001) cited that Mass Observation found evidence of anti-Semitism among more than 55 per cent of respondents in one survey, suggesting that Britons could divorce their opposition to Hitler from their anti-Jewish sentiments. A Home Intelligence report in 1943 (SxMOA1/1/8/3/26, FR 1648) stated there was "much latent anti-Semitism":

The Manchester *Daily Dispatch*, for instance, published a letter in which it was suggested Jewish names predominated in black market prosecutions, army dodging trials, clothing coupon rackets, petrol ramps and the like, the writer suggesting that the Jews should be put in their place.

An investigator reported this letter was widely discussed and quoted various remarks, including "there's no doubt they (the Jews) have too much power", "stinking lot of cowards they are, the Jews" and "Jews shops are always stocked up". An accompanying survey of Mass Observation's national panel of observers – credited in the report as: "a section of the population more intelligent and better informed than the average" – revealed that only 25 per cent of them felt "favourable" towards Jews and even as late as January 1944 another Mass Observation survey, cited in Hylton (2001), revealed that 24 per cent of the population wanted stricter controls on the activities of British Fascists but only two per cent saw the need for curbs on anti-Semitism. Societies and clubs openly excluded Jews and the author Douglas Reed used anti-Semitic themes in his novels, including *Insanity Fair,* published in 1938, the storyline for which had Jews taking over London. Interestingly, Reed ended the war as the foreign editor for Kemsley Newspapers, the publishers of Manchester's *Evening Chronicle* and, among other newspapers, the *Sunday Times,* despite his association with extreme anti-Semitic organisations.

Paradoxically, the bombing of the capital initially centred on the East End, which before the war had provided a geographical foundation for the anti-Semitic Sir Oswald Mosley's British Union of Fascists. This was a poor area largely comprising Victorian slums and so densely populated that 200,000 people lived in Stepney, for example, at an average of 12 people per dwelling (Stansky, 2007). "Everybody is worried about the feeling in the East End," Nicolson (1970:112) wrote in his diary on 17 September, "where there is much bitterness. It is said that even the King and Queen were booed the other day when they visited the destroyed areas." There was, according to Gardiner (2010), profound anger in the bombed areas of Stepney, West Ham, Poplar and London Docks that did not spill over into total panic, but was a long way removed from the popular image of the wisecracking Cockney undaunted by the destruction. Bernard Kops, a boy in the East End, recalled the awfulness of seeking an undignified and cramped shelter on London Tube platforms: "Some people feel a certain nostalgia for those days, recall a poetic dream about the Blitz. They talk about those days as if they were time of true communal spirit. Not to me. It was the beginning of an era of utter terror, of fear and horror" (Longmate, 1981:66). Calder (1969:187) stated that certain versions of the Blitz suggested "it was a mean and pusillanimous Londoner indeed who did not emerge from the debris with a wisecrack on his lips". He noted, however, that it was often hysteria that produced the witty remarks and often the purveyors of this humour were found sobbing uncontrollably a few hours later. Sansom

(1947) cited an anecdote where an elderly woman refused to leave her stew-pot she was stirring amid the ruins of her bombed-out house. To humour her, a stretcher-bearer agreed to taste her food only to find the pan was full of plaster and bricks.

When Coventry was badly bombed on 14 November, the *Daily Express* ("A Very Gallant City", 1940) reported the city was stricken "but keeps its courage and sanity". Knightley (2002:262) disagreed: "In fact, the German attack created panic. Thousands fled from the town in an unorganised rout. The army wanted to impose martial law, and an official report described the general mood by repeating what a survivor said: "Coventry is finished." Three Mass Observation inspectors, who had toured several bombed areas, were shocked by what they discovered in Coventry the evening after the raid. They reported (SxMOA1/1/5/11/17, FR 495):

> There were more open signs of hysteria, terror, neurosis, observed in one evening than during the whole of the past two months together in all areas. Women were seen to cry, to scream, to tremble all over, to faint in the street, to attack a fireman, and so on. The overwhelmingly dominant feeling on Friday was the feeling of utter helplessness… There were several signs of suppressed panic as darkness approached. In two cases people were seen to be fighting to get on to cars, which they thought would take them out into the country, though in fact, the drivers insisted, the cars were just going up the road to the garage.

Calder (1969) reported that one psychiatrist estimated that children who stayed in Bristol were eight times more likely to be psychologically disturbed than those who were evacuated and there are other disturbing statistics testifying to the mental strain the bombing imposed. There was a 100 per cent rise in the number of teenage girls arrested in the three years after 1939, more infants than usual were suffocated in their cots or choked on their food, more children were killed on the roads even though there were fewer cars and more children drowned. Paradoxically, the suicide rate fell.

Crime

If the rich were not in it to the same extent as the poor, the criminal underclass did not embrace togetherness either. Reported crimes rose from 303,711 in England and Wales in 1939 to 478,394 in 1945 and the number of people convicted went up 54 per cent (Hylton, 2001) Police numbers in England and Wales fell from 82,232 to 59,574 during the war, and the average age rose as younger constables were conscripted, but the high number of convictions points to a significant increase in criminal acts and to the numbers attracted by crime. Duncan Campbell, a former crime correspondent for *The Guardian*, said on the BBC Radio 4 programme *Bandits of the Blitz* (2010): "In many ways the war was a criminal watershed. Hundreds of emergency regulations protected the nation but many were seen as petty, even ludicrous, and led to a loss of respect for the law."

Prostitution boomed - in the West End they were known as 'Piccadilly warriors' - and many were new entrants to the oldest profession. In genteel Leamington Spa there were so many newcomers that pre-war prostitutes were forced to move out, claiming there were "too many gifted bloody amateurs here for a decent professional to get a living" (Hylton, 2001:120). The imposition of rationing and the consequent black market led to a rise in pilfering from work, threefold in Birkenhead docks during 1940, and shortly after the outbreak of war 500 policemen had to be sent to France to stop mass thefts from the British Expeditionary Force (Ponting, 1990). There were looters raiding bombed out houses in search of recoverable booty and Gardiner (2010:323) wrote that on 8 March 1941 a notorious incident occurred when two 110-pound bombs hit the *Café de Paris*, in the West End, when it was packed with Canadian nurses and young officers on leave. The ballroom and dining room, copied from the ill-fated Titanic, were underground and advertised as "London's safest restaurant", but the restaurant suffered a direct hit by two 50-kilo bombs at 9.45pm, killing 34 people, including the band leader Ken "Snakehips" Johnson, and seriously wounding 60 more. Delays by the emergency services led to an inquiry and several unsavoury incidents, including rings and jewellery being stripped from dead bodies by thieves. One survivor, a Mrs Blair-Hickman, recalled:

I saw somebody creeping around in a vague sort of dreamlike way, and this man came up, and he felt around. He felt my hand, which was lying relaxed... and I found, I realised later, that what he'd done was take a ring off my finger. He must have done that to quite a lot of people (Fitzgibbon, 1970:258).

Fitzgibbon noted that there were many forms of theft during the Blitz, the most innocuous being the fireman who stole a bottle of whisky or brandy from a burning pub. The men from Heavy Rescue "made a habit of pocketing valuables and breaking open gas meters" while professional criminals had plenty of opportunity to further their careers in the dark of the blackout (Fitzgibbon, 1970:259).

Manchester in 1940

Manchester and Salford entered the Second World War with a combined population of around a million. The census of the cities in 1931 counted 766,378 and 223,438 people respectively and, although the 1941 poll was not undertaken because of the hostilities, those numbers grew by the time war was declared (Fielding, 1988). There was a significant Catholic presence, amounting to 130,000 or 13 per cent in 1930, including around 800 Italians in Ancoats, an area just north of the city centre, while Bill Williams stated there was a 40,000-strong Jewish community in Manchester in 1933, although this also grew before the war as 8,000 refugees came to the city to escape Nazism from Germany, Austria and Czechoslovakia, most of them Jews (Williams, 2011). The city attracted immigrants, according to Hayes (1905) in 1840, because of its tolerance towards foreigners:

> Our foreign trade brings us into contact with most nationalities, and makes us probably more cosmopolitan in our views... Manchester makes no distinction as to creed or race. She opens her portals and offers an equal chance to all those who wish to settle here to trade and get gain (Cited in Williams, 2011:2).

This may have been the case in the mid nineteenth century, yet in the 1930s the membership of the British Union of Fascists was sufficiently large in Manchester that Mosley considered moving his headquarters from London to the city. The support for the BUF dissipated rapidly on the outbreak of war and a swing in the city's sentiments by June 1940 might be detected in that riots broke out in Little Italy in Ancoats when Mussolini allied with Germany and invaded France.

Manchester's Blitz arrived on the night of 22-23 December 1940, a Sunday night and Monday morning, when 149 aircraft of *Luftflotte 3* and 121 of *Luftflotte 2* dropped 272 tons of high-explosive bombs and 37,152 incendiaries (Ramsey, 1988). The attacks, concentrating on the western side of the city, the docks and industrial areas of Trafford Park and Salford, lasted from 7.45 pm to 1.20 am and again from 2 am to 6.55 am. Guided to the target area by fires still burning in Liverpool and Birkenhead from raids the previous night, more than 400 fires were started, 100 of which were serious, and within two hours the glare of the fires was visible to crews flying over London. The very large number of incendiary bombs dropped on the city and a shortage of civilian defence staff, who had been transferred to help in Liverpool the previous day, presented a multitude of problems and although there was no shortage of water it was not possible to extinguish them all before nightfall the following evening.[2] Trafford Park was particularly badly affected and the main bus station and both the city's main railways stations, Central and London Road (now Manchester Piccadilly), were hit. Fletcher (1946:62) wrote:

---

[2] Manchester sent 200 fire fighters to Liverpool to deal with aftermath of the bombing on December 20 and 21.

At times another Coventry seemed to be threatened and people living near Withy Grove [where the *Evening Chronicle* was based] risked death by deserting their own surface and Anderson shelters to seek greater protection afforded them beneath the largest of all provincial newspaper offices. Difficult as conditions were, none could be refused shelter that night and the refugees crowded on to the benches while the cramped sub-editors went about their job preparing for the morning's newspapers.

The following night, 23-24 December, 171 aircraft of *Luftflotte 3* dropped 195 tons of high explosive and 7,020 incendiary bombs between 7.15 pm and midnight bringing the Mancunian casualty list, according to the Imperial War Museum North, to an estimated 684 people dead and 2,364 wounded. Of the famous buildings in the centre of Manchester, the following were severely damaged: Free Trade Hall; Victoria Buildings; Rates Office; Cross Street Chapel; Manchester Cathedral; Chetham's Hospital; Masonic Temple; Corn Exchange; St. Anne's Church; City Hall; Smithfield Market and the Gaiety Theatre. Within a mile of Albert Square, 31.3 acres were in ruins, 165 warehouses, 150 offices, five banks and 200 other business premises were either destroyed or severely damaged (Hardy, Cooper and Hochland, 1986). Salford, a city bordering Manchester, was also very seriously damaged by the bombing, with 215 killed and 910 wounded, and Stretford, the domestic area closest to the factories and warehouses of Trafford Park, suffered an estimated 73 deaths (Masterton and Cliff, 2002). The human cost at Christmas 1940 was also reflected in the homeless: 6,000 people in Manchester; 5,000 in Salford; 4,000 in Stretford.

The effect was profound. Home Intelligence inspectors visited the city a matter of days later and reported (SxMOA1/1/6/1/7, FR 538): "Going from Liverpool to Manchester was like going from an atmosphere of reasonable cheerfulness into an atmosphere of barely restrained depression." The report noted that the city was plagued by rumour, there was "constant talk about air raids", much staring at bombed-out buildings and visible alarm when sirens sounded. There was little singing, whistling or laughing in the streets, a higher degree of gas mask carrying and, at night, Manchester's city centre was virtually empty. The inspectors did acknowledge that plenty of Mancunians were "determined and courageous" but talks with the city's senior sociologists and social workers also pointed to "a considerable private opinion of real depression and despair". They added: "Manchester people are definitely on edge, are afraid of the next raid, are beginning really to worry about the future with a feeling of crime semi-despair [sic]. All this is under the surface."

This report contradicted the propaganda message of "carrying on" and unity of purpose but was mirrored by other contemporary reports. Bill Naughton, a Mancunian lorry driver reporting for Mass Observation, wrote of a "Blitz complex" in January 1941 in the days after the Manchester bombings that manifested in absenteeism from work (SxMOA1/1/6/3/26, FR 620). He reported that his own firm, a distributor of fruit and vegetables, was operating at 20 per cent of the pre-Blitz norm, partly because of the bomb damage that disrupted transport but mainly because of the attitudes of the employees. He reported that "sharp extremes of mental and moral feelings were manifest" and followed geographical lines. Those who lived outside Manchester were philosophical about the damage to their damaged city-centre businesses, those whose homes were closer to the blitzed areas were near to total dejection. Naughton wrote: "In the bombed areas where homes, personal belongings and relatives were lost, the morale was shockingly low. I visited three rest centres... the misery and despair of the people were past description."

The scale of destruction did not strike Rita Maloney, a 20-year-old female clerical worker in Manchester, until she cycled to work on 24 December to find Piccadilly, one of Manchester's main squares, cordoned off and saw local landmarks on fire. She wrote (SxMOA1/1/6/1/7, FR 538): "I didn't realise the sight would affect me so much that I was near to tears. We were all quiet at work, shaken by the sight of so much damage... None of us worked again, and early in the afternoon we were paid and sent home until Monday. I was glad to get away from town." She went on articulate the sense of despair many of her fellow Mancunians felt, and the anger and distrust directed at the media:

> You will hear a lot of talk of Manchester carrying on. I suppose we are, as well as any other town at any rate, but as one who lives here, it's a rather weary carrying on. When we heard the BBC's summing up of our Blitz, making it sound rather like a village which had had a stick of bombs dropped on it, along with many others, we wondered how true the reports on Coventry and Liverpool were, and all the other towns. We are carrying on and "taking it" because we've got to, but we aren't very happy about it.

The reports in Manchester's local newspapers did not reflect Mrs. Maloney's mood. On 27 December 1940, *the Evening Chronicle* ("Manchester gets down to work behind boards", 1940) reported that the city "may be scarred and in some parts battered, but the people, after the Christmas respite, returned to work with determination." The *Manchester Guardian*'s autopsy of the aftermath of the Blitz ("Manchester's Rest Centres", 1941) was equally upbeat, reporting: "At all centres visited the catering arrangements seem to be admirable. In every shelter in the city turkey was served for Christmas Day dinner." The Home Intelligence inspectors, who visited the city, were scathing: "This, like many other press versions, is alas untrue" (SxMOA1/1/6/1/7, FR 538).

Reporting the Blitz

Manchester was Britain's second press centre for most of the Twentieth Century and would have become the principal one in the event of irreparable damage to Fleet Street during the war. Every national newspaper had a print centre there except *The Times* and the *Financial Times* and the city was so important for the press in Britain that when the Berry brothers, Lords Camrose and Kemsley, formed Allied Northern Newspapers in 1924 its Withy Grove site was described as Europe's largest single print hub, employing 3,000 people (Waterhouse, 2004). "Manchester is far and away the largest newspaper centre outside London," Camrose (1947:116) wrote. "Indeed, it closely rivals the metropolis itself." Provincial newspapers played a part in creating this centre, spearheaded by the *Manchester Guardian*, which began life as a regional newspaper but by 1939 had a national audience. The *Guardian's* circulation was modest (51,000 in 1939, rising to 140,000 in 1951), but its influence was far greater.[3] Its editor, W. P. Crozier, met Churchill on a regular basis - Ayerst (1971) stated there are records of 16 meetings between October 1939, when they met for the first time, and October 1943 - and Lord Halifax, the Foreign Secretary from February 1938 until December 1940, said he read the *Manchester Guardian* every day (Margach, 1978). The profits of its sister paper, the *Manchester Evening News*, sustained the loss making *Manchester Guardian* and perhaps that is a reason why the former did not submit circulation numbers before the Second World War. Even its audited figure for 1945, 250,000, is suspiciously rounded but the newspaper rightly described itself as "the oldest established and leading evening journal in Manchester" (Seymour-Ure, 1997, pp. 274-6). The *Evening Chronicle* sold more than 200,000 copies a day in the build-up to the war and in 1945 was licensed as selling 224,000. Its title page boasted "the largest evening sale in the provinces".

The reporting of Manchester's bombing was compromised by the censor and by the self-censorship of editors and reporters, and a study of the three newspapers reveals there was a wholesale attempt to massage the truth for propaganda purposes. A Home Intelligence report in February 1941 (SxMOA1/1/6/2/3, FR 568) quoted a remark "(private of course) by a famous columnist". It read: "Journalists report the cheers. No one dare report the tears." This was borne out by Manchester's newspapers from December 1940 to February 1941. There was more than one raid on Manchester, although reports suggested otherwise; casualties were worse than reported; the destruction to homes and the city's infrastructure was greater; efforts were made to increase the success of air defences; shortcomings in fire fighting were virtually ignored; heroes were plentiful and promoted; the *Luftwaffe's* success were dismissed as rare and it was civilian rather than industrial targets that were

---

[3] 1910-1939 figures taken from T. B. Browne's Advertiser's ABC 1910-40; 1951 figures from the Audit Bureau of Circulations, cited in Butler and Sloman (1975).

hit. All were distortions designed to maintain morale and demonise the enemy.

So was there anything in the editions to suggest that the government-inspired message of "we can take it" was not the whole picture? The most obvious indication, as has been listed earlier, was crime. Court reporting is a staple item in every newspaper because it forms easily and regularly acquired copy and because, as Keeble (2005:173) noted, "courts are a marvellous source of human interest and crime stories". The *Manchester Guardian, Manchester Evening News* and the *Evening Chronicle* gave significant amounts of space to reporting the courts, devoting approximately a page in the case of the evening newspapers and around half a page in the *Guardian*. In a time when much of the news was subject to censorship and travel and communication were complicated by air raids and bomb damage, the attraction of guaranteed news stories that could be reported without restriction, other than those that normally applied to court reporting, was obvious.

All three newspapers reported court cases at length without making the link between the special circumstances of war and the degree of lawlessness they provoked. Hylton (2001, p 154) wrote: "There were new classes of offence for people to commit in a heavily regulated wartime society, and the opportunity to commit them was enhanced by the cover of the blackout and the substantial reduction in police numbers." Gardiner, a social historian, said on the Radio 4 programme *Bandits of the Blitz* (2010) that looting was extremely widespread, to the despair of the authorities:

For example, the Reverend John Markham, who was a vicar in Walworth and a chief air-raid warden. He reckoned the minute a bomb fell in his area it was essential that he and his wardens get there not just to look for the injured but to protect property. There were instances where he had to leave a property overnight and he returned to find it stripped out.

There was what we might call ambulance chasers today, just honing in where something happened. When he found bodies he would take them to a crypt in his church and get a warden to guard them because if he didn't somebody would go through their pockets and remove their watch, their money, their ID, anything of value.

This was reflected in the reports in Manchester's newspapers, most notably a week after the city's Blitz, when the *Guardian* reported the comments of Noel B. Goldie, the Recorder at Manchester Quarter Sessions ("Manchester breeding young criminals", 1941). The judicial officer noted there were 56 youths before him on indictable offences and said, "something had to be done":

I have no doubt that in the first instance it was due to a lack of parental control, but I have a strong suspicion that receivers in this great city are using youths for the purpose of committing these most serious offences... We are, in Manchester at the moment breeding a race of young criminals.

A week later the *Manchester Evening News* contributed to this debate ("Young crime trebles since September", 1941), quoting Goldie: "It is not merely an increase in petty pilfering. We are now getting serious crimes such as breaking and entering. And the boys who are responsible show complete hardness when they are caught." Below the story were other headlines: "50-mile joy ride in van", "Roaming town like wild things", "Gas meters robbed in bombed houses" and "Father suspected own son". All the accused were aged between nine and 14.

Later that month the *Manchester Evening News* columnist Eileen Elias commented:

> The gangsters are here. No, this is not something from an American film. Police, parents and magistrates wish it were. It is just a plain statement of fact about the country today in the midst of war.
>
> For juvenile crime is on the increase. In Manchester alone during the past three months it has trebled. Never before have we been faced with so serious a problem in the life of young Britain (The gangsters are here, 1941).

Other than references to breaks in education and the lack of parental control caused by absentee parents, including called-up fathers, no link was made to the effect of raids on young attitudes. However, speaking on the Channel 5 television programme *Secrets of the Blitz* (2011), Roy Lee, a teenager in 1940, articulated the sense of life's pointlessness once his best friend Matthew was killed in the Manchester Blitz:

> When he went my clock stopped ticking. I remember saying to myself: "That's it. No matter what happens now it could be me tomorrow." I made up my mind there and then to live for me and my mum and to hell with everyone else.

Lee and his friends would wait for the all clear and then loot bombed-out buildings. He added:

> Obviously money was the first thing you looked for, and then, of course, there was always food, packets of tea and this, that and the other, anything that had been blown up in people's kitchens. You never handed it back. Anything that was worthwhile we just stuck in our pockets and away we'd go.

Lee lived in Manchester but his case was not exceptional. In *The Blitz* Gardiner (2010:324) said that looting was the "largely unspoken, unacknowledged underside of the 'blitz spirit', the fissure that crazed the pulling together to face a common enemy - and it was widespread." This fissure was not acknowledged by Manchester's newspapers - the reports of Recorder Goldie's comments notwithstanding - although they did report on many court cases without meeting one of Randall's maxim's of good reporting: "Hold up the mirror to society, reflecting its virtues and vices and also debunking its cherished myths" (Randall, 2000:3). Had reporters properly examined the image in the mirror they would have noticed it was not just youths who were reacting to the war by disregarding the law but people who normally would be regarded as pillars of the society. So it was a war reserve policeman (aged 34) and a customs office watcher (46) who were convicted of stealing 12 bottles of whisky, a 30-year-old soldier who was given a three-month prison sentence for looting and a 39-year-old shop keeper charged with stealing £4 10 shillings in cash and a £20 cash register from a bombed out inn ("Whisky stolen from docks", 1940; "Looting after air raid", 1940; "Looting charges", 1941). An Air Raid Patrol officer was imprisoned for "neglecting duty", beginning his one-month's sentence to the words of the Manchester Stipendiary Magistrate, who said: "If you had lived under a different regime you might have been shot" ("ARP rescue man gaoled for neglecting duty", 1941). Violent crime did not end with the violence of the bomb either and during the eight-week study period of this chapter the *Evening Chronicle* reported two soldiers would be executed for domestic murders ("Soldier's execution date", 1940). Finally there was a report of a political execution when it was announced Charles Albert van den Kieboom, a 26-year-old Dutch clerk, would hang at Pentonville Prison for spying ("Third Nazi spy executed", 1940). He was the third spy to be executed in seven days, following Jose Waldberg and Karl Meir to the gallows. All three were found in possession of a wireless transmitter.

Letters to the Editor

There are feedback loops that ensure there is a two-way communication between newspapers and their audience, but the most overt come in the readers' letters column. These form an important part of a newspaper in that they, as Richardson (2008:56) argued, "enable both the press and the readership to keep an ear to the ground and listen in to some of the leading themes of local conversation". All readers' letters are subject to the gate-keeping of journalists, however, and with newspapers actively promoting the notion of togetherness not many letters straying from this theme in a letter would have been allowed to pass by the gatekeepers.

Not that the *Manchester Guardian* formed an un-passable wall against criticism of the government. For instance, the government's suppression of the Communist *Daily Worker* in January 1941 prompted a series of letters for and against the ban provoked by the *Guardian*'s editorial on the subject. That concluded: "The *Daily Worker* did not believe in the war or in democracy; its only aim was to confuse and weaken. We can well spare it" ("The *Daily Worker*", 1940). This was a surprising stance given the *Guardian*'s stance on pre-war freedoms in Nazi Germany and most readers condemned the editorial. The comments included: "It is a step which the executive of a democratic country should never take", ("The Right of Criticism", 1941); "We have taken a perilous step towards the totalitarian concept of journalism", ("A Blow at Freedom of the Press", 1941); "Criticism has been driven underground", ("The Right of Public Criticism", 1941); and "Why use a Coalition steam-hammer to crack a Communist nut?", ("Some Probable Effects", 1941.) Crozier, the editor, was forced to defend the *Guardian*'s position, stating: "We would hold strongly that freedom to criticise the executive is as vital in time of war as it is in peace," before adding the rider "subject to the inevitable abridgements that a virtual state of siege may impose". Later in his response he wrote that the suppression of the *Daily Worker* was a "choice of evils" ("Risks of Stifling Criticism", 1941).

The *Guardian*'s eagerness to criticise was overstated by Crozier, but the readers were less inhibited (or the censors were more willing to allow them to be). In December 1940 a letter noted that the shortage of workers in munitions and aeroplane factories had not prevented advertisements in a London newspaper requesting two footmen, at least 5ft 10in tall, for "a noblemen's establishment" and another two footmen to join a "large staff" in London and Windsor. This, the writer, wrote was "deeply shocking" ("Service and Sahibs", 1941). Three days later another letter condemned the sentence of 10 years handed down to two young policemen for looting. "I read the news with feelings of horror at the severe sentence," it read, "and have since watched the press for some sign of charity and mercy, which I have failed to notice" ("Crime and punishment", 1941). On 30 December 1940 seven students wrote a letter about the conditions sheltering in London's tube stations. "Do the authorities really think that 12 sanitary buckets are sufficient for 2,000 people?" they asked ("Shelter conditions in Tube stations", 1940). These letters point to dis-satisfaction and hint at a lack of common purpose but were not followed up with any vigour by the press.

Home Intelligence reported (SxMOA1/1/5/5/32, FR 126) that "serious, long letters" were published only in *The Times,* the *Daily Telegraph* and the *Manchester Guardian,* and the *Manchester Evening News,* which comprised six pages compared to the Guardian's 10, gave less space to readers' views, averaging two a week over the study period. There was little sense of criticism of the authorities and no letter referred to the Manchester Blitz until 2 January and they thanked a team of women voluntary helpers for their work in a rest centre and a Mr Eastwood, a greengrocer, who had given his keys of his shop to a local rector so that the homeless could have "the run of the shop" (1941). There were only hints at social divisions, the first signed by "Query" (1941), who asked of a woman who employed two maids: "Would she not be more patriotic is she were merely to do all her own housework and thereby release two women for whole-time national work?" In February "Share Alike" (1941) from Levenshulme (south east Manchester) wrote that he was pleased to see the

Manchester Evening News "had the courage to criticise landlords who refuse to make a contribution towards the cost of long ladders to protect their own property". Given that the newspaper had neglected to confront the authorities over their lack of preparation for, and reaction to, the Blitz, it was difficult to detect courage in tackling nameless landlords.

The *Evening Chronicle* also had relatively few letters and hardly any were critical. Some had an almost child-like belief in official communiqués and press propaganda, particularly a correspondent named as "Chins Up" (1940), who wrote:

> Reading that Germans living in the much bombed Rhineland and Rhur industrial towns don't bother to go to their shelter now in RAF raids because they have learned that British pilots stick to industrial targets, and that when the warning of an RAF raid is given factory workers quit their jobs and move into residential districts for their safety, one wonders why, in the view of the *Luftwaffe*'s methods, we should take such care to restrict the RAF to military targets. The only way to reply to the Nazi tactics is bombs and more bombs.

Readers' letters are, of course, subject to the gate keeping referred to above and there could have been other, less belligerent and believing, letters that did not make it to print. "Chins Up" could also have been a journalist asked to push the newspaper's particular point of view by an alternative means, but a publication would rapidly lose credibility if letters were consistently too far removed from the prevailing mood. On 1 January, for example, "Chins Up" was followed by an un-named correspondent (1941), who wrote: "By far the largest majority of the pubic are indignant that we do not serve the enemies with similar raids to those suffered by our towns and cities." Ten days later "Common Sense" (1941) wrote: "They should have the same medicine," adding, "we have been told the number of air raid casualties in this county. Has Germany published her figures?" These letters pointed to a desire for retribution that Hastings (2011:493) claimed was a result of government propaganda:

> Only a limited number of British and American people gave much thought to the fate of Germany beneath air bombardment, partly because their governments persistently deceived them about the nature of the campaign: the reality of area bombing, the targeting of cities, was concealed beneath verbiage about industrial installations.

The only hint of criticism of the local authorities in the *Evening Chronicle*'s letters column, came on 24 January 1941 when a correspondent questioned the assertion that bombed-out families had been rehoused. The correspondent said he knew of one family who had been moved in with other people "making a total of 10 in one house, with three small bedrooms".

Conclusion

Even before the war started the *Daily Mirror* was promoting a message of togetherness. "Cheerfulness was the keynote of Britain's people in the hours of crisis yesterday," it printed in August 1939. It added: "We've always come smilin' through" ("Britain smiles and prepares", 1939) This theme became the default position of newspapers but there was a more nuanced reaction to the war that included frowns and despair. People managed because there was no alternative. London was bombed heavily first and the "Cheerful Cockney" became the template by which the populations in other cities would judge themselves. Home Intelligence reported (SxMOA1/1/5/9, Box 1) that people outside London had an exaggerated impression of the damage being inflicted on the capital but believed that "if London can take it, so can we". Calder (1991:142) noted:

> That civilian morale survived exposure to conditions often as frightful as those of battle is what guarantees, mythically, that the British people, as a whole, deserved to save Europe and defeat Hitler. Because they held out and Hitler was eventually defeated, one cannot counterfactually select from contemporary reports by careful observers, not for publication, ... all the remarks and glimpses of behaviour that suggest poor and volatile morale.

With such a determined effort to emphasise and even manufacture good news, it is not a surprise that no newspaper properly examined the drift towards lawlessness by a significant number of people bombed out of their normal patterns of behaviour. This chapter has shown that crime was reported and statistics published but the link between the effects of the war and criminal activity was never established. While it would be overstating the case to say there was large-scale opposition to the war, the country had suffered deep divisions in the 1930s and these did not disappear under the threat of invasion. Crime rose, industrial relations were strained and social tension grew. The Blitz exposed shortcomings at local level that and the host of regulations that encouraged many to disobey or disregard. There were alternative views, but an occasional letter to the editor apart, they were neglected by the newspapers. Marie Price, from Liverpool, remembered an atmosphere that differed from what she read on the press and saw in the newsreels:

> Churchill was telling us how brave we all were and that we would never surrender. I tell you something - the people of Liverpool would have surrendered overnight if they could have. It's all right for people in

authority, down in their steel-lined dugouts, but we were there and it was just too awful (cited in Levine, 2006:142).

Circulations rose during the war but so did the disillusionment with newspapers and, despite the bombing, Ponting (1990) cited surveys that indicated that the lack of interest in the war rose from 10 per cent in spring 1940 to nearly a third by the end of that year. Curran and Seaton (2003:126) summed up the mood in the civilian ranks not so much as "all in this together" as "us" against "them": "The opposition was as much to the unbelievable bureaucracy of British administration as to the Nazis themselves." As newspapers did not challenge the administration, nor give a platform to concerned, they lost the confidence of their readers.

References

Government Reports

Mass Observation Archive. UK. Brighton: University of Sussex.
Shipway, G. W, *Diaries 1939-65,* 17th January 1941.
SxMOA1/1/5/9, Box 1, *Propaganda and Morale 1939-42*, 18th
    September, 1940.
SxMOA1/1/5/5/32, FR 126, *Report on the Press*, May 1940.
SxMOA1/1/5/9, Box 1, *Propaganda and Morale 1939-42*, 18th
    September, 1940.
SxMOA1/1/5/11/17, FR 495, *Coventry*, 18th November, 1940.
SxMOA1/1/6/1/7, FR 538, *Liverpool and Manchester,* January, 1941.
SxMOA1/1/6/3/26, FR 620, *Manchester Airs Raids*, March, 1941.
SxMOA1/1/8/3/26, FR 1648, *Recent Trends in Anti-Semitism*, March,
    1943.

Newspaper Articles

'Germans Torpedo Germans'. 1940, July, 4. *Daily Express*:1.
'A Very Gallant City'. 1940, November, 16. *Daily Express*:1.
'Britain Smiles and Prepares'. 1939, August, 25. *Daily Mirror.* 16-17.
'Soldier's Execution Date'. 1940. December, 20. *Evening Chronicle*:4.
'Manchester Gets Down to Work Behind Boards'. 1940, December, 27.
    Evening Chronicle:1.
'Your own opinion…' 1940, December, 27. *Evening Chronicle*:2.
'Your own opinion…' 1941, January, 1. *Evening Chronicle*:2.
'Your own opinion…' 1941, January, 11. *Evening Chronicle*:2.
'Your own opinion…' 1941, January, 24. *Evening Chronicle*:2.

'Third Nazi Spy Executed'. 1940, December, 17. *Manchester Evening News*:1.

'Letter'. (1940. December, 21). *Manchester Evening News*:2.

'Letters'. (1941, January, 2). *Manchester Evening News*:2.

'Young Crime Trebles Since September'. 1941. January, 9. *Manchester Evening News*:6.

'The Gangsters are Here'. 1941, January 20. *Manchester Evening News*:2

'ARP Rescue Man Gaoled for Neglecting Duty'. 1941, January, 29. *Manchester Evening News*:6.

'Letters'. 1941, February, 5. *Manchester Evening News*:2.

'Service and Sahibs'. 1940, December, 16. *Manchester Guardian*:8.

'Crime and punishment'. 1940, December, 19. *Manchester Guardian*:10.

'Shelter Conditions in Tube Stations'. 1940, December, 30. *Manchester Guardian*:8.

'Whisky Stolen from Docks'. 1940, December, 30. *Manchester Guardian*:2.

'Looting After Air Raid'. 1940 December, 31. *Manchester Guardian*:10.

'Manchester Breeding Young Criminals'. 1941, January, 1. *Manchester Guardian*:2.

'Looting Charges'. 1941, January 2. *Manchester Guardian*:3.

'Manchester's Rest Centres'. 1941, January 2. *Manchester Guardian*:6.

Sutherland, G. A. 1941, January, 2. 'Pacifists and Broadcasting'. *Manchester Guardian*:8.

'The Daily Worker'. 1941, January, 22. *Manchester Guardian*:4.

'The Right of Criticism'. 1941, January, 27. *Manchester Guardian*:8.

'A Blow at Freedom of the Press'. 1941, January, 28. *Manchester Guardian*:10.

'Risks of Stifling Criticism'. 1941, February, 1. *Manchester Guardian*:4.

'The Right of Public Criticism'. 1941, February, 4. *Manchester Guardian*:10.

'Some Probable Effects'. 1941, February, 6. *Manchester Guardian*:10.

Secondary Sources

Ayerst, D. (1971). *The Manchester Guardian: Biography of a Newspaper*. UK. London: Guardian Newspapers.

Bandits of the Blitz, prod. by Liz Carney. BBC Radio 4, Broadcast 8 September, 2010.

BBC, *WW2 People's War* [Online]. Available: http://www.bbc.co.uk/ww2peopleswar.

Bingham, A. (2004). *Gender, Modernity and the Popular Press in Inter-war Britain*. UK. Oxford: Clarendon. British Library [Online]. Available http://www.bl.uk.

Butler, D. and Sloman, A. (eds.), (1975). *British Political Facts 1900-1975*.

5th edn. UK. London: Macmillan.

Calder, A. (1969). *The People's War: Britain 1939-45*. UK. London: Cape.

Calder, A. (1991). *The Myth of the Blitz*. UK. London: Jonathan Cape.

Calder, R. (1941). *Carry on London*. UK. London: English Universities Press.

Viscount C. (1947). *British Newspapers and their Controllers*. UK. London: Cassell.

Curran, J. and Seaton, J. (2003). *Power Without Responsibility: Press, Broadcasting and the Internet in Britain*, 6th edn. UK. London: Routledge

De Felice, P. (1998). 'Reconstructing Manchester's Little Italy', *Manchester Region History Review*, 12:54-65.

Fielding, S. J. (1988). 'The Irish Catholics of Manchester and Salford: Aspects of their Religious and Political History, 1890-1939'. Doctoral thesis, University of Warwick, United Kingdom.

Fitzgibbon, C. (1970).*The Blitz*. UK. London: Macdonald.

Fletcher, L. (1946). *They Never Failed: The Story of the Provincial Press in Wartime*. UK. London: Newspaper Society.

Gammon, E. E. (2011). *A House to Remember: 10 Rillington Place*. UK. Cirencester: Memoirs.

Gannon, F. R. (1971). *The British Press and Germany 1936-9*. UK. Oxford, Clarendon.

Gardiner, J. (2010). *The Blitz: The British Under Attack*. UK. London: Harper.

Hardy, C., Cooper, I. and Hochland, H. (1986). *Manchester at War*. UK. Bowdon: Archive.

Hastings, M. (2011). *All Hell Let Loose: The World at War 1939-45*. UK. London: Harper.

HMSO (1940, 1942). *Hansard*. London, United Kingdom: HMSO.

Hylton, S. (2010). *A History of Manchester*. 2nd edn, UK. Andover: Phillimore.

Hylton, S. (2001)*Their Darkest Hour: The Hidden History of the Home Front 1939-1945*. UK. Stroud: Sutton.

Ikle, F. C. (1950). 'Reconstruction and population density in war-damaged cities', *Journal of the American Institute of Planners*, 16, 3:131-39.

Imperial War Museum North, *Manchester Blitz* [Online]. Available: http://www.iwm.org.uk/server/show/ConWebDoc.2790.

Jones, E., Woolven, R., Durodie, B. and Wessley, S. (2004). 'Civilian morale during the Second World War: Responses to Air Raids Re-examined', *Social History of Medicine*, 17, 3:463-79.

Keeble, R. (2005). *The Newspapers Handbook*. 3rd edn, UK. London: Routledge.

Kirkup, J. (2011, October 5). 'David Cameron and the bulldog spirit: can the Prime Minister become an economic war leader?' Retrieved from (http://blogs.telegraph.co.uk/news/jameskirkup/100109176/david-cameron-and-the-bulldog-spirit-can-the-prime-minister-become-an-economic-war-leader/

Knightley, P. (2002). *The First Casualty: The War Correspondent as Hero and Myth-Maker from The Crimea to Iraq.* 3rd edn. UK. London: John Hopkins.

Levine, J. (ed.), (2006). *Forgotten Voices of the Blitz and the Battle of Britain.* UK. London: Ebury.

Longmate, N. (ed.), (1981). *The Home Front: An Anthology 1938-1945.* UK. London: Chatto and Windus.

Maconie, S. (2007). *Pies and Prejudice: In Search of the North.* UK. London: Ebury.

Margach, J. (1978). *The Abuse of Power: The War between Downing Street and the Media.* UK. London: W.H. Allen.

Masterton, V. and Cliff, K. (2002). *Stretford: An Illustrated History.* UK. Derby: Breedon Books.

Nicolson, H.(1970). *Diaries and Letters 1939-1945.* UK. London: Fontana.

O'Brien, T. H. (1955). *Civil Defence.* UK. London: HMSO.

Ponting, C. (1990). *1940: Myth and Reality.* UK. London: Sphere.

Randall, D. (2000). *The Universal Journalist,* 2nd edn. UK. London: Pluto.

Ramsey, W. (ed.), (1988). *The Blitz Then and Now,* vol. 2. UK. London: Battle of Britain Prints International.

Reed, D. (1938) *Insanity Fair.* UK. London: Cape.

Richardson, J. (2008). 'Readers' Letters' in *Pulling Newspapers Apart: Analysing Print Journalism*, by Franklin, B. (ed.). UK. London: Routledge:56-66.

Sansom, W. (1947). *Westminster at War.* UK. London: Faber.
'Secrets of the Blitz', dir. by Steve Humphries. Channel 5, broadcast on 20 January, 2011.

Seymour-Ure, C. (1997). *The British Press and Broadcasting Since 1945,* 2nd edn. UK. Oxford: Blackwell.

Stansky, P. (2007). *The First Day of the Blitz.* UK. London: Yale University Press.

Stockley, N. [Online]. Available: neilstockley.blogspot.com

Wahl-Jorgensen, K. (2002). 'Understanding the Conditions for Public Discourse: Four Rules for Selecting Letters to the Editor', *Journalism studies,* 3:1:69-81.

Styan, J. (2004, June, 17). 'Wartime Hardships: Rationing in London'. Retrieved from http://www.bbc.co.uk/history/ww2peopleswar/stories/98/a2756298.shtml

Waterhouse, R. (2004). *The Other Fleet Street.* UK. Altrincham.

Watson, S. E. R. (1980). 'The Ministry of Information and the Home Front in Britain, 1939-1942', Doctoral thesis, University of London.

Williams, B. (2011). *Jews and Other Foreigners: Manchester and the Rescue of the Victims of European Fascism, 1933-40*. UK. Manchester: Manchester University Press.

Williams, K. (2010). *Get Me a Murder a Day: A history of Media and Communication in Britain*. 2nd edn. UK. London: Arnold.

Chapter 7

Canadian Media Coverage of the War: Conditions and Constraints[1]

Aimé-Jules Bizimana
Université du Québec en Outaouais, Canada

Introduction

During the Second World War, hundreds of Canadian and foreign war correspondents reported on the military events on the fronts. On December 10, 1939, Gillis Purcell of the Canadian Press (CP) and Robert T. Bowman of the CBC were the first Canadian war correspondents dispatched to sail to England with the First Canadian Contingent under the command of General Andrew G. L. McNaughton. However, the captain of the flagship *Aquitania* refused to allow Bowman and his technician, Arthur W. Holmes of the CBC, on board until authorities in Ottawa intervened (Powley, 1975:5). This refusal shows the "natural" resistance of armies to allowing war correspondents on the front, suspecting them of the "original sin of indiscretion." During the First World War, British authorities allowed only six war correspondents, and nonetheless kept them far from the trenches. As a Dominion, Canada was allowed only one correspondent, who represented the members of the Canadian Press Limited (Bizimana, 2009:21-43).

The initial reserve at the beginning of the war gave way to a greater but more controlled acceptance of war correspondents on the front. From 1939 to 1945, nearly 120 Canadian war correspondents were accredited to cover Canadian Forces operations for the written press and the radio, still in its infancy[2]. The Canadian Press and the two English and French news networks (CBC and Radio-Canada) were the most active. With a priority guaranteed because of its vast member network, the CP employed about twenty war

---

[1] A French version of this chapter has been published by the Quebec journal *Bulletin d'histoire politique* (vol. 21, n°3, printemps 2013).
[2] The figure of 120 war correspondents is an estimation from various lists of which that established by Powell (1994).

correspondents, including five at the Normandy Landings. During the war, Ross Munro was the face of the CP's exhaustive coverage. The CBC/Radio-Canada Overseas Unit was made up of about thirty correspondents and technicians. Matthew Halton (CBC) and Marcel Ouimet (Radio-Canada) became renowned for the most outstanding coverage on their two networks. Radio's ability to transmit the sounds of war meant it was used as an instrument of propaganda (Eck, 1985). Canadian newspapers, however, were not to be outdone, with the continuing presence of papers like the *Toronto Star* and the *Montreal Standard*.

All journalists accredited by the army and circulating in a war zone were subject to military censorship. Canadian Army Public Relations was in charge of accreditation, the provisioning, and the surveillance of correspondents in the field. For the Canadian army, the Dieppe raid in 1942 played a double role: it acted as a barometer for censorship, and for the relationship between information and the war effort. Consequently, war correspondents were supervised by the army to prevent the disclosure of information that could be useful to the enemy, to preserve troop morale, and to rally the Canadian public to the national war effort. More than in any previous war, the Canadian and Allied military posture literally succeeded in putting information 'in uniform[3]' transforming press representatives into an effective amplifier for the war effort. After presenting the censorship system in Canada and the war correspondent accreditation process on the front, this chapter will analyze how the censorship of war information worked, the role of Canadian Army Public Relations, and the coverage of large-scale Canadian military operations.

Press Censorship in Canada

From the start of the conflict, and as was the case during the First World War, political authorities and the Canadian press agreed on the necessity of censoring information. Two texts were created for this purpose: the *Censorship Regulations* on September 1, 1939, and the *Defense of Canada Regulations* on September 3, 1939. The former would be revoked in January 1940, and the latter would serve as a reference document for the duration of the conflict. A Censorship Co-ordination Committee was formed on September, 3, 1939, and was replaced on May, 13, 1942, by the Directorate of Censorship under the responsibility of the Department of National War Services.

---

[3] The expression is used in its primary sense of "information in the colours and orders of the army" and not in the sense of information uniformization outlined by French historian Marc Ferro (1991).

In accordance with the *Defense of Canada Regulations*, the Directorate of Censorship regularly gave confidential directions to editors-in-chief of newspapers and directors of radio stations. Published in March 1940, the first press and broadcasting censorship manual explained the objectives of the Canadian State in its mission to control information and defend national interests (Privy Council Office, fonds, 1940). This manual was followed by a number of updates containing separate directions aimed specifically at newspapers and radio stations. Station directors had to keep watch on gossip and political discussions (Radio-Canada, 1941:6).

After having planned to implement "costly, objectionable, and inefficient" (DND 72/295) censorship, the Canadian government finally decided to adopt a voluntary system, counting on press leaders to work with them, despite the uncertainty of such a practice. British (with their D-Notices) and American censors also used a voluntary system.

Censorship was aimed not only at military information or other indiscretions that could be used by the enemy but also at any voices strongly opposed to the war effort. The press in Canada generally cooperated with the federal authorities, despite some confusion about how to implement the administration of censorship and some criticism (Beauregard, 1998, pp. 38-41). In this time of national crisis, the restrictions imposed by the Mackenzie King government on the freedom of the press and of opinion were generally well received by a Canadian press concerned with showing patriotic solidarity. However, the system imposed upon accredited correspondents on the front was more restrictive.

The Accreditation and Surveillance of War Correspondents

In order to obtain permission to cover the conflict, each representative of a press organization had to make a request to the High Commissioner's Committee for Wartime Publicity in order to obtain a correspondent licence. The licence was granted after the journalist's background and identity were verified. The number of correspondents was set by the committee in consultation with the press.

Accredited war correspondents signed to indicate they would submit to military discipline and orders and respect the rules in a little twenty-page booklet. This booklet, that acted as a licence, was countersigned by a staff officer. The Canadian Military Headquarters (CMHQ) in London kept a register of all the accredited press representatives. Besides regular journalists, visiting correspondents were also accredited for short stays on the front. During the war journalists were strictly forbidden to be accredited by a foreign military without the approval of the Canadian Headquarters.

Like their colleagues of the Great War, the war correspondents of 1939–1945 had to wear the military uniform provided by the army with the inscription *CANADA WAR CORRESPONDENT* on both shoulders. Ground Rules also stated that they had to wear an armband on their right arm with *PRESS* on it, but this rule was rarely followed. On the front, they generally lived in a press camp and were fed and transported by the army, which collected fees from their press organizations. Correspondents had the assimilated rank of captain but were not authorized to carry arms[4]. The Department of National Defence [DND] in Ottawa even prepared rules similar to those for foreign correspondents in view of accrediting journalists in Canada in case of an attack on Canadian territory (DND, DHH, 111.6.003 (D1); Bizimana, 2007:308-309).

Whereas voluntary censorship was used in Canada, the Canadian army followed the example of other nations at war and imposed obligatory press censorship on the front. In their official licence, journalists had to sign the following declaration:

> I hereby undertake to submit for censorship all books, articles or other material concerning the force to which I am accredited, written by me during the period of hostilities, whether or not I remain an accredited war correspondent. I further undertake to abide by the decision of the censorship authorities concerned. (Clark, fond, May 24 1941:22)

Sketches, photographs, and films made by journalists with the authorization of a commander were also subject to military censorship, as was journalists' private correspondence. Once reports had been checked, they were stamped with an official censorship seal marked "Passed for Publication" and indicating the date and the name and number of the field press censor.

At the start of the war, Canadian war correspondents had to submit their reports to British censorship, usually through the Ministry of Information in London. This was a handicap for Francophone correspondents, who had to translate their reports before submitting them to the British censors. From the 1943 invasion of Italy on, there was a Canadian military censorship team at the Allied Force Headquarters in Algiers in North Africa. The N° 1 Canadian Field Press Censorship Unit was deployed in June 1944 on the North-Western front (DND, DHH, 157.4C2009 [D6]). A total of three field press censorship units were operational in English and French under Allied command until the end of the war.

In areas of operation, war correspondents were placed under the supervision of an officer from Canadian Army Public Relations. At the start of the war, this task was given to the Public Relations Officer (PRO) from the

---

[4] The ban against carrying arms was momentarily lifted upon entry into Germany (Bizimana, 2007:306).

Canadian Military Headquarters. Starting in 1943, the PRO was replaced by the Deputy Director of Public Relations (DDPR) at the Canadian Headquarters in London and the Assistant Deputy of Public Relations (ADPR) with the First Canadian Army. Correspondents had to address any questions about covering the conflict to these military officials and go through them to communicate with high-ranking Canadians. Visiting an area of operation required written permission from a public relations officer, who also had to escort war correspondents in the field and resolve any disputes concerning them. Public relations officers acted as go-betweens linking correspondents and commanders, accompanied correspondents, and performed military press censorship. Their many coordination and monitoring duties made them a vital part of the information front during the Second World War.

In general, censorship on the front affected military information that could benefit the enemy. In the daily reports of military censors, the censored news concerned troop movement and tactics, operational orders, the names of forces before they were officially announced, and the exact numbers of formations (DND 157.4C2009). There were sometimes differences of opinion between officers and journalists, who liked to remind the military that censorship was supposed to be applied for security reasons only and that General Eisenhower had promised allied war correspondents there would be no political censorship[5].

Bad news and alarming news were constantly censored during the war, as is evident in the restrictions on the press during the difficult operations at Dieppe, at Anzio, at Arnhem, and in the Ardennes (Bizimana, 2007:312-325). In *The Information Front*, Tim Balzer (2011) also mentions that negative and embarrassing news was sometimes censored by Canadian political and military authorities.

In a 1942 survey by the Gallup Organization, 56% of Canadians responded that they were satisfied (36% unsatisfied, 8% undecided) with the censorship of war news in Canada. For the question, "Do you think Ottawa gives the public enough information on torpedo attacks in the St. Lawrence River?" the level of satisfaction in Canada was 46% (40% unsatisfied, 14% undecided). In Quebec, only 30% of respondents, Anglophone and Francophone, said they were satisfied, whereas 58% were unsatisfied, and 12% undecided[6].

---

[5] Letter from Powley to Major F.M. Payne in the Library and Archives of Canada, Matthew Halton fonds, MG R-10120, Series I-9-E, folder: Interviews-Research-Powley.
[6] Amongst men, the rates are 52% satisfied, 41% unsatisfied, and 7% undecided. Among women, the rates are 60% satisfied, 31% unsatisfied, and 9% undecided. Cf. La censure et les nouvelles de guerre, *La Presse*, Sept. 19, 1942:22.

Military Public Relations

At the beginning of the war, in 1939, Canadian war correspondents were accredited by the British War Office in London due to the absence of a Canadian service in charge of press relations. A Public Relations Office was created at the Canadian Military Headquarters (CMHQ) in London in January 1940 under the direction of Captain William G. Abel. Its main function was to publicize the Canadian Army's activities at the front and to make the press' work easier. The office also served as a meeting place for visiting Canadian journalists and accredited war correspondents as well as ensured that the press coverage followed the security regulations (DND, DHH, Report No. 2). Furthermore, the office collaborated with the National Film Board of Canada to produce Canadian Army newsreels.

The Canadian Corps also employed Gillis Purcell as public relations officer at its headquarters. Purcell was commissioned as a captain after being a Canadian Press correspondent at the very beginning of the war. Ross Munro, a CP war correspondent and the only journalist at that time to permanently live with the troops, also worked at the Canadian Corps Headquarters. It is important to note that, at the beginning, the CBC/Radio-Canada team was located in the BBC building and not at army headquarters.

James Spence, who was British, worked as a third press officer for the High Commissioner of Canada in London, Vincent Massey, as well as for the Canadian Air Force and Navy. Nevertheless, Purcell and Spence did not collaborate much with William Abel at the main military headquarters in London. This lack of collaboration between public relation services was due to inter-departmental and interpersonal rivalries and to the Canadian government's wait-and-see attitude in terms of implementing a coordination authority (Balzer, 2011:22-23).

Because Canadian troops had long waiting periods in England and there was a lack of large-scale operations, the amount of service done by the Public Relations Office was narrow during its first few years. The number of accredited Canadian war correspondents was limited and the Public Relations Office at the CMHQ only had one photographer and one cameraman. When Canadian troops finally saw action, a large-scale organization was created to fight the battle of information with the Canadian Army along with the journalists. Furthermore, from 1940–1945, the public relations organization greatly surpassed the role of the Canadian War Records Office led by Max Aitken (Lord Beaverbrook) during the Great War. As we are going to see below, the first big Canadian military operation turned out to be disastrous on both military and information fronts.

Press Coverage of Dieppe

On August 19, 1942, nine war correspondents were accredited to cover the Canadian troops during Operation Jubilee at Dieppe. Four Canadians were amongst them: Robert T. Bowman from the CBC, Ross Munro from the Canadian Press, Frederick Griffin from the *Toronto Star*, and Wallace Reyburn from the *Montreal Standard*[7]. Munro and Reyburn, along with British correspondent Alexander B. Austin from the *London Daily Herald*, were the only correspondents that were able to make it ashore with the troops. Under intense fire, the coverage of the Dieppe raid was extremely dangerous, and several correspondents barely escaped death. This failed military operation, which caused many casualties and great material losses, led to one of the worst cases of information censorship during wartime.

During the first 24 hours, not a single report written by a war correspondent was published in Canada. Lord Mountbatten, Chief of Staff of Combined Operations ordered that eyewitness reports be blacked-out. Only official reports that were prepared in advance were published and they gave an incomplete and erroneous first look at the operation (Balzer, 2011:89-112; Bizimana, 2007:57-66, 316-321; Richard, 2002:47-65). Success in the operation was showing up in the newspaper headlines, and the dispatches included details on troop composition that were far from accurate. The day after the raid, the correspondents that had not been accredited for the operation were kept away from the troops returning from Dieppe. Bombarded with insistent demands from the press, William Abel, the senior PR Officer at the Canadian Military Headquarters, tried to intervene on behalf of the journalists but the permission to meet the incoming troops was refused by the Combined Operations Headquarters (DND fonds, Aug. 22, 1942). Since it had no authority over the operation, the Canadian Public Relations Office was no better informed than the non-accredited correspondents. The confidential messages between the Canadian Military Headquarters in London and the Department of National Defense in Ottawa showed the embarrassment of Canadian authorities. Strict British censorship led to the minimization of the participation of Canadian troops, who had actually contributed the most in terms of numbers to the operation at Dieppe (DND fonds, Aug. 27, 1942).

The correspondents' coverage emphasized the Canadian soldiers' heroism. The goal of censoring the information was to expurgate the stories by bowdlerizing very graphic description, as was revealed in an article by Wallace

---

[7] The total number of war correspondents accredited by the Combined Operations Headquarters was 22 (Canadians, British, and Americans).

Reyburn (1942) that was published in the *Montreal Standard* (Aug. 22:4). When the war correspondents returned to Canada, they still had to tell a heroic story in their public lectures.

At a lecture at the Montreal Forum, CP correspondent Ross Munro told a story about how the British commanded by Lord Lovat at Dieppe eliminated 150 German prisoners. The story was published by the *Montreal Gazette* before the Combined Operations Headquarters in London intervened and instructed Canadian censors to prevent further spread of the story. The Canadian Press tried its best to ban the story and Munro was forced to deny what he had said (Bizimana, 2007:321). The publication of the number of casualties at Dieppe was also delayed at the request of the British Ministry of Information. The official list of casualties was only made public on September 15, 1942, almost one month after Operation Jubilee. Munro later confirmed that British and Canadian authorities wanted the shock of the number of casualties to be softened for the Canadian public. Munro had stated his disapproval: "[I] feel it was one of the most flagrant abuses of censorship regulations during the war." (Purcell, 1946:131) Afterwards, military authorities in Ottawa and on the front tried to better supervise reporters in order to avoid bad management of press relations similar to what happened over the reporting of Dieppe.

Invasion of Sicily and Italy

The landing of Allied forces in Sicily in which the 1st Canadian Division participated in on July 10, 1943 (Operation Husky), was covered by four Canadian correspondents: Ross Munro (Canadian Press), Peter Stursberg (CBC), William A. Wilson (British United Press), and Lionel Shapiro (*Montreal Gazette*). In March 1943, a full-scale run-through was done between the Public Relations Office and the Canadian war correspondents during Spartan, an exercise operation. The Canadian General McNaughton recognized the importance of the war correspondents in informing the Canadian public and asked his staff to help these "valued colleagues." (DND, DHH, CMHQ Report No. 91)

In Sicily, the first news report published by a war correspondent is that of Ross Munro from the CP. This scoop was successful because Munro's story, which had to be shared by the press through an international pool, was dispatched to Canada without going through the usual route of Allied censorship. Sent to Europe by the CP in 1940, Munro had covered the short Canadian expedition in Spitsbergen, a Norwegian island in the Arctic, in 1941. His powerful coverage of Dieppe and his numerous scoops would bring him more fame than any other Canadian war correspondent.

In July 1943, Peter Stursberg from CBC also became famous because he recorded the bagpipes of the Seaforth Highlanders of Canada after the Canadians conquered the town of Agira (Stursberg, 1993:113-114; Powley,

1975:47-48). Stursberg had been sent back to the front after having to return to Algiers to be able to transmit reports of the landing in Sicily where there still was not any recording equipment. Stursberg (1993) wrote in his memoirs that the army's Public Relations Office, in which the majority of the officers had been newspaper journalists, had a tendency at the beginning to favor the Canadian Press and not the new medium of radio (p.101). Before arriving in Canada, the stories had to take a long route through Algiers and London.

The Italian Campaign was marked with several organizational and communications difficulties. Just as at Dieppe, only a limited number of correspondents had been accredited for the assault on Sicily, priority having gone to press organizations that had wide distribution. For this reason, the Canadian Press always had an advantage. However, this priority system was criticized on the number of correspondents chosen per press organization and the lack of importance accorded to French-language reporting (Balzer, 2011:130-140).

When troops landed in Sicily, a dozen other correspondents were impatiently waiting in the Mediterranean, in Algiers and Tunis, for the order to sail towards the island. The priority system of the Allied Force Headquarters did not take into account the different needs for English and French stations (CBC and Radio-Canada) since they only allotted one spot for public radio. A correspondent for nine French language newspapers associated with the Canadian Press since 1942, Maurice Desjardins went to Sicily via Tunis after the fall of Messina, the last step for the Italian Campaign. Desjardins, however, was far down on the list of favored CP correspondents since the agency gave precedence to the Anglophone correspondents in order to satisfy its larger clientele first. At that same time, a Francophone team from Radio-Canada, under the management of Marcel Ouimet, also arrived on site.

The brand-new Public Relations Group N°2 was not adequately equipped to transport correspondents. The enemy sank a ship carrying material, including jeeps, among others, that were supposed to be used by the correspondents. Furthermore, the correspondents complained about the lack of communications equipment to transmit their reports, delays because of the censorship and the absence of regular field briefings by military authorities. The war correspondents' complaints even made it into Canadian newspapers and caused embarrassment to the Canadian government (Malone, 1983:209). On August 14, 1943, *The Globe and Mail* published an article signed by Ralph Allen explaining the problems that the war correspondents had and blaming the inefficiency of the public relations detachment of the Canadian army (p.13). Reorganization was imperative.

After Sicily, the war correspondents landed next in the south of Italy with the 1st Canadian Division during Operation Baytown on September 3, 1943. Again, Ross Munro became famous for another scoop. Transported by ship, then by motorcycle and finally by plane to Syracuse, the first report of the landing made headlines in the papers (Powell, 1994, p. 46). This time, Radio-Canada had two correspondents: Matthew Halton, having recently been recruited by the CBC network, and Marcel Ouimet, having just landed in Italy to take care of coverage for the French-language network. Ouimet had his baptism by fire, but Halton had already covered the Desert War in North Africa for the *Toronto Star* (Halton, 1944). At the same time, Paul Dupuis and Paul Barette in London and Benoit Lafleur in Algiers made up the Radio-Canada team. In London, the CBC/Radio-Canada Overseas Unit also produced entertainment broadcasts and, through the BBC airwaves, news, specifically for Canadian troops in England. Between 1939 and 1945, Gérard Arthur, Gerry Wilmot, Jack Peach, Rooney Pelletier, Jacques DesBaillets, Édouard Baudry and Paul Dupuis were the main journalists for this service on the two networks.

The landing in Italy was generally marked by better public relations services with respect to working conditions for Canadian war correspondents. Following the difficulties the press had previously faced, Minister of Defense James L. Ralston had asked Colonel Richard Malone, until then on General Montgomery's staff, to take care of press relations and also to start a Canadian army newspaper, the *Maple Leaf*, which was launched in January 1944. Malone's arrival gave a second wind to the Public Relations detachment and contributed to improving the accredited correspondents' working conditions, thanks to the availability of adequate transport and communication resources. Of course, communication problems emerged at the beginning, such as when the front was moving quickly or when the press camp was located in small towns that had few resources.

However, the Italian Campaign was marked by an organization that was more efficient in assisting the press and in transmitting its stories to Canada. Among others, Malone had negotiated with the Allied Force Headquarters in Algiers, where censorship normally took place, so that the Canadians could manage their own censorship, transmission of reports and supervision of their war correspondents.

On the Italian front, CBC/Radio-Canada made good use of its recording van and portable equipment. In 1940, the CBC Overseas Unit had been equipped with its first armoured truck specifically developed for war reporting. Having this modern truck, nicknamed Big Betsy, the war correspondents of the English- and French-language networks had at their disposal a mobile studio equipped with turntables, portable microphones, batteries and a generator. This enabled them to simultaneously produce on-the-spot recordings and edit them on discs. Big Betsy primarily became famous with the recordings of the London Blitz bombings. Thanks to this equipment, Matthew Halton and Marcel Ouimet became the most well-known correspondents in Canadian households. Among other things, Marcel Ouimet was recognized for his famous reporting of San Marco, Italy, which was broadcast all over the world. As for Benoît

Lafleur and Peter Stursberg, they were able to obtain a recording of Pope Pius XII's speech after Rome was taken. "The unique contribution of radio reporting was its ability to record little pieces of war itself, send them quickly across oceans, and bring them to listeners who wanted to share them with the men who were doing the fighting," confirmed Marcel Ouimet after the war. (Documentation et archives *Radio-Canada*:3-4)

The CBC/Radio-Canada team counted on a team of experienced engineers to operate and maintain the recording equipment. They were also accredited as war correspondents. After Arthur W. Holmes, who in December 1939 had accompanied Robert T. Bowman, the very first CBC war correspondent, many more engineers followed from both networks[8].

Normandy Landings

The invasion of Normandy and the opening of the second front were covered by nine war correspondents attached to the Canadian forces[9]. On his fifth landing with the Canadian Army after Spitsbergen, Dieppe, Sicily, and Italy, Ross Munro added a worldwide scoop to his already substantial list of publications. Thanks to a British officer who tipped him off that a destroyer was headed to England, Munro was able to send the first bridgehead report (Knightley, 2004:352). He was the first but not the only one. The first group of published reports and photographs of the invasion were also Canadian. They came from Marcel Ouimet (Radio-Canada), Ronald Clark (British United Press), William Stewart (Canadian Press) and Ralph Allen (*The Globe and Mail*). Photographs were sent by Lieutenant Frank Dubervill and Sergeant Bill Grant (Canadian Army Film and Photo Unit).

Marcel Ouimet disembarked in the town of Bernières-sur-Mer with the Chaudière regiment, where he described the warm welcome from the people of Normandy. As a bilingual correspondent, he was number one on CBC/Radio-Canada's D-Day priority list. His colleague from the English network, Matthew Halton, and Charles Lynch (Reuters) were with the staff of the 3rd Canadian Division at Graye-sur-Mer. The first Canadian press camp was then established at Courseulles-sur-Mer.

In Normandy and later on the North-Western front, the war

---

[8] This included Anglophone engineers Albert Altherr, Paul F. Johnson, Lloyd Moore, Alec J. MacDonald, Harold Wadsworth, Clifford W. Speer, Laurence Marshall and Fred McCord as well as Francophone engineers Claude Dostie and Joseph Beauregard.
[9] Canadians Ross Munro and William Stewart (Canadian Press), Marcel Ouimet (*Radio-Canada*), Matthew Halton (CBC), Ralph Allen (*The Globe and Mail*), Lionel Shapiro (NANA), Charles Lynch (Reuters), Ronald W. Clark (British United Press) and the American Joseph Willicombe (*International News Service*).

correspondents were members of Public Relations Group No. 3 created by the Canadian Army to cover the second front. The group was led by Colonel Richard Malone, who was called back from the Italian front, but because he was absent on D-Day, French-Canadian Captain Placide Labelle commanded the PR group. A former writer for the *La Presse* newspaper, he supervised the PR detachment in the field on June 6, 1944. The PR Group No. 3 reported to the SHAEF and to the 21st Army Group while being responsible on their own for minding and censoring war correspondents in the Canadian areas of operation.

Started from scratch in 1940 with a small group of men with limited resources, the Canadian Army's PR organisation was at its peak from 1944 to 1945. Among its assets were staff and impressive resources divided among the three main sites: CMHQ in London, the Italian Front, and the North-Western Front. The efficient nature of the unit helped to build a better rapport with the Canadian war correspondents through briefings and regular communications as well as the quick transmission of reports and photographs thanks to better planning and improved communication equipment. By ensuring effective supervision of the press and favorable coverage of the Canadian Army, the Public Relations Office became a bona fide "publicity machine". (Balzer, 2011:50-85)

From the Normandy campaign to the liberation of Germany, the war correspondents went on to cover all of the Canadian Army's and Allied troops' major operations. Halton and Ouimet played the barrage of the Canadian canons over the airwaves, notably from Carpiquet, Caen the "Martyr City[10]", and Falaise. On August 25, 1944, Matthew Halton (CBC), Marcel Ouimet (Radio-Canada), Maurice Desjardins (CP), J.A.M Cook (Winnipeg Free Press), Allan Kent (Toronto Telegram) and Gerald Clark (Montreal Star) entered Paris with French General Leclerc's 2nd Armoured Division. The group was led by Colonel Malone, who earlier had negotiated with the US command to establish a transmission point in liberated Paris. They requisitioned the Scribe Hotel, where the Canadian correspondents were able to transmit the first reports of the liberation from the celebratory French capital (Malone, 1984, pp. 67-70). The Scribe Hotel would go on to become, until the end of the war, a large Allied press center and the major rendez-vous point for all the war correspondents.

After the liberation of Paris, press coverage continued at a rapid pace. Ross Munro (CP) and Frederick Griffin (*Toronto Star*) returned to the beaches of Dieppe on September 1, 1944, two years after the bloody raid of 1942. Matthew Halton and Marcel Ouimet were among the group covering the symbolic return of Canadian soldiers to Dieppe with General Henri D.G. Crerar.

---

[10] Radio report from Marcel Ouimet (Radio-Canada), July 10, 1944.

Arriving from Italy at almost the same time, Peter Stursberg (CBC) and Benoît Lafleur (Radio-Canada) followed the American forces from the landing in the south of France and reported on the activities of the French Resistance. A year earlier, Lafleur and Andrew Cowan (CBC) had reported about the French navy on board the submarine *Casabianca*, the destroyer *Le Terrible* and the cruiser *Jeanne d'Arc* (Cowan Andrew Gillespie Fonds, MG30-E298). Accredited by the French-Moroccan forces, Lafleur would be the only Canadian correspondent to cover events in Corsica.

The correspondents also followed the liberation of Belgium and Holland. Joining a British battalion, they arrived in Brussels on September 4, 1944—24 hours after the liberation. On September 17 of that year, Matthew Halton and Marcel Ouimet became the first to penetrate enemy territory after the American forces broke through the German front. With events accelerating on the various fronts, the Canadian journalists had to leave the Canadian troops and momentarily follow other Allied troops to cover the liberation of different capitals and other large cities. The symbolic significance of the liberation of a capital city was obviously of high journalistic interest to editors, who expected their correspondents to be on hand. However, for Richard Malone, the desire to follow the developments in the liberated areas did not override the fact that the Canadian war correspondents were supposed to be covering the Canadian Army, and so the correspondents' absence in the Canadian activities was not supposed to exceed one or two days (Balzer, 2011:65).

From October to November 1944, the Battle of the Scheldt in Holland held the attention of the war correspondents. With Matthew Halton in Canada to participate in the 7th Victory Bond Campaign, Marcel Ouiment was covering, for both the French and English Radio-Canada networks, the battle of Scheldt, which was supposed to open the Port of Antwerp to the Allies. Before leaving for Canada, Halton covered the failed Operation Market Garden in Arhem where his report was held back by the censors for three days.

With hundreds of Allied war correspondents spread across a number of fronts and operating very close to combat, there were inevitable risks associated with covering the war. During the Great War (1914-1918), a handful of journalists were accredited but were always held back from the trenches so the press had very few casualties among their ranks. During World War II, the first casualty among Canadian correspondents was Samuel S. Robertson from the Canadian Press. He was killed on the SS *Nerissa* after a German U-boat torpedoed the troopship in April 1941. During the Blitz in London, the CP office and Radio-Canada recording van was the target of German bombings, but there were no casualties. After having survived a torpedo attack en route to Algeria a month earlier, Édouard Baudry of Radio-Canada was shot and killed above Morocco while flying to Casablanca for the Churchill-Roosevelt conference in January 1943. In June 1944, the Château Morel in Bény-sur-mer, Normandy, where the Canadian press had set up, was heavily bombed. There were no casualties among the correspondents or public relations officers, but many lost their personal effects. In September 1944, William Kinmont of the *Toronto Star* was captured, along with a driver (Corporal Brown), by the Germans in Belgium. Kinmont was released at the end of war. Technician Clifford W. Speer was killed as a result of a collision between a Radio-Canada recording van and a military truck in May 1945 in London, only a few days after V-E Day. Throughout the war, a number of members of the PR detachment were also injured, taken prisoner or killed. The army's photographers and cameramen had the most dangerous job (Balzer, 2011:64).

In early 1945, numerous Canadian correspondents were granted furlough in Canada at the moment when Canadian troops were in the Nijmegen salient in Holland. After a meeting at the Windsor Hotel in Montreal on January 5, 1945, the Canadian Press War Correspondents Association (CPWCA) was created by a group of eight CP correspondents. Correspondent Ross Munro was designated president. After the war, the association would be called the Canadian War Correspondents Association (CWCA) and would include all the war correspondents accredited during the war and all the public relations officers (Powell, 1994:1; Bizimana, 2007:243-44).

The last Allied effort against Germany started in February 1945 in the west with Operation Veritable of the First Canadian Army in the Nijmegen salient. During a confidential briefing before the attack, General Crerar himself explained the details of the operation to Canadian war correspondents. Once again, the correspondents crossed the Rhine by hopping between the Canadian and Allied troops marching towards Berlin.

William Herbert (CBC) and Paul Barette (Radio-Canada) who had been in Italy until then, joined the press camp on the border between Holland and Germany at the heart of Operation Goldfalke - the secret transfer of Canadian troops from Italy to Holland. One of the major periods of Canadian military censorship was the holding back of information during the two months of the operation (Purcell, 1946:127). A new arrival to the front was Graham Spry from the *Ottawa Citizen*. At the same time, René Lévesque[11] was accredited by the American Army as a war correspondent and covered General Patton's Third Army and then General Patch's 7th Army. With Patch's forces, Lévesque was also a liaison officer with General Lattre de Tassigny's French 1st Army, which was integrated into the US 7th Army. Recruited by the Office of War Information (OWI), the official American propaganda department, René Lévesque went to London in May 1944 to work as an announcer for the French

---

[11] After the war, René Lévesque became a well-known reporter for Radio-Canada and later became Quebec's Prime Minister.

segment of the American Broadcasting Station in Europe (ABSIE) (Bizimana, 2007:150-5, 245-284). Léo Cadieux was also accredited at the end of August 1944 to write for the Francophone papers *La Presse* and *La Patrie*. Former assistant manager of the Canadian Army's Public Relations Office in Ottawa, Cadieux would only stay three months in Paris.

At the beginning of 1945, the war correspondents discovered the concentration camps. How were they to translate to their readers and listeners the horror of the camps and the discovery of mass-scale genocide? It was an insurmountable challenge for the press. Faced with how immense and surreal the Holocaust was, many correspondents would realize how difficult it was to report unspeakable atrocities without being accused of monstrous propaganda. Part of the blame lay with the Allied propaganda and their invented stories of German atrocities from World War I (Knightley, 2004:359-360). The Canadian war correspondents would go on to report on the discovery of concentration camps in Belgium, Holland, and Germany.

In late April 1945, the Canadian correspondents were at the American-Soviet junction on the Elbe. On May 5, they saw the German capitulation on the Canadian front before General Charles Foulkes in Wageningen, Holland.

Gerald Clark of the Montreal Standard was the only Canadian correspondent among the seventeen Allied war correspondents designated by the SHAEF to cover the official surrender ceremony of the Wehrmacht before General Dwight D. Eisenhower in Rheims. As the Canadian representative, Clark was also responsible for reporting for the CBC (Clark, 1995:97). Ross Munro (CP) and Matthew Halton (CBC) were chosen to cover the surrender ceremony in Berlin organized by the Soviet headquarters staff. Two months after the surrender in Germany, a dozen correspondents entered Berlin with a Canadian battalion that was part of the British forces that had occupied the German capital. With the end of the war in Europe, William Stewart of the Canadian Press was sent to the Pacific in May 1945. The following month, the dropping of atomic bombs on Hiroshima and Nagasaki put an end to World War II. When Japan surrendered, Stewart was with released Canadian prisoners in Hong Kong.

Conclusion

Living in press camps near the front and often accredited during the first waves of the attacks during the landings, the war correspondents indubitably worked under perilous conditions. Almost every journalist was in at least one situation that could have cost him his life. With only three deaths - two correspondents (Canadian Press and Radio-Canada) and one technician (Radio-Canada) - Canadian casualties were only a very small fraction of the Allied reporters killed during the war.

In every army, the role of war correspondent was essential. The Canadian army made extra efforts, gradually but resolutely, to help the press with transmitting war news. Evidently, the information diffused by the Canadians was strongly framed by the censorship at home and on the front. Based on the British model, and operating under an Allied command, a well-oiled information and press reports control system was implemented in the field with the assistance of the military censors from the Public Relations detachment. Military indiscretions and strategies that could have been of interest to the enemy, as well as any demoralizing and embarrassing news such as command errors, had to be omitted from the press agencies' news bulletins, from newspapers, and from the radio. With each unfavourable situation for the Allies, such as Dieppe, stricter censorship was applied to the press in the field.

The war correspondents' attitude toward the war also contributed to the patriotic nature of their journalism. With few exceptions, it was certainly extremely difficult to defy the military censorship without risking immediate disapproval from the authorities and expulsion from the theater of operations. "No we weren't free but I never felt I was a PR agent for the government," Ross Munro confirmed after the war (Thompson, 1990:69). Entirely consumed by a war that threatened the vital interest of Canada and her Allies and under powerful military control, the uniformed war correspondents also practiced self-censorship to keep negative and damaging news about the Canadian Army from being published and sabotaging the war effort.

References

Print References

Allen, R. (1943). War Correspondent Beset with Troubles. *The Globe and Mail*, August 14, 1943:13.

Balzer, T. (2011). *The Information Front: The Canadian Army and News Management during the Second World War*. Vancouver: UBC Press, coll. Studies in Canadian Military History.

Beauregard, C. (1998). *Guerre et Censure au Canada 1939-1945*. Sillery: Septentrion.

Bizimana, A-J. (2007). Le contrôle de l'information. In *De Marcel Ouimet à René Lévesque : les correspondants de guerre canadiens-français durant la Deuxième Guerre mondiale*. Montréal : VLB Éditeur, coll. *Études québécoises*.

Bizimana, A-J. (Winter 2009). Le Canada et la Grande Guerre : les nouvelles du front. *Bulletin d'histoire politique [dossier spécial sur la Première Guerre mondiale], vol. 17, No. 2*.

Bizimana, A-J. (2012). René Lévesque, reporter de guerre. In Alexandre Stéphanescu et Éric Bédard (ed.), *René Lévesque : homme de la parole et de l'écrit*. Montréal : VLB Éditeur, coll. *Études québécoises*.

Clark, G. (1995). *No Mud on the Back Seat: Memoirs of a Reporter.* Canada, Montreal: Robert Davies Publishing.

Eck, H. (Ed.). (1985). *La guerre des ondes : histoire des radios de langue française pendant la Deuxième Guerre mondiale.* Canada, Montreal: Hurtubise.

Ferro, M. (1991). *L'information en uniforme.* France, Paris: Ramsay.

Halton, M. (1944). *Ten Years to Alamein.* Toronto: S. J. Reginald Saunders.

Knightley, P. (2004). *The First Casualty The War Correspondent as Hero and Myth Maker from Crimea to Iraq* (3rd ed.). USA, Baltimore: The Johns Hopkins University Press.

Malone, R. S. (1983). *A Portrait of War, 1939-1943.* Don Mills: Totem Press.

Malone, R. S. (1984). *A World in Flames 1944-1945.* Canada, Toronto: Collins.

Powell G. (1994). *Life and Times of the Canadian Press War Correspondents Association and the Canadian War Correspondents Association.* [Pamphlet : *An Informal Compact Record: 50th Anniversary (1945-1995)*].

Powley, A. E. (1975). *Broadcast from the Front: Canadian Radio Overseas in the Second World Wars.* Canada, Toronto: Hakkert.

Purcell, G. (1946). *Wartime Censorship in Canada.* (Master's dissertation). Canada, University of Toronto.

Reyburn, W. (1942). *The Montreal Standard*, August 22, 1942:4.

Richard, B. (2002). *La mémoire de Dieppe: radioscopie d'un mythe.* Canada. Montréal: VLB Éditeur.

Stursberg, P. (1993). *The Sound of War Memoirs of a CBC Correspondent.* Canada,Toronto: University of Toronto Press.

Thompson, E. (Summer 1990). Canadian Warcos in World War II: Professionalism, Patriotism and Propaganda. In *Mosaic*, vol. 23, n°3.

Archival References

Andrew Gillespie Cowan Fonds, MG30-E298, *CBC Overseas Unit and CBC International Service*, vol. 16, folder, *CBC War Correspondents.* Operation order from the French Navy to Benoit Lafleur and Andrew Cowan. [État-major général, N°74 E.M.G./CAB]. Library and Archives Canada [LAC].

Corresp & Reports on Evolution of Field Press Censorship, Canadian Field Press Censorship in the War. Apr/May 1945. Department of National Defence [DND], Directorate of History and Heritage [DHH], 157.4C2009 (D10).

Department of National Defence [DND] fonds. (Aug. 22, 1942) RG 24, vol. 12329, folder 4/Dieppe/1, Major W. G. Abel Memorandum. Library and Archives Canada. Library and Archives Canada.

Department of National Defence fonds. (Aug. 27, 1942) RG 24, vol. 12329, folder 4/Dieppe/1, Message to CANMILITRY from DEFENSOR, CGS 386. Library and Archives Canada.

Clark Gregory fonds (May 24 1941). *Regulations for Press Representatives with The Canadian Army in the United Kingdom.* R8258-0-8-E: Wartime Series, vol. 4, folders 4-9. Library and Archives Canada.

Matthew Halton fonds, Letter from Powley to Major F.M. Payne. MG R-10120, Series I-9-E, folder: Interviews-Research-Powley. Library and Archives Canada.

Ouimet, M. [CBC TIMES Copy]. *War Correspondents*, pp. 3-4. Documentation et archives *Radio-Canada*.

Press Conference Concerning Organization of First Cnd Army and Arrangements for Press Representatives. (Feb. 25, 1943) DND, DHH, CMHQ Report N. 91.

Press guidance notes & samples of trend copy. DND, DHH, 157.4C2009 (D6).

Privy Council Office fonds (1940). *Manuel concernant la censure de la presse et de la radiodiffusion*. RG2, vol. 5942, file 1. Library and Archives Canada.

Radio-Canada (October 1941). *Censure de la radiodiffusion. Manuel Codification des directives*. Documentation et archives Radio-Canada. Ottawa: Imprimeur du roi.

Regulations for War Correspondents Canadian Armed Forces (Home Forces) 1942, 1943. DND, DHH, 111.6.003 (D1).

Report on Censorship, A Narrative on the Organization, Activities and Demobilization of Censorship During the War of 1939-1945, 31 January 1946. DND, DHH, 72/295.

Work of Public Relations Officer, CMHQ. (Jan. 7, 1941). DND, DHH, Report N. 2.

Chapter 8

'Total War': Effects of World War II on the Live Music Industry in Cheshire and North Wales

Helen Southall
University of Chester, UK

"Warfare between 1939 and 1945 was thoroughly industrialized. The major combatants mobilized between a half and two-thirds of their industrial work-force, and devoted up to three-quarters of their national product to waging war. This was war waged on an unprecedented scale. [...] The sheer scale, however, was dictated by the shared belief that in total war states should exert their economic strength to the limit consistent with the survival of a minimum living standard on the home front." (Overy, 2000)

Introduction

Given the profound effect which World War II had on the economy of the UK as a whole, it would be surprising if specific areas of that economy – such as live music in the provinces – were not affected as well. How did 'total war' affect the live music industry on a local level? Evidence I have collected for a study of musicians active in and around Chester during the period suggests that the large number of military bases in the area, combined with the effects of other wartime factors such as conscription, rationing and the need to maintain both military and civilian morale, did indeed affect the size and nature of the market for live dance music locally. For instance, the large US Air Force base at Burtonwood was a source of work for local musicians, as well as an opportunity to mix with American musicians and music fans. As well as presenting information obtained through interviews with musicians and their relatives, I will also look briefly at what happened to the musicians and the bands after the war, when economic and social conditions changed again, at the same time as advances occurred in music-related technology.

No one as famous or influential as the Beatles emerged from Chester (although they did pass through). Much writing on popular music history focus's, quite reasonably, on what is new, unusual and revolutionary in a particular time or place. I argue that new, revolutionary and unusual things are best understood in context, and to understand the context of popular music in the British North West in the 1960s, it is necessary to look also at previous decades, and to avoid being seduced into only being interested in Liverpool. That in turn means looking at the profound effects that World War II had on local music scenes. I will focus on the area centred on Chester and North Wales.

Theoretical and Historical Background

A common way to study the history of popular music since the advent of commercial sound recording has been to focus on which artists were most successful in terms of record sales at a particular time, or perhaps in terms of their influence on the recordings of artists who followed them. While this is a perfectly valid approach, it does have its limitations, the most obvious being that a large proportion of the music that is played or composed does not get recorded at all. Recorded music (and its close cousin broadcast music) therefore offers at best a partial view of the music scene(s) active in a particular time or place.

The fact remains that however many recordings are made available via the Internet, even more music is and will remain ephemeral; it is there, and then it's gone beyond recall. This was certainly the case for most popular music performances at the time of World War II. Basing a history of popular music scenes at that time purely on the available recordings is therefore inappropriate. It is unfair to the memory and efforts of the people involved in the vast majority of musical activities, as well as being likely to give an inaccurate and incomplete view of the work of musicians and entertainers who did become well-known through recording and broadcasting, because it ignores most of the context and infrastructure that they worked within. Fortunately there is plenty of evidence of music making at that time which is more durable than the music itself, such as contemporary newspapers and periodicals, which are particularly useful for confirming facts, figures and locations.

In addition, the personal testimony of individuals who were directly involved in popular music performances has its own specific advantages, especially in giving viewpoints which contemporary published sources tended not to cover, such as that of part-time musicians in provincial towns and cities like Chester and Warrington. The vast majority of the evidence produced in this process (for me) was text and pictures, with only a few short recordings of music of any sort. To understand these, I use the Howard Becker's approach to looking at 'Jazz Places' and the concept of weak ties in social networks as described by Granovetter (1973).

Popular music in marginal fields

People are willing to pay for music as part of the ambience of a place or event. Consciously or not, they value and respond to background music in shops, restaurants and other public spaces. They are demonstrably willing to pay to have dance music available for social occasions and musical heroes to idolise, but from an economic point of view what usually matters is the availability of the music, rather than the physical presence of the musicians. The musicians themselves are equivalent in this model to agricultural labourers or baristas (or, according to session bass-player Herbie Flowers, truck drivers) (Turner, 2002). Interestingly, my field research has already revealed a strong 'craft industry' ethos among musicians who worked in Chester in the 1950s. It is worth noting that mechanisation of a craft industry is frequently blamed for the loss of traditional craft skills and their replacement by less skilled "operative" job roles. In this respect, the music industry appears to have gone the same way as watch-making and motor-cycle production. It is therefore proposed that the transition from dance bands to amplified pop groups and discos was, among many other things, a late stage of the industrial revolution, in which one of the few remaining craft industries was mechanised and automated. The landlords in this case are still, basically, landlords - but landlords as in land owners, not pub managers. The "farmers" (or would-be kiosk-owners) are the hotel proprietors, pub managers, NAAFI managers, or other entertainment venue operators. To them, music is one of the technologies they use in order to make their equivalent of a farm or kiosk more profitable, by encouraging people through the door in the first place, persuading them to linger and spend money on food and drinks once they arrive, and tempting them to return again in the future.

Wartime conditions increased the number of service personnel with no option but to live in or near Chester, thereby increasing the overall size of the local market. Wartime conditions also restricted things such as transport, free time and disposable income, producing a favourable environment for locally based live music in Chester during that period. The end of the war, followed later by the end of national service, reduced this advantage. These changes would have reduced the opportunities for part-time professional musicians in the area by themselves from the mid-1950s onwards. Also, the profitability of an entertainment venue providing music depends partly on how much providing that music actually costs. If a good proportion of the public are sufficiently well off to be paying for musical entertainment at all, and live acoustic music is basically the only option other than silence, competent musicians should find it relatively easy to find work, especially as larger venues will require large groups of musicians in order to physically fill the venue with sound. Those musicians (or groups) who manage to attract a large following for their specific product may be able to charge a premium, or pick and choose where they work, but there will still be plenty of opportunities for those who aren't individually famous.

On the other hand, if a venue barely makes a profit and is employing musicians to provide background music or dance music rather than as the focal point of its activities, technology which makes it possible to use recordings instead (on a juke-box or controlled by a DJ) changes the balance of power between promoters and musicians dramatically. Recordings of nationally famous or fashionable performers may be more attractive to customers than 'unknown' local musicians playing live - as well as being cheaper to provide, taking up less space, and requiring less personal management. If the local musicians want to continue to play at such venues, they may end up having to pay for the privilege - or at least having to take on the financial risk themselves, via a "door takings only" arrangement. While some venues may still make a virtue of the "novelty" of having live musicians on stage, and attract a dedicated audience for that reason, most will tend to go for the easier and more profitable approach of using recorded music.

Jazz Places

> Every artwork has to be someplace. Physical works, like paintings and sculptures, have to be someplace: a museum, a gallery, a home, and a public square. Music and dance and theater have to be performed someplace; a court a theater or concert hall, a private home, a public square or street. [...] Jazz has always been very dependent on the availability of places to perform it in. For much of its existence, jazz was played in bars and nightclubs and dance halls, places where the money to support the entire enterprise came mostly from the sale of alcohol and secondarily from the sale of tickets. So the availability of places for the performance of jazz depended on the viability and profitability of such places.
> (Becker, 2002)

In wartime, musicians also benefit from another source of income; the government. Entertainment has proven benefits for the maintenance of mental health and morale (Jones, 2012), and music has long been considered an essential part of military life. In World War II, British government support extended not only to entertaining the armed forces themselves, but also to various types of musical entertainment, both live and recorded, aimed at maintaining morale among the civilian population back home. In the British Army, for instance, an important role for military bands was entertaining the troops who were stationed for long periods in remote locations overseas, such as Egypt and the Sudan. In an era before satellite television and portable, high quality recorded music devices, regimental bands and dance bands were an essential component in the maintenance of morale away from home. Every regimental band also had its own dance band, whose function was mainly to play for regimental dances. They also provided public entertainment on the Home Front during the war when 'holidays at home' were encouraged. As saxophonist Les Stevenson put it, "You couldn't really go abroad, could you?" Army concert bands and dance bands therefore provided plenty of entertainment in local parks during holiday periods. Army dance bands were also available for civilian functions, charging the standard musicians' union rate for their services.

Wartime Jazz Places in the Chester Region

Chester is an important and long-established route centre, positioned on trade routes between North Wales, Ireland and the rest of the UK, and (like Liverpool) on the west coast route between the south of England and Scotland. The Western Command Headquarters was close to the city centre at Handbridge. Although there was a large complex of buildings already on the site, during the war these were augmented by wooden huts in the grounds to accommodate the extra staff. There was an army garrison at Chester Castle, and also in the nearby barracks beside the Race Course. Other army units were based at camps off Liverpool Road, at Saighton Camp, at the Dale Camp, and just outside Hoole. There was a military hospital a couple of miles North of the city centre at Mostyn.

Moving on to Air Force bases, there was a large RAF base at Sealand, again only a couple of miles from the city centre, as well as two large American bases, at Vicar's Cross (now the Rugby Club) and Hoole Bank (now the Hammond School). There were also many smaller bases dotted about the Cheshire countryside, including an RAF base at Hooton on the Wirral which was the base for the City of Chester fighter squadron. Even the Royal Navy had a base nearby, despite Chester's lack of a port for vessels larger than a pleasure boat or canal barge by this time. This was because the Naval College at Dartmouth was bombed during the war, and it was decided to move the entire institution to a safer location for the duration of the war. The Duke of Westminster's country house at Eaton Hall – again, just a couple of miles from the city centre – became the Royal Naval College in exile, as it were. After the war it became a college for British Army Officer Cadets doing their National Service. In addition to these larger bases, there were lots of small searchlight and anti-aircraft batteries. While each of those might only have a handful of men (or sometimes women) to operate them, all of these people had to live – and be entertained – in the local area as well. Many rooms, and entire houses, were commandeered as billets for personnel stationed in the area, including U.S. Forces personnel and civilian migrant workers working in war factories such as the bomber factory at Hawarden (now British Aerospace) or the munitions factories near Frodsham.[1]

Chester in the mid-twentieth century boasted a large number of public houses for the relatively small size of the city, and according to Len these were very popular with service personnel and factory workers based in the area.

---

[1] Harry Proctor was a young pianist living in Chester during the war. His band the Swing Seranaders played a memorable gig at a school on Helsby Hill which was used during the war as a dormitory for migrant workers who had come over (mostly from Ireland) to work in the factories nearby. The gig was on a Saturday night, and getting there and back was difficult, so the band arranged to spend the night at the venue. It turned out to be a sleepless night, as they were put in a room with some very loud snorers!

Chester also offered entertainment in the form of cinemas and theatres, and of course dancing venues such as Quaintways and Clemences in the city centre, and 'village hops' in village halls and the like. For service personnel, there were clubs such as the NAAFI and the American Red Cross in the city centre. American servicemen also made use of the Chester College gym[2] for dances, to which female ATS personnel billeted nearby were often invited. It wasn't always necessary for service personnel to leave their bases for entertainment however. The NAAFI (Navy, Army and Air Force Institute) or their US equivalents organised dances and entertainments for service personnel on base[3] (or at other locations such as hospitals, e.g. Moston Hospital), from booking the bands to providing the catering. All of these venues offered opportunities for local entertainers, and the more so since non-essential travel (including band tours) was strictly limited. It is important to remember that in the midst of all the upheaval, life on the Home Front went on. People were shunted around the country (and the world) with scant thought for their personal preferences or burgeoning musical careers,[4] but at the same time it is likely that local music scenes in some ways became even more local - or at least didn't overlap as much as they might have done otherwise - because of practical factors like fuel rationing and directed employment. For all of these reasons, local musicians in Chester – and presumably elsewhere in the country as well – had plenty of local opportunities for part-time musical employment during this period, even if they were required to work in non-musical occupations by day.

It should be noted that Chester musicians did not by any means limit themselves to playing in the city of Chester itself. Within the limitations imposed by wartime travel restrictions and post-war fuel rationing, they frequently travelled further afield. A good example of a venue which provided work for many local musicians is the US air base at Burtonwood, near Warrington, which will be discussed in more detail in the next section.

---

[2] Local youngsters who were interested in jazz weren't actually invited to these dances, but according to saxophonist Danny Morgan they often weren't turned away either, provided that they kept quiet and behaved themselves. This was Danny's first opportunity to see an American swing band at close range.

[3] e.g. Harry Proctor's Swing Serenaders played on several occasions at the US Army base at Delamere in Cheshire.

[4] For some young musicians, the start of World War II put at least a temporary end to their playing careers. Drummer Doug Hall had just got established with the Adelphi Dance Band when his call up papers arrived. He played his last gig with the Adelphi Dance Band at Tarporley on Saturday 1st September 1939, and on Monday morning he was marching to Chester station with the Cheshire Yeomanry, with the military band playing in front of the troops. He fought at Dunkirk and in Palestine, and did not return to the Chester music scene until after the end of the war.

Burtonwood

Musicians and bands from Chester and North Wales regularly travelled outside their hometowns to perform, often to entertain personnel at the many military bases in the area. One base, which was mentioned frequently in interviews, was at Burtonwood, near Warrington. A few large buildings still remain on the site, but looking at what remains today gives little idea of just how large it was – or how many people lived there – in its heyday in the nineteen-forties and fifties.

Burtonwood air base was originally built in 1939 as an aircraft repair depot for the RAF, but was taken over by the Ministry of Aircraft Production in 1942, before being operated by US Forces from 1940. The base was occupied continuously by American and British units - in spite of being divided by the M62 motorway in the early 1970s - until its final closure in 1993. Many of the remaining storage buildings continued in civilian use until the early 2000s, by which time much of the land not already underneath the motorway was the site of a large out-of-town retail development, including stores such as the furniture warehouse IKEA (Granfield and Bushell, 2010b).

Burtonwood played an important part in World War II, and also in the Berlin Airlift of 1948. The first US personnel arrived in June 1942. This was followed by the construction of six huge storage hangars with a combined area of 734,000 square feet, as well as hundreds of hastily- constructed huts to accommodate the US personnel at the base, which eventually grew from a few hundred in 1942 to more than 18,000 by the mid-1950s, effectively making it a small town in its own right. By that time it was the largest US military base outside the USA, with its own chapels, a hospital, schools and recreation facilities. From 1967 until the base closed in 1993, Burtonwood was a storage depot for the US Army in Europe.

For comparison, the town of Warrington today has a population of around 80,000, a that hasn't changed much since the 1950s, and Chester in 1951 had a population of approximately 45,000 (Anon., 2013a). In effect, an ex-patriot American population equal to nearly half the population of Chester was living at Burtonwood at its height - and Burtonwood was just one of many US military bases in the area. It's therefore not at all surprising that these bases had a noticeable effect on the social, cultural and business life of the area, although what is perhaps not so obvious is that this wasn't all one-way traffic, and local musicians benefitted from the enlarged entertainment market in their area, as well as from things like access to imported records and the American Forces Network radio broadcasts.

Even at the height of the war, American celebrities such as James Cagney, Bing Crosby and Bob Hope travelled to the UK to entertain US Forces personnel stationed at military bases, including Burtonwood. Burtonwood was also one of the venues where Glenn Miller's Army Air Force band played when it was in the UK in 1942 (Way, 1996).[5]

But Miller and his band only played a single night at Burtonwood. It's unlikely that even all the US service personnel based there at the time were able to be present at the performance, so although the band's influence and entertainment were spread more widely by radio broadcasts and recordings, as far as Burtonwood itself was concerned, an interesting question remains. Bearing in mind that large-scale dance hall entertainment using recorded music required technology which was, at that time, yet to be fully developed, who entertained the 18,000 personnel when the stars from back home weren't available – in other words, most of the time?

The Dennis Williams Quintet

As has already been suggested, the answer is that local bands and musicians were frequently employed to provide entertainment on base. According to interviews, the American bases in particular provided gigs that were popular sources of work, as they were well paid and generally enjoyable as well. There was therefore competition among bands to get these gigs, and bands used employment at bases such as Burtonwood as proof of competence and quality when advertising for work elsewhere, the implication being that not only were they sufficiently professional to provide an evening's entertainment in a large venue, they were also accepted to supply what was in essence American-style music to an American audience.

Their brochure includes a testimonial from the Base Commander at USAAF Burtonwood, as well as others from the USAF Officers' Club, Burtonwood, and a list of the more prestigious venues in the area such as Clemences Restaurant in Chester, the Grosvenor Ambassadors in Chester, the Castle Hotel in Bangor (North Wales), the Bulkeley Arms Hotel in Beaumaris (Anglesey), and the Royal Anglesey Yacht Club. This list gives an idea both of the level of professionalism a potential booker could expect from the quintet, and also their usual geographic range, running approximately from Warrington in the East to Anglesey in the far West of North Wales.

---

[5] Chester trumpet player Don Owens was a fan of the music played on the American Forces Network, including the Glenn Miller Army Air Force Band. The Miller band arrived in Britain in June 1944 and played at numerous venues around the UK before leaving for France in December of that year. (Miller, famously, never arrived in France, although the rest of the band did.) One day Don's mother came home from work and announced that Glenn Miller was going to be on the radio that evening. Don was sceptical at first, but it was true; the band had arrived in Britain and were broadcasting live that evening.

The brochure also emphasises the band's performances in national and regional dance band competitions, as more evidence of proficiency and professionalism. The band had in fact started out under the leadership of Syd Lawrence, who grew up near Chester and played his first professional gigs in the Chester area. When Lawrence left to pursue a successful full-time musical career (Gifford, 1998), the rest of the band carried on as a semi-professional Chester-based group, now led by saxophonist Dennis Williams. The band also included bass player Ces Davies, who went on to lead another resident band at Quaintways in Chester, and guitarist Frank Jeffes, who had spent his last few months of conscription with the RAF at the end of the war touring South Asia with an RAF concert party.[6]

But even a respected ensemble like the Dennis Williams Quintet would have been physically unable to provide all the entertainment required at venues like Burtonwood on their own. While musicians from larger cities like Manchester and Liverpool would undoubtedly also have been employed there as well, it should be remembered that Manchester and Liverpool were extremely busy entertainment markets in their own right; in the forties and fifties, at least, there was generally no need for musicians from the larger conurbations to travel into Cheshire and North Wales for work on a regular basis, as they were usually kept busy closer to home. Therefore, it shouldn't be a surprise, in pre-discotheque days, to find a substantial network of dance band musicians operating out of Chester (and also North Wales, especially Wrexham). The Dennis Williams Quintet, was just one band, and Burtonwood was just one venue - albeit a large one. However, both typify a type of market and musical product which were common in this period. The market changed as (for example) military mobilisation decreased after the war, and again with the end of National Service in the early 1960s. As discussed earlier with regard to the economics of running music venues, the increasing availability of hi-fi sound recording and reproduction also had a substantial effect.

Other Burtonwood stories

The following information is taken from interviews with other local musicians who had been active in the Chester and North Wales dance band scene, and help to put Burtonwood into context as an important venue in the region.

Trumpet player Tommy Jones remembers hearing the Western Base Sector Dance Orchestra, were based at Burtonwood near Warrington. He was too

---

[6] Jazz guitarist Frank Jeffes was in the RAF during the war, but it wasn't until after the war had finished that his musical ability brought him with opportunity travel as a professional musician: 'The war had finished and they didn't know what to do with us. They found out that I played at home...' Frank was directed to join the six-piece band backing a concert party, which travelled around India and Ceylon for six months or more in a DC4 Dakota aircraft.

young to get to know any of them at the time, being only about fourteen, but he was very impressed by the band, which included ex-professionals who had toured with bandleaders such as Harry James and Tommy Dorsey before they were called up. Jones joined the RAF in 1948 and was assigned to work as a telephone operator. He did manage to carry on playing his trumpet while in the RAF, where he was impressed by some of the other musicians in the bands he played with. One was a brilliant 18-year-old cornet player who was already earmarked for the RAF Regiment band. There were also a couple of ex-university lads in their early twenties, and a bassoonist who had previously studied at the Royal College of Music. In later years Jones played at Burtonwood with his own bands. This was after the war, but food rationing was if anything even tighter by then. He always enjoyed playing for the Americans because they were an appreciative audience, and also the food was always 'amazing'. Egg sandwiches were still a luxury off base, but at Burtonwood they were easily obtained, and overflowing with two or three eggs each.

Jones' anecdotes suggest that as well as bolstering the market for musicians who were already active in the region's dance bands, the influx of American service personnel into the UK brought with it influences and opportunities which young enthusiasts in the area would probably not have encountered in peacetime. Similarly, conscription into the British forces both during and after the war brought with it its own opportunities for many. For instance, when Don Owens was called up for his National Service he decided to join an Army band, as he saw this as an opportunity to get a good practical education in music that would include jazz and dance band styles, which were simply not acknowledged in British civilian education institutions at that time. His trumpet teacher was a local ex-military bandmaster called Ernie Martin. Martin helped Owens to get a position in the 11th Hussars Band, where he was posted first to Germany, and then to Malaya during the Malayan Emergency. After leaving the Army, he returned to Chester and started gigging with Billy Brickland, who he describes as 'a very charming, kindly man', as well as Wilf Field and Billy Gibbons. Gibbons recommended Owens to Leon Sait, who led the resident band at the River Park Ballroom. All the arrangements for this band were written by Dave Pearce and Sait himself. The band's unusual sound was well-received, even by members of big touring bands who heard it. As well as the residency at the River Park Ballroom, the Sait band played regular Sunday gigs at Burtonwood, which Owens described as interesting and very well paid.

Moving across the River Dee to Wrexham (North Wales), Ray Irving started his band-leading career in 1948, just after Irving and most of his musicians had been de-mobbed from the Royal Welch Fusiliers. Over the next thirty years or so Ray's band provided experience and employment to numerous local musicians. They were the resident band at the Queen's Ballroom, Rhyl, from 1948 to 1951. The band made its first broadcast in 1949, and during its time as the Queen's Ballroom Orchestra shared the bill with top touring bands including those of Ted Heath, Joe Loss, Geraldo, Cyril Stapleton, Ray Ellington, Ambrose and the Squadronaires. In the mid-1950s, Irving and his band played at American bases in the area, including Burtonwood, where they shared the bill with American artists including Count Basie, Bob Hope and Les Brown. They also played the 'university circuit', including gigs at Manchester, Keele, Bangor and Aberystwyth. In the 1960s and 70s the band played at society functions in Wales and the borders, and continued to appear occasionally on television.

As well as showing how far afield Burtonwood's band bookers went to obtain entertainment for the base, Irving's story illustrates the extent to which local bands interacted directly with big-name bands and artists when they were in the area, often playing opposite them in a similar capacity to the support acts at modern rock and pop gigs. While it is certainly the case that musicians in the British regions were influenced by recordings and radio broadcasts, many also had the opportunity to meet the artists who had inspired them in the flesh and to observe them in action, when they could look for answers to the sort of questions which matter to practitioners more than they usually do to critics and theorists, such as 'What reeds is he using?', 'How does he hit those high notes all evening without getting a nose-bleed?' or 'How does he voice those chord when accompanying a singer?'. In other words, the distinction between well-known full-time musicians and their local, part-time equivalents was not clear-cut. They frequently worked at the same venues on the same evenings, and there was a substantial overlap between the social networks of the individuals concerned.

The connection with the nascent university circuit is also interesting. Although the Robbins report, which led to the expansion of the British higher education, was not published until 1963, many of the institutions, which became part of the resulting wave of new universities, were already in existence as technical colleges or university colleges[7], and like military bases they also housed large groups of young people in need of entertainment. The infrastructure for the university circuit, which became an important part of British popular music in later years, therefore had its roots in the dance band era.

---

[7] For instance, the University of Keele was first established as the University College of North Staffordshire in 1949, when it was founded in the grounds of the Sneyd Estate near Stoke-on-Trent. Like Eaton Hall near Chester, Sneyd Hall had been requisitioned for military use during the war, and the new university college took over the pre-fabricated Army structures in the grounds as well as the ancestral home of the Sneyd family as its first buildings. It is likely that musicians who had previously entertained the troops based there moved on fairly seamlessly to entertaining the students at the same venues.

A Social Network of Musicians

A large number of musicians were involved in playing with dance bands in Chester and North Wales at both civilian and military venues. Like every other organisation during the war, the dance bands had to cope with people coming and going at the whim of the call-up system. This probably reinforced the existing preference for reliance on stock arrangements and good sight-readers, and bands tended to have 'chairs' to be filled so that the necessary dance music could be played to an adequate standard, rather than indispensible star personalities. In Chester, bandleader Wilf Field was among those who stayed behind and did the coping, because he was in 'reserved occupation[8]' as a draftsman. His job at a company making aircraft components kept him out of the fighting, although he was required to do fire watching at night. His son Gordon remembers sitting high up with his father, watching the bombers over Liverpool.

Obviously the war had other effects on Field's band-leading activities. Clothes rationing meant that band uniforms weren't available, so Field compromised by insisting that his musicians all wore the same tie emblazoned with his initials 'WF'. And although the large numbers of service personnel stationed locally provided extra business for bands such as Field's, actually getting to and from the gig could be challenging; Field's son recalls that his father found being driven fast along the dark Cheshire lanes in an American army jeep rather hair-raising, especially as the headlights had to be covered to show only narrow slits of light on the road ahead. Getting a band together – especially a dance band or 'big band' requiring between seven and fifteen musicians – was an activity which required a lot of contacts, especially in an era before mobile phones and e-mails when contacting musicians at short notice was more difficult. Evidence provided by Gordon Field included his father's 1955 Musicians' Union pocket diary, which Field used as an address book and contact list. Field's 1955 diary, though obviously from a decade later, is evidence of the systematic approach, which Field developed to ensure he could contact the musicians he needed, when he needed them. By that time he was running not one but three or four separate bands, quite often with two or more out working on the same evenings, so making sure that the right people turned up in the right places, correctly equipped and attired for the job in hand, was a considerable feat of organisation - and still one which he did in addition to his full-time job as a draftsman. In the language of social network analysis, the list

---

[8] Musicians who were too young or too old to be called up also found themselves at an unexpected advantage. For instance, Pianist Colin Gibson sometimes played the organ in church while still a schoolboy, because so many older musicians were away in the forces.

of contacts Field used to help him achieve this would be known as 'weak ties', of the sort described by Granovetter in Boston in the 1970s – that is, people who are not necessarily close friends or relatives, but whose primary reason for staying in touch is that they can help one another, usually on a work or business basis.

The evidence from Field's diary, when combined with that from interviews and other materials collected for this study, shows that this network of musicians was remarkably long lasting and resilient. The majority of musicians in Field's address list are also mentioned by the other musicians I interviewed, or shown in the photographs and press cuttings which they loaned me. It is particularly interesting to note that the list in Field's 1955 diary overlaps to a very large extent with the musicians who took part in the 'Soundings of Chester Jazz' concert, which took place nearly ten years later.

Resident Bands and Musical Lineage

Although rock 'n' roll and skiffle were already making inroads into the British popular music scene by the mid-1950s, new ballrooms were still opening in the late 1950s, complete with resident big bands providing waltzes, foxtrots, quick-steps and Latin tunes for ballroom dancing in styles more commonly associated with the war years. Although this may seem counterintuitive, there was a good commercial reason; cinema chains such as the Rank Organisation were suffering drops in demand due to new diversions such as television, and were looking for other things to do with their large buildings; many were turned into dance halls, and operated successfully in that form for some years, before eventually that market fell away as well, and they were finally demolished or turned into bingo halls. The opening night programme in the photograph is from the Majestic Ballroom in Chester, an example of just such a venue.

The resident band at the new Majestic Ballroom was led by Roy Williams, a former Royal Marines bandsman and representative for the Schillinger system of composition and musical harmony (Simpson, 2008). Other members of the band included Stan Thomas, who had played professionally with Ken Mackintosh's band the Royal Navy Blue Mariners. Stan had been a prisoner of war in Japan in Nagasaki when the atomic bomb was dropped there, and suffered continuing health problems as a result. Arrangements were done by Dave Pearce and Roy Williams. A recording exists of the Majestic Ballroom Orchestra which was made in the following year (1958), and is an interesting reminder of the war, as well as a portent of things to come, as it was made on a portable tape recorder which was itself a result of wartime technological innovations. As has already been alluded to in the section on dance band economics, related hi-fi sound reproduction technology eventually led to demise of many commercial dance bands.

This late 1950s ballroom opening might be seen as the tail end of the previous trend, rather than the youthful beginnings of the next one. However, this was the world that the skiffle groups, rock 'n' roll bands and rhythm and blues musicians of the coming generation grew up in. This is the sort of entertainment their parents or older brothers and sisters enjoyed - or provided. Elvis Costello, Pete Townsend and the Bee Gees all had fathers in the dance band business (Cook, Hughes, & Bilyeu, 2009; Kelts, 2012; Leigh, 2011) Even Bert Weedon, whose guitar tutor book 'Play in a Day' influenced innumerable young guitarists (including Townsend) was an integral part of the dance band world, having played at with major bands including Ted Heath, Mantovani and the Squadronnaires, before becoming a featured soloist with the BBC Show Band (Anon., 2012).

The Chester Jazz Scene - post-war and beyond

The Chester music scene in the 1950s wasn't just about dance bands by any means; the stylistic basis of the music was jazz, purveyed in various forms. The Wall City Jazz band was formed in 1952/3 and still plays at the Mill Hotel in Chester on Monday nights as at 2013. The Wall City Band was and is a sort of traditional jazz band, but not as purist as some; they certainly aren't above playing swing or blues numbers if the audience or that night's personnel like the idea. In general, there doesn't seem to have been the antipathy between 'trad' and 'modern' jazz musicians among my interviewees, which was reported elsewhere. In general, if the jazz scene around Chester had a dominant philosophy, it seems to have been pragmatism.[9]

However, it's also the case that by the mid-1960s - just as the Beatles started to reach the peak of their commercial success - some of the local musicians were starting to focus on playing high quality jazz for its own sake, rather than purely on a commercial basis. An example of this is provided by the 'Soundings of Chester Jazz' concert, which took place in Chester in 1964.[10] It is interesting

---

[9] Several interviewees reported having given up music temporarily at the busiest points in their full-time work career, and returning years later when work and family commitments became more manageable again, by which time the motivation was definitely social and musical rather than financial. It would be interesting to look at this from the point of view of ancillary parts of the live music industry, such as music shops, who by the nineteen-nineties would have had a significant market for replacement instruments, accessories and consumables for reed and brass instruments among men who were by this stage reasonably prosperous retirees, rather the schoolboys and teenagers they had been when they first became involved in music. I say 'men' here quite deliberately; other than some vocalists and a few pianists, the proportion of women involved in professional or semi-professional dance bands in the nineteen-forties and fifties was very small. The reasons for this would be material for another chapter on their own.

[10] According to the programme for the event, "The Jazz Music Group is a formal name for what is really a very informal gathering of Chester Jazz Musicians. Although we all differ in our approach to jazz, and, essentially, give and individual meaning to jazz, there are two points about which we agree. Firstly, a sincere and passionate belief in good jazz music and secondly a desire

to note that almost all of the musicians who took part in this event in 1964 are also listed in Wilf Field's address list from 1955, which would seem to counteract any suggestion that this was a completely separate set of people from the commercially-oriented bands organised by Field. What seems more likely is that the musical environment - and the musicians' own personal and family circumstances - had altered, and this had affected where, when and how the musicians chose or were able to perform.

No longer 'Pop', but Part of the Furniture...

Although Glenn Miller disappeared en route to France in 1944, his music is still frequently played - live, as well as in recorded form - today in 2013. Use of the 'Glenn Miller Orchestra' name is tightly controlled, with three fully professional bands working in different parts of the world at the time of writing (Anon., 2013b). In addition, original arrangements and transcriptions are widely and legally available, and played all over the world by ensembles including school and conservatoire bands, military bands, and local semi-professional big bands and dance bands. The music is now usually marketed as nostalgia, and often aimed at those old enough to remember it when it was popular dance music, or (to a lesser extent) younger people who have developed an interest in ballroom dancing as a result of television shows such as Strictly Come Dancing.

An example of such a nostalgia event was the 'Christmas at the Base' dinner-dance which was organised at Burtonwood by the Burtonwood Association (Granfield & Bushell, 2010a) in 2003. Many of those present were former US Servicemen and women and their families who had once been based at Burtonwood, and who had travelled back to the UK for the occasion. Interestingly, the entertainment was once again provided by a local band - the Norman Roy Orchestra - that included several of my interviewees as musicians (as well as the author playing lead alto).

---

to play, as individuals and as groups, good jazz and good music. Initially, the group started as a big 'rehearsal' band embracing musicians of all styles meeting occasionally on Sunday mornings to play big band jazz scores. From this beginning, it was decided to present a concert of jazz, which would serve the dual purpose of giving the musicians something tangible to work for and allow the public a chance to see and hear what is happening to the art of jazz in Chester.
The delicate flower of jazz has flourished in Chester and, in the post-war years particularly, some bands and musicians have proved their worth on the National scene. What is regrettable is that the jazz musicians of Chester are working with little or no recognition in their own city. We hope that the activities of the Group, including this concert, will rectify this. The music in this concert covers all styles of jazz, from traditional and mainstream to modern with groups of all sizes from trios to the Big Band and includes a number of original scores and arrangements by members of the Group.
We welcome you to what is an exciting occasion for us. We are sure that it will be a stimulating and we hope delightful evening for you. After all, we want this concert to be the first of a series, not an isolated occasion."

Between the time when big band jazz and swing were popular music, and recent years when they have been more likely to be categorised as nostalgia, live local dance bands were part of the musical furniture. Their activities overlapped with, influenced, and were influenced by their musical and cultural surroundings.

Conclusions

There was a busy live jazz and dance music scene in the Chester area from the late 1920s to at least the late 1950s, which then moved venues rather than dying out entirely. Some bands and venues survived well into the 1970s and beyond, even though dance band music was no longer 'popular' among the young. In this chapter I have described some of my research on how and why this was the case.

While there is undoubtedly a lot of truth in popular music histories which credit changes in prosperity and social attitudes after the war, as well as the baby boom, with catalysing the explosion of new music and popular culture in the 1960s and beyond, they do have weaknesses. However, apparently unexceptional live music scenes such as this are important and worthy of study, both because of their effect on the development of new artists and musical trends, and also because of the light which such studies shine on the lives and activities of a range of ordinary people in a particular time and place.

References

Anon. (2012). *Influential guitarist Bert Weedon Dies*. BBC News: Entertainment & Arts. Retrieved 31st May 2013, 2013, from http://www.bbc.co.uk/news/entertainment-arts-17781762.
Anon. (2013a). *Census Reports. A Vision of Britain Through Time*. Retrieved 17th June, 2013, from https://vision.port.ac.uk/census/.
Anon. (2013b). *Licensed Territories. The Famous Glenn Miller Orchestra*. Retrieved 17th June, 2013, from http://glennmillerorchestra.com/licensed-territories/.
Becker, H. S. (2002). *Jazz Places*. Retrieved from http://buffaloreport.com/020401beckerjazzplaces.html.
Cook, H., Hughes, A. M., & Bilyeu, M. (2009). *Tales of the Brothers Gibb*. UK. Omnibus Press.
Gifford, D. (1998, Thursday, 7th May). Obituary: Syd Lawrence, The Independent. Retrieved from http://www.independent.co.uk/news/obituaries/obituary-syd-lawrence-1160896.html.

Granfield, L. & Bushell, C. (2010a). *RAF Burtonwood*. Retrieved 3rd August, 2012, from http://www.rafburtonwood.org/.

Granfield, L. & Bushell, C. (2010b). *RAF Burtonwood - Potted History*. Retrieved 6th June, 2013, from http://www.rafburtonwood.org/history.html.

Granovetter, M. (1973). 'The Strength of Weak Ties'. *The American Journal of Sociology*, 78(6), 1360-1380.

Jones, E. (2012). *Morale, Psychological Wellbeing of UK Armed Forces and Entertainment: A Report for the British Forces Foundation*. King's Centre for Military Health Research, King's College London.

Kelts, R. (2012, October 9th 2012). *Pete Townsend's War, The New Yorker*. Retrieved from http://www.newyorker.com/online/blogs/culture/2012/10/pete-townshends-war.html.

Leigh, S. (2011, Thursday, 1st December 2011). *Ross MacManus: Singer, trumpeter and father of Elvis Costello*. The Independent. Retrieved from http://www.independent.co.uk/news/obituaries/ross-macmanus-singer-trumpeter-and-father-of-elvis-costello- 6270103.html.

Overy, R. (2000). 'Total War II: The Second World War'. In C. Townshend (Ed.), *The Oxford History of Modern War*. USA, Oxford, New York: Oxford University Press. (pp.138-157).

Simpson, D. L. (2008). *My Introduction to the Schillinger System*. Retrieved from http://josephschillinger.wordpress.com/introductio/.

Turner, A. W. (2002). *Herbie Flowers. Glitter Suits and Platform Boots*. Retrieved 14th March, 2009, from http://www.alwynwturner.com/glitter/flowers.html.

Way, C. (1996). *Glenn Miller in Britain: Then and Now: After the Battle*. UK. Battle of Britain Prints.

Chapter 9

'Every German had a bloody Leica'. Heinrich von der Becke's 'Negro' and Other Photographs of Colonial POW's in WW2.

Brian Machin
University of Chester, UK

They made us line up in five ranks. They counted us. With the remains of formations from other sectors which were already there when we arrived, we were about five thousand. A senior officer, with a whole cohort of fellow high-ups reviewed us. Other conquerors photographed us. They have a mania for snapshots; already, on the way there, I don't know how many soldiers had turned their cameras on our column - they all have cameras; it must be the German tourist tradition flourishing on French soil.
(Robert Guerlain, *A Prisoner in Germany*, 1944)

Sometimes German soldiers and reporters added insult to injury by photographing or filming captured black soldiers. The blacks were presented as exotic curiosities in the weekly newsreels and in documentaries about the campaign, as in Sieg im Westen, where black soldiers had to perform a strange dance shown towards the end of the film. Books published shortly after the campaign juxtaposed unflattering photos of black soldiers with photos of well-groomed German soldiers. Witnesses and surviving photos indicate that some German soldiers and guards took pride in posing with black POW's for a picture.
(Raffael Scheck, *Hitler's African Victims*, 2006)

Introduction

As part of a much larger project dealing with the experiences of a black British soldier in World War 2, I have come across very few images of Black British soldiers. Those that do exist are in the main standard portraits of smiling young men in new uniforms taken in studios and sent home to families. There are some group portraits of battalions or companies with a black face present -

there were at least two black paratroopers recorded as present in the Arnhem fighting, and in Cornelius Ryan's book about the D-Day raid on Pegasus Bridge we read of three black soldiers in the glider-borne force (Ryan, 1995). We also see the occasional black British face in army public relations material. As the indigenous black population of Britain was probably less than 20,000 in 1939, then that is probably sufficient explanation in itself for the scarcity of such images.

In looking for images of black British soldiers, I actually encountered many more images of black French colonial soldiers – about one in ten French soldiers was of colonial origin, mostly North or West African. While there are images of African men in French recruiting material, more often than not, any photographs I found were taken by Germans. I have concentrated on 1940 as that is the locus of my larger study and the campaign in France produced the majority of photographs of black colonial soldiers.

A complicating factor to the task of finding pictures of Black British soldiers is that the British military, unlike that of the United States, did not segregate races, at least not in British based units. They did, of course, separate those that they considered colonial troops and there was considerable debate about the use of African or Caribbean troops in combat roles. As David Killingray (2010), in *Fighting for Britain*, put it,

> Military thinking about the use and employment of African troops had moved on slightly since the First World War but the expectation was that African colonial forces would be used exclusively within Africa and that such operations would require substantial support from a large labour corps. The course of the war in Europe, the role of African troops in defeating the Italians in East Africa, the military and labour demands placed on Africa for the North African campaign, and the Japanese threat to India in 1942-43 determined that African soldiers would play a much more prominent role overseas than was demanded of them in the Great War (Killingray, 2010).

In France, the recruitment of African troops had been practiced since the 1830s and indeed, conscription was introduced in all French colonies in 1919. These soldiers were always intended to be employed on the French mainland and indeed in 1937, the French High Command planned to deploy 162,000 men from French West Africa and it is estimated by Nancy Ellen Lawler that some 150,000 were actually deployed in the European Theatre at the fall of France in June 1940 (Lawler, 1992: 27). There is some dispute over the actual casualty rates suffered by west African *Tirailleurs* but these were similar to if not greater than French metropolitan units and the ratio of killed to wounded and prisoners was higher. Colloquially at least, these men could expect to be placed in the thick of the fighting and to be treated harshly if they managed to surrender – in itself a difficult task for any soldier in the heat of battle; for a black African soldier an extremely hazardous one.

This chapter intends to say something about the uses such photographs were put to by the Nazi regime in the second world war. Much more specifically it looks at particular photographs of black French colonial soldiers taken in very different circumstances and for widely differing reasons. As such, it will only be able to touch on certain contextual issues such as the attitude of the Third Reich towards black African soldiers and the place of photography in the Nazi regime. All the photographs were taken between 1940 and 1942, some by professional photographers working in Propaganda Kompanies (PK) of the Wehrmacht (German Army) and responsible to the Propaganda Ministry headed by Joseph Goebbels, others were taken by ordinary German soldiers.

Propaganda Kompanies

In 1940, the French colonial soldier was photographed in several different ideological contexts, both by professionals working directly for the Nazi propaganda ministry and by ordinary soldiers with cameras. The very fact that the Propaganda Kompanies (PK), the military arm of the German propaganda ministry, had incorporated trained photographers, journalists and artists since 1938 brought an approach to the work produced that was different both to the professional work they produced prior to military service and to the kind of snapshot that ordinary soldiers were taking.

The relationship between the PK and the Propaganda Ministry was not straightforward. On the one hand the PK members were producing official propaganda material, but also material of their own. There was competition between the requirements of military propaganda and state propaganda (Cooper, 1989). This against the background of a widespread amateur ethos in Germany as a whole. As early as 1933, Joseph Goebbels called upon, "an army of millions of amateur photographers to educate the nation according to the principles of National Socialist propaganda".[1] Of course many amateur photographers joined the military. To complicate matters, the Nazi regime encouraged soldiers to take photographs and send them home to encourage morale – with the usual taboos of not depicting German dead or wounded and most certainly not atrocities. An appeal published in the journal *Photofreund* at the beginning of the war added force to this demand: "At this time it is the unconditional duty of every soldier to keep his camera in action".[2]

---

[1] See, Starl, *Knipser. Die Bildgeschichte der privaten Fotografie in Deutschland und Österreich von 1880 bis 1980*, Cited in Bopp, 2012.

[2] *ibid* Staril, cited by Bopp.

Finding Photographs

The photographs have been found in various archives or in online collections for sale, often in the USA, as well as battlefield mementoes captured by Allied troops. They don't fall easily into discrete categories, but there is a distinction to be made between those taken by the PK in direct accord with and as a result of orders to produce specific, racially aggressive and offensive images, and, later on in 1940 and 1941, what I have termed 'ethnographic' propaganda – images of colonial soldiers intended to illustrate the general inferiority of colonial troops and that of the French regime which recruited and controlled them. Secondly, we encounter images taken mainly by soldiers in an amateur context, in which the purpose of the photograph is varied, often as souvenir, representing the colonial soldier as 'exotic', or an object of interest, amusement or even derision. Included in this latter group are the grimmer battlefield snapshots of surrendering black soldiers, often seeming to presage future disaster; indeed one encounters several pictures of corpses.

I will use the term 'snapshot' - not by chance a term with its origins in rifle shooting - for such photographs both to avoid confusion and to distinguish them from professional photographs taken by trained and experienced individuals in the course of their military role. That distinction was made explicit by soldiers themselves at the beginning of the last century - for example, an album in the Army Museum in London bears the title "Photographs and Snapshots during the South African War 1901-1902" (Struk, 2011:26). The distinction seems to have been about the time taken to expose the picture rather than the genre of the subject.

There is a third group, even less distinct; photographs taken by professionals or soldiers which occasionally present difficulty in reading the image in a straightforward manner. In looking at such images in particular I wish to highlight the tension inherent in both the role of the photographer and the meaning signified by the image.

Soldiers have taken cameras to war almost since the camera was invented, but the American firm Kodak had marketed a folding pocket camera in 1888 with their now familiar slogan, "You press the button; We do the rest". This idea of 'point and shoot' as distinct from the laborious processes associated with the long exposure, the plate camera and the official portrait will be more important as we explore the context of specific photographs.

Cameras on the Battlefield

Although armies on all sides explicitly banned the use of cameras in military areas, camera manufacturers marketed cameras to soldiers in an equally explicit way. Kodak had also marketed a small folding camera in 1915 - the Vest Pocket Autographic - as "The Soldier's Camera". 1.75 million had been sold by 1919.

Kodak even urged soldiers to, "Make your own private record of the war" and in WW1, thousands of ordinary individuals did just that. Newspapers ran competitions for snapshots of the war and openly solicited photographs from military personnel, despite official policy and pronouncements to the contrary. In 'Learning to Photograph War' the second chapter of 'Private Pictures', her book on soldiers' photographs, Janina Struk (2011:33) says,

> The *Daily Mirror* was not the only newspaper to disregard Press Bureau instructions. Within two days of the newspaper's appeal to soldiers for their pictures, the *Daily Sketch* and the *Daily Mail* had followed suit and pledged even bigger cash prizes to soldier-photographers in exchange for their snapshots.

Struk (2011) goes on to quote advice from a military contributor to *Amateur Photographer* magazine in 1916, "Don't ever photograph the horrible...you will find war quite horrible enough, without perpetuating the seamy side of it" (Struk, 2011:33).

Enough 'seamy' pictures from WW1 and later wars exist to indicate that advice wasn't always followed – although again, there is a distinction that must be made between 'professional' images taken by photographers and reproduced as 'souvenirs' of the horrors of war and those snapshots taken by individual soldiers with their own cameras. As Struk says, very few of the latter type tend to emerge in the silence following conflict. She notes (Struk, 2011:69), "a kind of confusion", prevalent in a lot of First World War albums she views,

> The macabre scenes found in these (American) soldiers' albums do not portray epic scenes of war, they are not well composed scenes of suffering, the kind of photographs that would be taken by a photojournalist less interested in the rotting corpses of the dead than the misery of the living. They have a different, but equally powerful message, that of stillness, emptiness, and a silence.

In looking at the Second World War, we have to remind ourselves of a world without the instant digital transmission and dissemination of images. Even in 2003, at the trials of British soldiers accused of the murder of Iraqi detainee Baha Mousa, we find many of the offending photographs were taken on 'disposable' cameras and the prints discovered by the staff of high street photo processors. The general public and even families of soldiers often remain unaware of the details of military experience. Veterans may bring home souvenirs and mementoes that often remain hidden for the rest of their lives. They cannot bring home the atmosphere of brutalisation and dehumanisation which accompany war. Photographs of enemy corpses may function as a secret link with that past arena, a reminder of horrors past but not forgotten, even if the individual is not the author of that image.

Suvendrini Perera, is writing a book entitled, 'Old Atrocities, New Media'[3]. She says,

Triumphal images from the battlefield are not new. Trophy images have always been circulated but, historically, in limited or secretive ways. With new digital technologies, however, images of terror multiply and mutate. This is the dark side of social media, and it raises questions about how trophy images travel, and to what effect.[4]

As Perera argues, in her book-in-progress, modern digital media embodies a paradox: it allows us to capture more intimate images than ever before and, at the same time, circulate them more widely across public as well as private domains. Whereas previously the battlefield atrocity photograph might be passed around between a small circle of comrades; reproduced and kept as a talisman or souvenir, we can now see such images instantly streamed across the internet where their use and consumption cannot be tightly controlled.

Harry Rignold, appointed as the first official British War Office Cameraman in September 1939, was to find all manner of tight controls when he tried to obtain access to the British Expeditionary Force's activities. Being 'official', Rignold was subject to military discipline and strictures; simply put, he was unable to avoid the pressure of military regulations as civilian war correspondents, particularly neutral ones, were able to do. Furthermore, Rignold, an experienced documentary cameraman, was responsible not only for producing footage intended for instructional films, technical evaluations and historical record, but also for newsreels – a job that was better suited to professional newsreel cameramen. As McGlade (2010:20) recounts,

When the first 2700 feet (30 mins) of film of the BEF's embarkation and landing arrived, it was to prove a disaster and was quickly seized on by the newsreel companies, labelled inferior in quality and accused of giving a very sorry picture of Britain's war effort. A further 4000 feet arriving a week later was described in an official government report as, 'so amateurish and failed so hopelessly to depict our war effort, that al the newsreels returned the footage to the Ministry of Information.

Not so in Poland, where, according to Stephen Bach in his biography, *Leni*, the celebrated film maker Leni Riefenstahl was photographed in the town of Konskie in Poland, wearing military uniform - some claim this was a *Waffen SS*

---

[3] See, http://www.curtin.edu.au/research/aapi/projects/suvendrini-perera.cfm.
[4] See, Lewis, (15/7/2013) Retrieved from http://news.curtin.edu.au/cite/stories/

uniform - and even carrying a pistol. This may not be so remarkable given that she was apparently there as a war correspondent and as such she would have been a member of the military forces and subject to their discipline. She was apparently present when 30 Jews were executed in retaliation for an attack on German soldiers. She claims to have remonstrated with the soldiers, only stopping when forced to at gunpoint (Bach, 2008).

Clive James (2008) claims there were photographs of her taken that day, looking distraught, but she always claimed not to have realised that the victims were Jews (James, 2008). The Polish campaign was seen as a fruitful testing ground for the working relationship between front-line troops and the propaganda makers and indeed, by the time the Germans invaded France in May 1940, the apparatus had moved into high gear.

As an example of the commitment to the organisation of war reporting, during August of 1941, the SS-Kriegsberichter-Kompanie alone was expanded to Abteilung (battalion) strength. Waffen-SS expansion continued to grow throughout the war, and in December 1943 the reporters unit again expanded, this time to regimental size. It also received an honour title at this point, becoming known as SS-Standarte 'Kurt Eggers'.

The first Propaganda Kompanies had been formed in 1938. A *Propagandatrupp* originally consisted of three men; journalist, cameraman and driver, there were several *truppen* making up a *zug* or platoon, and several platoons made up a *Kompanie*. Members were soldiers first and had to complete some form of basic military training. They worked alongside front-line troops and reported directly to their headquarters that applied censorship at local level. Their work was passed to the Wehrmacht High Command and further censored before being submitted to the office of the Propaganda Ministry. Here, the work might be further altered before being submitted to the newspapers and other outlets, which had the option of accepting or rejecting it. The system worked the other way, orders and requirements were frequently passed from the Propaganda Ministry, indeed Goebbels himself, to the PK's and *Kriegsberichters* in the field.

In addition to the ubiquitous PK, German soldiers appear to have been much more likely to possess cameras and to use them both on the battlefield and off it. This may be simply due to the fact that Germany had a thriving camera and optical manufacturing industry and that cameras were much more of a consumer object here than in the rest of Europe. It is estimated that seven million Germans owned a camera in 1936 (Struk, 2011:97). As I have already stated, German soldiers were encouraged to send photographs back home for use in newspapers and other publications and photographs were often reproduced and distributed. On the other hand, British and French soldiers were, as they had been in the First World War, expressly forbidden to use any form of recording apparatus while on active service and particularly in a battle zone. The prohibition extended from cameras to the keeping of diaries and scrapbooks.

Of course, the introduction of the 35mm Leica camera in Germany stimulated an industry in good quality portable cameras that didn't exist on anything like the same scale in Britain or America. Although the Kodak Retina camera of 1934 had begun the 35mm film cassette revolution, these cameras were not widely available in Britain. In Germany Leica models were also comparatively expensive luxury items, but there were several other camera manufacturers in Germany such as Zeiss who also made excellent quality lenses. For example, in 1932 the German company Ihagee began production of the Kine Exakta camera – the first 35mm SLR[5]. It was smaller and more compact than previous SLR designs although it still used roll-film and a waist-high viewfinder. The camera was very popular and Ihagee sold hundreds of thousands in different variants.

That doesn't mean British and French soldiers didn't take photographs or record their experiences, but the manner in which that material has emerged into the public gaze has been profoundly different. I have copies of a series of photographs taken by members of the Propaganda Kompanies during the 1940 campaign - they are housed at the Bundesarchiv in Germany and available online, albeit as low resolution proofs.

The one that takes my attention immediately in the group is a photograph of a black French prisoner of war by Heinrich von der It depicts a black African soldier, almost certainly an African *Tirailleur* of a French colonial regiment. He is sitting on the ground, on grass; he is self-evidently a prisoner; there are no weapons visible in the frame, nor does he wear any other equipment; webbing belts or haversack. The soldier's helmet is still firmly on his head. This is a Model 1926 *Casque Adrian* with a Colonial Infantry anchor and grenade badges on the front. He is wearing puttees,- the rolled leggings or gaiters familiar from uniforms of the first world war - and at least two pairs of similar puttees presumably belonging to other POW's can be seen behind him. He is looking up at the camera, and the cameraman would seem to be looking down, as if standing, or perhaps crouching slightly from above, but close enough to his eye line to capture his face under the rim of the helmet.

His right hand clasping the leather strap of what is probably a water canteen and the left hand is not visible, but in his lap behind the right, also holding the strap. He is wearing a greatcoat, the breast of which is secured with one button across the chest. There may be numbers emblazoned on the collar patches, as was common in the uniform of the day, and the best I can make of them is a '53' or a '58' which would tell us his regiment, but they are difficult to see at this resolution. There was no 58th Regiment d'Infanterie Coloniale, which would place this man in the 53rd Regiment. But it is the soldier's face that immediately

---

[5] The Kine Exakta was introduced in 1936.

takes the attention. The whites of his eyes are very prominent. His mouth is open, the chin thrust forward somewhat and the light on his nose makes a prominent shape as does his lower lip. The upper lip barely registers as a smudge of grey, but the impression is one of a slack jaw as if breathing hard. His chin merges into the upturned collar of his greatcoat, and the head is sunk somewhat in its depths.

What also takes my attention is the dark tone of his face. Apart from the areas on the bridge of his nose and lower lip, the centre of interest in the frame is the whites of his eyes and the upturned pupils, reduced here to the same tone as the rest of his face so all that registers is two white crescents. It may be the low resolution of the copy, but there are no other facial features that emerge from the concentrated area of darkness under the rim of the helmet, which appears to be slightly overexposed in contrast. He gives every appearance of exhaustion and dejection, and it is impossible not to register suspicion and fear in his expression.

What I see here is a tension that is not wholly due to the situation of the subject. I have alluded to the German treatment of black POW's as somewhat less than decent and most certainly not carried out in strict accordance with the rules of the Geneva Convention. I will come to that, but for now, I see the tension between the composition and the subject matter. This is a portrait, not a snapshot and carries all the traits and hallmarks of a portrait in the sense of despair it conveys that cannot be accidental.

This portrait was taken by a man who was no stranger to photographing black people. Heinrich von der Becke had been a press photographer since 1925 and from 1935 until his conscription into the army, he worked for the Max Schirner press agency, well known for sports photography. In fact von der Becke took many of the now famous images of Jesse Owens and other athletes at the Berlin Olympics of 1936. Von der Becke had initially served in the anti-tank company of an infantry regiment throughout the Polish campaign, but was then recruited into the Propaganda Kompanies.

What I see in the von der Becke portrait is both propaganda image and a portrait of an exhausted human being who has lost hope and is perhaps unsure whether this photograph may be a prelude to his own death.

The original caption for this photograph, that unfortunately does not tell us where it was first published, is, '*Englands Hilfsvölker. Erstaunt und etwas ängstlich sieht der Neger den Photographen an*'. This translates roughly as "England's international aid. Surprised and somewhat anxious look of the Negro at the photographer". This is clearly a propaganda caption expressed in the form of racial slurs. Contrast the later and much milder Bundesarchiv description, '*Westfeldzug (Frankreich).- Kriegsgefangener französischer Soldat aus den französischen Kolonien (Kolonialsoldat), auf dem Boden sitzend*'. This translates as, 'Campaign in the

West (France) -. POW French soldier from the French colonies (colonial soldier), sitting on the ground.'[6]

Hilfsvölker is one of those German words it is difficult to translate exactly, being a composite of the words for 'help' and 'people'. Some commentators have suggested there is more of the slave than the 'help' even though the phrase is often given as helper'. The sense here is certainly the same as applied to France in other propaganda of the time; that England has sunk so low as to need help from such 'auxiliary tribes'.

When Cy Grant, a Guyanan navigator in the RAF, was captured in 1943, his picture was taken and used in the German newspaper, the *Volkischer Beobachter,* with the title, *Ein Mitglied der Royal Air Force von unbestimmbarer Rasse* - "Member of the Royal Air Force of indeterminate race", with the similar insinuation that England was scraping the bottom of the barrel for aircrew (Grant, 2006:x).

Of course, it is difficult for us to see this image in that light – it is not known where the photograph was first published – if at all. Seventy years have intervened and this portrait is less an image of a degenerate race than it is an illustration of the uses of portraiture in propaganda. I don't know if it signified that to von der Becke either

Figure 2: Personal collection W.T. Barbour – reproduced with kind permission.

– a man well used to photographing black people and in particular, their grace, beauty and athleticism. There are published photographs by von der Becke of Owens not only competing, but relaxing alongside the white German long jumper Luz Long – a picture that caused a stir in the ranks of the Nazi hierarchy. Owens is also pictured with Louise Stokes, a black sprinter. Stokes, along with Tydie Pickett, also black, was picked for the US 440 yards relay team. But at the last minute was replaced by white athletes.

Indeed, von der Becke was so friendly with Owens that he is said to have arranged a meeting with Adolf Dassler, a manufacturer of training shoes and longstanding Nazi party member. Dassler, later the founder of the Adidas empire, reputedly persuaded the German athletics coach, Joe Waitzer, to get Owens to use the shoes (Adidas archive) but there are many versions of how

---

[6] Bundesarchiv, Bild 146-2004-0202 / Becke, Heinrich von der /June 1940. Indeed, a further note to these photographs states: "For documentary purposes the German Federal Archive often retained the original image captions, which may be erroneous, biased, obsolete or politically extreme".

this actually happened. What is certain is that von der Becke and Owens maintained contact and met several times after the war. There are photographs of the two men together in 1973, taken by von der Becke's son.

The other photograph I wish to consider here is not a portrait, nor does it look like one. It has not appeared in any propaganda material that I know of and has not been published at all in fact. The photograph (Figure 2) is in landscape format rather than portrait - it shows a full-length prone black soldier - also a Tirailleur judging by the uniform and accouterments. He is lying on his front; head and shoulders raised off the ground and looking up, not at the photographer, but at someone else, who appears by the man's frightened gaze, to be behind and above the photographer, who may well be kneeling or crouching to take the photograph.

This man is bareheaded, he is wearing the tunic and leather webbing equipment standard for Tirailleurs of the period. He also has puttees over his uniform trousers, but his feet are cut off by the edge of the frame. I assume from the pose and the fact that not only is he wearing his webbing equipment, but also, a long bayonet in the scabbard which protrudes between the tail of his tunic, which is buttoned together at the back. It is therefore probable that he is either wounded or recently captured as this, along with any other weapons and webbing equipment would certainly have been removed by the Germans who captured or wounded him, before he was rounded up with other prisoners of war.

This photograph was picked up by Sergeant Major W.T. Barbour in Normandy when he was serving in the 3rd Irish Guards in 1944 and sent to me by his daughter, Diane. She had this to say about the photograph:

He told me he'd picked up these German photos from an abandoned trench in Normandy; could have been from dead German(s); but he isn't squeamish or evasive, so perhaps the former is true.

As a child I remember being upset by the one of the black soldier on the ground - his eyes! - but of course my understanding at the time wasn't sophisticated enough to work out circumstances. Fortunately my father never hid away paraphernalia or avoided the topic of war. It was very much 'there' all the time. He told myself and siblings everything pretty much as he remembers it happening, with the caveat that his memories are just that, his - and that others have quite often a totally different perspective. His explanation is that a memory is like a snapshot - that he may have been watching some other detail compared to the man next to him, that some memories are out of focus, some blurred, whilst others never were developed properly. (To that I would add the phenomena of photo-shopped; I would imagine some memories are edited.) He married a German woman some 20 years after the war ended so we as a family have an unusual but very frank perspective on the war and how it affected the individuals we knew....

I can tell you now the impact on me. I was very young when I first saw his 'captured' photos. I had a basic knowledge but not the maturity etc. to understand why I did not like to look at that one in particular. Men pictured in uniforms were everyday to me, this was not, it was unsettling, disturbing, the story within unfinished.[7]

Perhaps there is here, in the same momentary sense as a shutter release is pressed, of hatred or supremacy, a wish to express dominance over a feared enemy; an enemy who, so your newspaper said yesterday, would cut off your head with a machete and, in all probability eat the remains. We have contemporary accounts of such fears and I quote them later. But a weak and helpless wounded enemy is just that, and we can't imagine this man being dangerous any more than the naked detainees photographed in Abu Ghraib pose a threat to their captors. Of course, such photographs are often taken and crimes perpetrated by rear echelon soldiers who are taking advantage of diminished and helpless captives, expressing their frustration at not being seen as fighting troops.

Battlefield atrocities – and photographs of the results – occur often in or just after the heat of the moment and for less deliberate, but no less reprehensible reasons. Soldiers who took such snapshots had no other audience in mind when they took such photographs, except fellow soldiers. 'Action' photographs are rare in battlefield photography from the period and I am interested in this image because in all the many images I have seen, this is the only one that shows the black soldier alive but helpless. There are photographs of dead and bloated corpses of black French soldiers, there are photographs of them surrendering, or humiliated by being forced to dance or sing for the camera, but none where the photograph has been taken in the act of subordination, of diminishment as it were.

It is interesting that the soldier in this picture retains his bayonet. The German troops engaged in combat against *tirailleurs* retained a dread of the 'coupe-coupe', the long, machete type knife that Tirailleurs Sénégelais traditionally carried. Raffael Scheck says, "German war diaries often took note of the *coupe-coupes* of captured Tirailleurs. Many Germans automatically assumed that the blacks were using their *coupe-coupes* for illegitimate purposes such as the mutilation of German prisoners or corpses" (Scheck, 2006:71). The fact that the weapon was usually carried in an inconspicuous sheath gave rise to a fear of this weapon well beyond its capabilities and the entire notion of black troops as savage and somehow illegitimate combatants arose.

In this case, the visible weapon is not a *coupe coupe*, *but* the bayonet for a Berthier rifle - a model issued to colonial troops. The bayonet is some 16 inches

---

[7] D. Barbour, personal communication, September, 10th 2011.

long and already out of date as an assault weapon; it was too long and ungainly for trench warfare and close combat. By this time modern bayonets were shorter and tended to be used as general purpose tool, but the French armaments industry had simply not manufactured enough modern weapons to equip all of its troops and so colonial troops used WW1 vintage rifles and equipment.

The German fear of the black soldier was borne from a long and complex process of racial habituation. Raffael Scheck (2006:113) concludes:

> ...the massacres of black Africans were authorised by the traditional stigmatization of black men in arms in German public discourse and the massive racist propaganda of the Nazi media during the campaign. That the vast majority of abuses happened after this propaganda campaign was launched by Goebbels, with Hitler's approval, is certainly no coincidence.

The photograph of the wounded *tirailleur* fills me with dread, the dread of impending disaster. I am reminded immediately of Roland Barthes' well-known meditation on Alexander Gardner's portrait of Lewis Payne.

Payne was charged with murder in association with the plot that killed President Lincoln. In the photograph, Payne is shackled - his wrists forced apart by a steel bar - and reclining against a cast iron panel, which is actually the gun turret of the ironclad monitor (gunship) that he was confined upon, staring out at the photographer.

Barthes captions the photograph: *"He is dead and he is going to die"*. Payne is long dead when Barthes views the photograph, but in the image Payne still waits to die. A famously strange juxtaposition of tenses this; he is dead (this has already happened), he is going to die (this will happen). For Barthes, at the root of every photograph is this *"catastrophe which has already occurred"*. Indeed, he has much the same to say about the photograph of his mother, Henriette as a five-year-old child, which was the catalyst for writing *Camera Lucida*, his seminal essay on photography in 48 fragments.[8]

Interestingly enough, many commentators assume the portrait of Payne was taken on or just before the day he was hanged, but it was actually taken several months before in April 1865, on or around Payne's 21st birthday. Gardner actually took some ten portraits of Paine and six of them show him against a canvas awning on the deck of the ship. He was a powerfully built, tall man and towers above the sentry guarding him, glowering at the camera in the other photographs. One observer commentates on the fact that he is 'menacingly free of handcuffs'.[9]

---

[8] See, Barthes (1982).
[9] Metropolitan Museum of Art catalogue entry to a photograph of Lewis Payne. Accession Number: 2005.100.97. Retrieved from http://www.metmuseum.org/

What five years earlier had been a taboo subject had now become a profitable one. And a conveniently manageable one, too. Those at Antietam were photographed as they lay; ten months later Gardner and his assistants moved bodies around Gettysburg like so many props, assembling scenes they wanted to record.

And of course we note the vast difference in time frame between Gardner's' use of the cumbersome wet collodion process, with limited plate life, slow shutter speeds and long exposures and the perhaps one-sixtieth or even hundredths of a second it takes to capture the battlefield images of 1940.

It is not entirely by chance of course that Gardner should feature in this essay. He has the reputation, long mistakenly attributed to his one-time employer and gallery owner Matthew Brady, of being the first person to take photographs of dead soldiers on the battlefield - in this case in the aftermath of the Civil War battle of Antietam in September 1862. Roger Fenton, often dubbed the first war photographer, had of course taken photographs of the Crimean War battlefields as early as 1855, but he was under strict instructions from the War Office to avoid making images of the dead, the maimed and the ill. Similarly in 1940, the soldiers and correspondents of both sides were expressly forbidden from taking photographs of the dead and wounded. Yet taking photographs of the enemy's dead and wounded was another thing altogether.

In an interview for the Imperial War Museum Archive in 1984, ex AFPU cameraman Dick Leatherbarrow, who landed on Juno Beach (Marwill, 2000) with the Canadian forces said,

My most ghastly memory...most vivid memory...I saw a body in the most bizarre and gruesome form I have ever seen...the head was blown off but in a sitting up position and the movement of the arms still taking place... something as gruesome as that I couldn't see the point of photographing it...not that I had the opportunity under fire. I mean, I had photographed dead Germans and civilians after that, (Leatherbarrow was part of the AFPU unit that covered the discovery of Belsen), but that one isolated incident was something I feel myself that if I had all the time in the world to do it I would have rejected it, you know because the whole thing was beyond... well who would have wanted it? What purpose would it serve, taking a close up of that... I'd just like someone to tell me what the justification for that would be.

Sergeant Major Barbour's captured German album does contain one image of a dead soldier (Figure 3). This is also a tirailleur from the same period as the first two - but this man is clearly dead. He is recently dead - there is no visible evidence of a wound, but the side of his face visible to us is mottled and perhaps bloody. There doesn't seem to be any post mortem bloating or decomposition as is plainly evident in Gardner's pictures of the three and four day old corpses at Antietam and

Figure 3: Personal collection W.T. Barbour
– reproduced with kind permission.

Gettysburg. This photograph - a snapshot - is badly framed, perhaps hurriedly. The man's legs - one curiously bare, the other hidden beneath swathes of greatcoat - are cut off by the bottom edge of the photograph - which is rendered in the decorative manner of the time, as if to imitate an ornate frame. The larger part of the picture is occupied by empty, rough ground, littered with stones and other detritus, as if the photographer has stepped too near the body, and then had to step back to compose the photograph in the viewfinder.

We have to note here that cameras of the time were perfectly capable of taking very sharp images with fast shutter speeds and short exposure times, with 35mm film which could be blown up to large prints. But they were not modern cameras in the sense that the photographer had to use a rangefinder on top of the camera to estimate the distance from lens to subject and for composition purposes. The Leica II introduced in 1932 brought a coupled rangefinder and viewfinder, so that the photographer could compose an image using an eyepiece engraved with 'safe' lines to aid composition. The 'through the lens' camera with a light meter that we are used to today even in simple cameras was not a technology available in a widespread form until the 1960s.

The man's helmet has come off, perhaps as he fell - at first I would assume that the bare legs might indicate death from blast - men were often killed and left unmarked, even naked, by the blast from artillery explosions. I then moved to the possibility of his having been wounded - in the leg perhaps and receiving treatment, then later dying of his wounds. However, my attention is drawn to what Barthes might call the *punctum* - (literally, that which pierces us, the spear point of the photograph) of his wrists. His wrists appear to be manacled together - what appears to be a chain adorns the left wrist and the bar of a handcuff the right. At first I thought this may be explained by some form of identity bracelet and perhaps a watch, but there is a definite right angle to one of the wrist adornments and the hands are at an odd angle which would lead me to believe they were fastened together in some fashion at the wrist.

Handcuffing prisoners of war was, if not specifically forbidden by the Geneva Convention, certainly a breach of the protocol surrounding the treatment of POW's. In retaliation for commando raids in the Channel Islands, the Germans manacled some allied prisoners for a period of time in 1942 - and Canadian POW's from Dieppe were certainly handcuffed, apparently in retaliation for the same punishment having been meted out to German POW's, but this was most certainly not common practice nor was it a permanent or regular state of affairs (Dancocks, 1983).

When these photographs, along with the others in the assortment found by Mr. Barbour were first put online in a world war two discussion forum, there were debates over whether the two men were the same figure; some sort of gruesome 'before and after'. There is no contextual evidence to support that theory, except the fact that they were in the same collection of photographs found on a dead German.

Petra Bopp (2012) puts it succinctly: "Our soldiers are keen photographers, they take a lot of pictures," the owner of a photo lab told one of his female customers in 1941, as he added photographs by the soldier named Georg into a sample book (Musterbuch) of front-line images that could be ordered by every member of the company. The subject matter of this sample book was described as destroyed villages, farmsteads and sub-humans in Poland, while in France, Georgs camera had captured images of ruins and ethnic types. The image of the enemy was, therefore, not only disseminated by journalistic propaganda in the daily newspapers and magazines; pictures taken by soldiers were also widely used by camera shops and the photographic trade to promote their products".[10]

That these photographs were souvenirs of the war is not in doubt; the wallet contained about fifty photographs of varying types, some can be found in the collection of General Erwin Rommel, then commander of the 7th Panzer Division, currently held in the National Archives in Washington. Such reproduction and redistribution appears to have been common; soldiers would obtain copies of well-known photographs from processors back home and pass them around much like postcards. Some are familiar propaganda images, such as parading German troops in Paris, but others bear the unmistakable stamp of amateur authorship.

Indeed, it may have been the presence of Rommel that drew both PK and amateur photographers to the area, as he was known as an amateur photographer and to encourage the depiction of his exploits. Rommel was

---

[10] Petra Bopp: Lecture presented at the symposium for the opening of the exhibit 'Strangers in focus', Legermuseum Delft, 26th April 2012.

reportedly given a Leica III camera by Goebbels personally, before the 1940 campaign. While Rommel's exploits with his 'Ghost Division' were often disapproved of by higher military authorities, Goebbels was perhaps exploiting Rommel's self-publicising for his own ends - indeed several photographs from the 'Rommel Collection' crop up in propaganda contexts.

In fact, Rommel would recreate his part in the battles of the Somme later in 1940. In his biography of Rommel, David Irving has this account: "The Nazi propaganda minister, Goebbels, asked him to collaborate on a big army film about the campaign, Victory in the West (*Sieg im Westen*). Rommel spent part of August re-enacting for the movie cameras the Spook Division's crossing of the Somme. He had a great time playing movie director, and he schooled his troops in acting techniques. A battalion of French black troops was hauled out of the prison camps to stage the surrender of a village. Again, this time for the cameras, Rommel's tanks charged, guns blazing. He told the blacks to come out toward the tanks with their hands up and looking scared; but the men over-acted, rolled the whites of their eyes, and screamed with terror. Rommel cut the cameras, and patiently explained through interpreters that actors had to show their emotions more subtly than that. The battle scenes were finally filmed on such an epic and reckless scale that several more lives were lost, though through no fault of Rommel's. "No expense has been spared to show it as it really was," he wrote on the last day of shooting. "There were blacks in it again today. The fellows had a whale of a time and thoroughly enjoyed putting up their hands all over again" (Irving, 1999:59).

There is no reference to this incident in Rommel's own memoirs, although these were selectively edited by Basil Liddell Hart, a great admirer of Rommel, but Irving does recount this story more than once.

There are however several stills extant in the 'Rommel Collection' from this reconstruction; a few showing the *Tirailleur* POW's running with hands up, tanks crashing through the wall of the Chateau le Quesnoy. The re-enactments were filmed by Hans Ertl, who had worked with Leni Riefenstahl on several films and was reassigned from PK Kompanie 501 by Lt.Colonel Dr.Kurt Hesse, a friend of Rommel's. Hesse was head of Wehrmacht Propaganda Section V, which dealt exclusively with the army, much to the annoyance of Goebbels' Propaganda Ministry, which wanted all footage shot by PK units sent directly to them (Graham, 1989).

Ertl was ordered specifically to recreate the tank battles of the Somme that hadn't initially received enough newsreel coverage. There is a photograph showing a cameraman, perhaps Ertl himself, standing on the back of a tank with a movie camera, the position of which matches footage included in the propaganda film, *Sieg im Westen*. The scenes with surrendering *Tirailleurs* did not make it into the final edit of the film.

Without going into too much detail, the black colonial soldiers of France's army fought hard and suffered casualties equal to, if not greater than their white, metropolitan counterparts. Raffael Scheck's book mentions several incidents involving the 53rd RICMS - perhaps the regiment that von der Becke's, 'somewhat anxious' 'negro' belonged to?

In Hangest-sur Somme, some captured Tirailleurs and a French second-lieutenant were shot by Germans in black uniforms, most likely members of Rommel's 7th Panzer Division". (the personnel of German armoured units wore black uniforms). In fact, Scheck (2006) estimates from various sources that some 2-300 black prisoners of war were murdered by German forces operating in the Somme area on 5/6th June. "The 53rd Regiment d'Infanterie Mixte Sénégelais was virtually annihilated in Airaines, suffering close to 90% casualties (Scheck, 2006:27).

There are many such accounts in Scheck's impeccably researched book, which seems notable in its attempts to quantify the extent of the crimes and avoid any hint of hysteria. He concludes that the German forces, including many ordinary Wehrmacht units, not just SS forces, massacred several thousand North and West African soldiers *after* combat had taken place in June 1940 (Scheck, 2006:54-57).

While this chapter has no room to discuss in detail the historical antecedents of the negative racial attitude of German forces towards black French soldiers on the battlefield; an order from Colonel Walter Nehring, Guderian's Chief of Staff (Echenberg, 1985:369) is typical of the few written sources of the period which survive:

It has been established that French colonial soldiers have mutilated in bestial fashion our German wounded. Towards these native soldiers, all kindness would be an error. It is rigorously forbidden to send these prisoners towards the rear without a guard. They are to be treated with the greatest rigour.

Whatever we think of it, this is a tactical instruction, made on the battlefield; Scheck establishes that there was not necessarily much hard evidence in the shape of such written orders to back up the notion of an organised policy of extermination or ill-treatment. There is much more solid background evidence of the general Nazi attitude towards black colonial soldiers - those from West Africa in particular, and it comes not through combat sources but from instructions on the representation of such forces. On 23rd May, Rolf Kratzer, deputy chief of the propaganda division of the Wehrmacht High Command - *not* the propaganda ministry, issued a request (Graham, 1989:6),

All Propaganda Companies are to look for opportunities for shots comparing good-looking German soldiers with especially brutish Senegal negroes and other coloured prisoners. A sharp racial contrast is important. Shipment of material urgent.

Then, at the end of May 1940, at a staff conference in the Propaganda Ministry, Goebbels ordered a sharpening of the media campaign against France and her use of colonial troops; in particular the deployment of black soldiers, who were derided as *Kultur Vorkämpfer* or 'Cultural Champions'. The aim of course being to discredit the French regime for using such inferior races to fight for them. The distinction was made by one of Goebbels's staff between Black Africans; "Negroes, niggers, inhabitants of the jungle" and North Africans, who, it was pointed out had played a part in Franco's campaign in the Spanish Civil War (Scheck, 2006:103).

One image which may be seen as a direct reply to that request for propaganda *is* a poster headed with the words, "Franzosische Kulturvorkämpfer - France's Cultural Champions". This is from a poster divided into four, each with a photograph - head and shoulders - of a French colonial soldier - in three cases black and probably West African, in the fourth, probably north African. Here the images appear to have been selected for their exaggerated 'racial' characteristics, large lips, noses and foreheads, and elongated jaws. The text reads,

'In the Name of Civilization.' France, infiltrated by Jews and Negroes, pushed its black Beasts on us for the third time. It must be that last time. It will be that last time!!

On 30th May Goebbels held another conference during which he demanded an even more ruthless tone against France. He encouraged journalists to revive memories of the Black Horror campaign (the French occupation of the Rhineland between the wars where black soldiers were used as garrison troops and accused of rape and murder on a large scale). He called the French a people of, 'niggerized sadists' and requested that the German people become full of anger and hate against France within a fortnight (Scheck, 2006:103).

The SS newspaper, *Das Schwarze Korps*, as might be expected, went even further, accusing black soldiers of cannibalism and describing them as,

Beings who derive a cultic joy from murder and mutilation (as authentic reports from the front prove), to whom the satisfaction of drives means a service to God and who stand on a level of development not much higher than the gorilla.[11]

The scale of massacres of French African troops in June 1940 would tend to indicate that Goebbels' tirade was reasonably effective. Indeed, Scheck details incidents in which white officers were singled out for brutality and even summary execution for merely being in command of Tirailleur units (Scheck,

---

[11] Edition of June 6th, 1940 in Scheck, 2006:122,

2006:25-26). Tirailleurs themselves recount ill treatment and shootings on these forced marches and even once they arrived in prison camps (Lawler, 1992:94-99). There are some ominous images for sale on both German and US auction sites of surrendering colonial POW's, often badly composed, badly exposed and all the more authentic seeming for that.

While the casualty figures for colonial troops are a subject of much debate and not the focus of this chapter, it is certainly clear that black colonial soldiers expected to be treated harshly by the Germans if captured. Raffael Scheck details the treatment of these men. About 10,000 of them were killed in the fighting and there is general agreement that some 2-3,000 were certainly massacred by various German units, both SS and ordinary Wehrmacht, after surrendering.

The Bundesarchiv and other collections contain photographs of long columns of French POW's being marched away to Germany. There are particular photographs of black West and North African and also Asian prisoners in a variety of situations, some evidently photographed in action and others which appear to be posed. Most make fairly obvious propaganda of the sort discussed above; at times the tone seems hysterical and forced to modern ears. A photograph of French black and white POW's standing together, was originally titled, 'Does this white Frenchman really look upon the thickly masked black as his brother?' The black POW in question is merely wearing a balaclava.[12]

It is one thing to shoot POW's in or after the heat of the moment - and there are endless discussions to be had about how long that 'moment' is - and killing those prisoners long after that moment has passed, or even using them as extras in propaganda films. David Killingray details the rigours and hardships undergone by French African POW's in German hands (Killingray, 1996). There is a scene at the end of *Sieg Im Westen* which shows Tirailleurs dancing and singing, tribal scarification marks clearly shown on their faces. Mossi soldiers from Burkina Faso who wore such marks were apparently singled out for such treatment (Lawler, 1992:101).

The images from the camps that have found their way into the archives take a physiognomic approach, imitative of anthropological studies, in which individual soldiers become subjects of 'scientific' scrutiny in order to emphasise their racial features and therefore differences.

The types of photograph from POW camps echo almost exactly those employed in a German propaganda book, *The POW in Germany*, published in 1915 and authored by Alexander Backhaus, an agricultural professor employed by the War Ministry. The comments Backhaus and other popular writers such as A.Korbitz in 'Types from the German POW Camps', emphasise 'brutal'

---

[12] Bundesarchiv, Bild 140-2001-02427/Schulze / June 1940.

features and 'savage' expressions. Indeed one passage from Backhaus' book could be lifted straight to 1940; "These…pictures demonstrate …the kind of riff-raff that Germany must fight and what the 'Champions of Freedom and Civilisation' lead into the field against the "German barbarians"', (Evans, 2004).

One typical image of 1940 taken by PK Ulrich-Scherl; depicting a dozen colonial soldiers of the different racial types to be found in the camp, is accompanied by a typical commentary: The 'saviour of France,' in captivity. Just as they did during the war 1914/18, France has used its auxiliary coloured people again. Murder and mistreatment of defenceless prisoners, arson and looting of the civilian population in the area of operations. This is a monstrous accusation against France, and is the result of nefarious doings of the colonial troops that the French not only tolerate but also encourage.[13]

'Again', was an easy word to reach for. Clearly, German propaganda didn't just call upon memories of the 'Black Horror of the Rhine' from the 1920s, but reached further back for effortlessly adaptable stereotypes.

Killingray (1996) also documents the improving treatment of the African POW's once Red Cross parcels began to appear in the camps in late 1940. Also, the Vichy regime, although it tended later in the war to reflect Nazi attitudes towards colonial POW's, was able to have some effect in ameliorating conditions in the camps. We therefore receive published images of friendly fraternisation between camp guards and Germans. In one much reproduced image from the Bundesarchiv collection, a *Tirailleur Sénégalais*, in his traditional red fez or *chéchia*, accepts a light from two grinning military policemen[14]. The title is a mild mannered, "Friend and foe - two military policmen of the Protection Force".

In another image, two African POW's sit inside a makeshift stockade, roped off from the smiling civilians who are looking at the camera, happy to be included in this circus of sorts that has come to their town, as indeed is their guard. Only the West African soldier is glowering into the camera, his discomfort expressed in anger, and signifying perhaps some form of passive resistance.[15] As so often, only the caption exists; in this case the almost benevolent, 'French prisoners of war (mostly colonial soldiers) with a German sentry.'

Benignly captioned or not, the work of the Propaganda Kompanies in respect of their depiction of black soldiers was heavily censored and several levels removed from their immediate influence. It is impossible to read intention into such depictions, but it seems clear to me that no matter how

---

[13] Bundesarchiv, Bild L83-L0509/ Ulrich-Scherl/ May 1940.

[14] Bundesarchiv, Bild 121-0417/ Unknown author/ 1940.

[15] Bundesarchiv, Bild 121-0430/ Unknown author/ May-June 1940.

specific orders were to make depictions of a certain kind, the influence of the individual photographer cannot be dismissed.

The German propaganda organisation possessed an access to and a control over image making which was unparalleled on the Allied side. I would also assert that the organisation of the propaganda mechanisms meant that the personal photographs of soldiers could be and were utilised for publicity, press and propaganda purposes. Again, a strange contrast emerges from the drive by those propaganda agencies to obtain pictures from the front set against the strict military instructions not to take photographs or use any recording apparatus at the front.

My assertion is also that the Propaganda Kompanies, being integrated into the military structure and in fact embedded with them, to use a more modern term, before the commencement of hostilities, were ideally placed to be able to react quickly to the demands of the propaganda ministry and to produce images which could be used in propaganda on a very efficient basis. The genius of this system was to enroll artists, writers and other creative people into a system whereby they plied their trade with all the conscientiousness and ability they possessed, but then to put that in the direct service of state propaganda.

Also, and perhaps more importantly; as enlisted soldiers, they were bound to empathise, if not sympathise with the everyday experiences of the soldiers they were working with. It isn't easy to criticise comrades who may well have supported you through the excesses of combat. If it isn't easy to criticise comrades, it is certainly not an easy thing to photograph atrocities they may have committed.

The PK were also politically and ideologically motivated, if not indoctrinated; they were given strict and swift instructions on what sorts of images to collect and where to send them, as can be seen from the orders mentioned above. The fact is that these men were not photo-journalists in isolation, they were members of a military organisation with all that entails; subject to military discipline, organised in military fashion, using modern equipment, wearing uniform, holding rank and crucially, often carrying weapons.

And yet, I think it is perfectly possible to detect the influence of the artist as photographer in the depiction offered by some of these images. In my opinion this gives rise to a tension between the propaganda title, the context the image was received in and the skills of the photographer in a way that was unparalleled in any Allied depictions

Therefore my comment about, von der Becke's 'negro' earlier may be unfair. While I think it is certainly possible to identify certain professional elements to his work, the sharpness of the image, the correct exposure, the composition above all, it might be more accurate to refer to 'Goebbels's negro'.

If we want to put a photograph back into the context of experience, social experience, social memory, we have to respect the laws of memory. We have to situate the printed photograph so that it acquires something of the surprising conclusiveness of that which was and is.[16]

References

Bach, S. (2008). *Leni - the Life and Work of Leni Riefenstahl.* USA, New York: Vintage.

Barthes, R. (1982). *Camera Lucida - Reflections on Photography.* UK. London: Jonathan Cape.

Berger, J. (2009). *About Looking.* UK. London: Bloomsbury.

Bopp, P. (2012). Lecture presented at the symposium for the opening of the *exhibit 'Strangers in Focus'*, Legermuseum Delft, 26th April.

Cooper C. G. (1989). 'Sieg im Westen' (1941): Interservice and Bureaucratic Propaganda Rivalries in Nazi Germany', *Historical Journal of Film, Radio and Television*, 9:1.

Dancocks, D. G, (1983) *In Enemy Hands: Canadian Prisoners of War, 1939-45.* Edmonton: Hurtig Publishers. www.canadiansoldiers.com/procedures/prisoners.htm.

Echenberg, M. (1985). 'Morts pour la France, The African soldier in France during the Second World War'. *Journal of African History*, Vol.26 no.4:369.

Evans, A. D. (2004). 'Anthropology and Photography in German and Austrian POW Camps in WW1'. In, *Colonialist Photography: Imag(in)ing Race and Place.* Hight, E. M. and Sampson, G. D. (eds.). USA, New York: Routledge.

Guerlain, R, (1944) *A Prisoner in Germany.* UK. London, Macmillan & Co.

Grant, C. (2006). *A Member of the Royal Air Force of Indeterminate Race.* UK. Bognor Regis: Woodfield Publishing.

Irving, D. (1999). *Rommel – The Trail of the Fox.* Ware. Wordsworth Military Library.

James, C. (2008). *Cultural Amnesia: Necessary Memories From History and the Arts.* UK. London: Norton & Co.

Killingray, D. (1996). 'Africans and African Americans in Enemy Hands' in *Prisoners of War and Their Captors.* Moore, B. and Fedorowich, K. (eds.). UK. Oxford: Berg Publisher.

Killingray, D. (2010). *Fighting for Britain.* UK. London: Boydell &

---

[16] See, Berger (2009).

Brewer Ltd.

Lawler, N. E. (1992). *Soldiers of Misfortune*. USA. Ohio: Ohio University Press.

Lewis, A. *Bringing them Home: Domesticating Images from the War on Terror* 15/7/2013) Retrieved from, http://news.curtin.edu.au/cite/stories/

Marwill, J. (2000). 'Photography at War', *History Today*, Vol.50:6.

McGlade, F. (2010). *History of the British Army Film & Photographic Unit in the Second World War*. UK. Solihull: Helion & Co.

Petra Bopp, Lecture presented at the symposium for the opening of the exhibit '*Strangers in Focus*', Legermuseum Delft, 26. April 2012.

Ryan, C. (1995). *A Bridge Too Far*. UK. London: Simon & Schuster.

Scheck, R. (2006). *Hitler's African Victims*. USA. New York: Cambridge University Press.

Starl, T. *Knipser. Die Bildgeschichte der privaten Fotografie in Deutschland und Österreich von 1880 bis 1980*, Munich/Berlin, 1985, p.19. Cited in Struk. J, (2011). *Private Pictures*. UK. London: Tauris & Co.

www.ingramcontent.com/pod-product-compliance
Lightning Source LLC
Chambersburg PA
CBHW052044090426
42739CB00010B/2043